INDIVIDUAL VOLUNTARY ARRANGEMENTS

ELGAR CORPORATE AND INSOLVENCY LAW AND PRACTICE

Series Editors: Andrew Keay, *Professor of Corporate and Commercial Law, University of Leeds, UK* and *Chief Insolvency and Companies Court Judge* Nicholas Briggs

The Elgar Corporate and Insolvency Law and Practice series is a library of works by leading practitioners and scholars covering discrete areas of law in the field. Each title will be analytical in approach, highlighting and unpicking the legal issues that are most critical and relevant to practice. Designed to be detailed, focused reference works, the books in this series aim to offer an authoritative statement on the law and practice in key topics within the fields of company law, corporate governance, corporate insolvency and personal insolvency.

Presented in a format that allows for ease of navigation to a particular point of law, each title in the series is written by specialists in their respective fields, often with insight either from private practice or from an academic perspective.

Titles in the series include:

Creditor Treatment in Corporate Insolvency Law
Kayode Akintola

Insolvency Practitioners
Appointment, Duties, Powers and Liability
Hugh Sims QC, Rachel Lai, Neil Levy, Stefan Ramel, Holly Doyle, James Hannant and Samuel Parsons

Cross-Border Protocols in Insolvencies of Multinational Enterprise Groups
Ilya Kokorin and Bob Wessels

The European Restructuring Directive
Gerard McCormack

Corporate Governance and Insolvency
Accountability and Transparency
Andrew Keay, Peter Walton and Joseph Curl QC

Individual Voluntary Arrangements
Law and Practice
Alaric Watson

INDIVIDUAL VOLUNTARY ARRANGEMENTS

Law and Practice

ALARIC WATSON

Barrister, Gatehouse Chambers, UK

ELGAR CORPORATE AND INSOLVENCY LAW AND PRACTICE

Edward Elgar
PUBLISHING

Cheltenham, UK • Northampton, MA, USA

Published by
Edward Elgar Publishing Limited
The Lypiatts
15 Lansdown Road
Cheltenham
Glos GL50 2JA
UK

Edward Elgar Publishing, Inc.
William Pratt House
9 Dewey Court
Northampton
Massachusetts 01060
USA

A catalogue record for this book
is available from the British Library

Library of Congress Control Number: 2022932884

This book is available electronically in the **Elgar**online
Law subject collection
http://dx.doi.org/10.4337/9781802205237

ISBN 978 1 80220 522 0 (cased)
ISBN 978 1 80220 523 7 (eBook)

Printed and bound by CPI Group (UK) Ltd, Croydon, CR0 4YY

For Pippa

CONTENTS

EXTENDED CONTENTS

PART III   INITIATING PROCEDURES

6   INTERIM ORDERS

7   THE ALTERNATIVE PROCEDURE

ABOUT THE AUTHOR

Alaric Watson is a barrister practising at Gatehouse Chambers, Gray's Inn, specialising in insolvency law, as well as general commercial litigation and employment law. He was called to the Bar in 1997. Prior to turning to the law, he was an academic, studying and teaching the history of the Roman Empire.

PREFACE

There is no concise, readable, reliable textbook dedicated to the law of individual voluntary arrangements (IVAs). This book is intended to fill that gap. It is aimed at practitioners, but I hope it will also find a readership among students and those who might be contemplating or are actually involved in an IVA and, more generally, among those who take an interest in how our law (and, in this context, insolvency law in particular) operates and affects our lives. It is intended to provide both a practical guide to the statutory regime and the case law that interprets it and also a commentary on the policies and trends that have helped to shape this area of the law as it operates today.

The law as stated in this book is current as at 31 August 2021.

An earlier and much more concise version of the material that makes up this book was shown to Stephen Baister, David Milman and John Tribe (with whom I was collaborating on another project at the time). I am very grateful to all of them for their comments on that earlier draft, and in particular to Stephen, who took the time to read through some later versions of parts of this text for me as well. I am also grateful to my partner, Pippa Hill, for her tireless support and her comments and suggestions. Needless to say, whatever errors and infelicities remain in the present work are down to me alone.

Alaric Watson
September 2021

ABBREVIATIONS

BA 1914	Bankruptcy Act 1914
BPC	Business and Property Courts of England and Wales
CDDA 1986	Company Directors Disqualification Act 1986
COA 1979	Charging Orders Act 1979
COMI	Centre of main interests
Cork Report	*Report of the Review Committee on Insolvency Law and Practice* (1982) Cmnd 8558
CPR	Civil Procedure Rules 1998
CRTPA 1999	Contracts (Rights of Third Parties) Act 1999
CVA	Company voluntary arrangement
DA 2015	Deregulation Act 2015
DAA 1914	Deeds of Arrangement Act 1914
DPO 1986	Administration of Insolvent Estates of Deceased Persons Order 1986 (SI 1986/1999)
DRO	Debt relief order
EA 2002	Enterprise Act 2002
EC Regulation	EC Regulation on Insolvency Proceedings 2000/1346
ECHR	European Convention on Human Rights and Fundamental Freedoms
ERRA 2013	Enterprise and Regulatory Reform Act 2013
EU Regulation	EU Regulation on Insolvency Proceedings, Reg. 2015/848, OJ L141/19 (aka the 'Recast Regulation')
EUWAA 2020	European Union (Withdrawal Agreement) Act 2020
FCA	Financial Conduct Authority
HMLR	Her Majesty's Land Registry
HMRC	Her Majesty's Revenue and Customs
IA 1986	Insolvency Act 1986
IA 2000	Insolvency Act 2000
IAEUER 2019	Insolvency (Amendment) (EU Exit) Regulations 2019 (SI 2019/146)

ICAEW	Institute of Chartered Accountants of England and Wales
IP	Insolvency practitioner
IPA	Insolvency Practitioners Association
IPD	Practice Direction on Insolvency Proceedings (July 2020) [2020] BPIR 1211
IPO 1994	Insolvent Partnerships Order 1994 (SI 1994/2421)
IPR 2005	Insolvency Practitioners Regulations 2005 (SI 2005/524)
IR 1986	Insolvency Rules 1986 (SI 1986/1925)
IR 2016	Insolvency (England and Wales) Rules 2016 (SI 2016/1024)
IVA	Individual voluntary arrangement
OR	Official Receiver
PVA	Partnership voluntary arrangement
R3	The Association of Business Recovery Professionals
RPB	Recognised professional body
SBEEA 2015	Small Business, Enterprise and Employment Act 2015
SI	Statutory instrument
SIP	Statement of Insolvency Practice
Standard Conditions	R3 Standard IVA Conditions (Version 4, January 2018)
TCEA 2007	Tribunals, Courts and Enforcement Act 2007

TABLE OF CASES

TABLE OF LEGISLATION

UK STATUTORY INSTRUMENTS

EUROPEAN LEGISLATION

PART I

OVERVIEW

1

INTRODUCTION

A. SCOPE OF THIS WORK

1.01 This book is concerned with the law of England and Wales pertaining to the personal insolvency regime known as the individual voluntary arrangement (IVA). It is primarily aimed at practitioners working in the field of insolvency and those who, while not necessarily operating in that field, need to understand more about the nature, effect and procedures of IVAs.

1.02 The IVA is a formal statute-based debt relief mechanism available to individual debtors that was first introduced by the Insolvency Act 1986 (IA 1986) as an alternative to bankruptcy. The IVA procedure aims to provide a mechanism, broadly contractual in nature, underpinned by statutory rules, whereby an individual can enter into a binding arrangement with their creditors as a whole without having to deal with each creditor individually.[1] The scheme is designed to be relatively 'court-lite': although the court exercises an overarching control function and remains the arbiter of disputes, it has little involvement in the normal course of the process.[2] Rather, the entire process

---

1   This is the effect of s 260(2) of IA 1986. See further below [2.14].
2   Other than in relation to interim orders, on which see Chapter 6 below.

comes under the guidance and supervision of a qualified licensed Insolvency Practitioner (IP) throughout, initially in the role of nominee and, following the approval of the arrangement, as supervisor; the office holder is, in turn, ultimately answerable to and under the control of the court.

A similar, albeit subtly different, statutory debt relief mechanism is available **1.03** to individual debtors in Northern Ireland;[3] in Scotland there is an equivalent regime, although it is placed on a rather different footing;[4] both are outside the scope of this work. A comparable regime, essentially analogous to the IVA, also exists for companies under IA 1986, known as a company voluntary arrangement (CVA).[5] This work is not concerned with CVAs, as such; but, although there are necessarily a number of differences between the two regimes, the case law in relation to CVAs is often highly relevant to IVAs (and vice versa), so that this case law necessarily forms an important source for the interpretation of the law pertaining to IVAs.

IVAs may be entered into by the individual partners of an insolvent partner- **1.04** ship, as an alternative to bankruptcy. Where the partners propose their own IVAs, the partnership itself may also enter into a parallel voluntary arrange- ment, known as a partnership voluntary arrangement (PVA).[6] The two pro- cesses work in tandem, in much the same way as a partnership may be wound up and the individual partners made bankrupt in tandem. The mechanisms and procedures involved in dealing with such IVAs are broadly the same as those that pertain to individuals not involved in a partnership, as described in this work, with the additional complications inherent in the overlying partner- ship structure and the parallel PVA proceedings.[7] PVAs, as such, are outside the scope of this work.

The work is divided into five parts. Part I provides an overview of the IVA **1.05** regime and analyses the context in which it operates while the remaining four parts examine different aspects or stages of the IVA regime in turn. Part II explains how the proposal and accompanying documents are put together and

---

3   Under Part 8, Chapter 2 of the Insolvency (Northern Ireland) Order 1989 (NISI 1989/2405). On the signif- icance of the differences between the two jurisdictions, see *Bank of Ireland Mortgage Bank v Sheridan* [2015] NICh 12; [2015] BPIR 1001.

4   IA 1986, s 440(2)(b); see the Debt Arrangement and Attachment (Scotland) Act 2002 and various statutory instruments made thereunder and/or in connection with the Bankruptcy (Scotland) Act 2016.

5   IA 1986, Part 1. (Although, when originally enacted, the Parts of IA 1986 were designated by Roman numerals, the modern convention, adopted in this book, is to use Arabic numerals.)

6   Under Part 1 of IA 1986, as modified by the Insolvent Partnership Order 1994, SI 1994/2421 (IPO 1994), art 4 and Sch 1 (as amended).

7   IPO 1994, art 5.

what they need to cover; Part III considers the two alternative routes open to the debtor to initiate the procedure (either with or without an interim order) and explains the differences between them; Part IV analyses the procedures involved in the creditors' decision and how this may be challenged; Part V examines the implementation and supervision of the IVA and when and how it may come to an end.

B. THE LEGAL FRAMEWORK

1. Legislative and regulatory infrastructure

(a) The core statutory provisions

1.06 The legislative infrastructure for IVAs is principally located in IA 1986, supplemented by a set of bespoke rules, currently located in the Insolvency (England and Wales) Rules 2016 (IR 2016).[8] This statutory framework has been modified on a number of occasions since IA 1986 first came into force, in particular by the Insolvency Act 2000 (IA 2000), by the Enterprise Act 2002 (EA 2002) and then by the legislative reforms of 2015 brought in by the Deregulation Act 2015 (DA 2015) and the Small Business, Enterprise and Employment Act 2015 (SBEEA 2015). The nature and impact of these reforms will be considered in their appropriate context later in this book.

(i) The Insolvency Act

1.07 The primary statutory provisions governing the IVA procedure are located in Part 8 of IA 1986, comprising sections 252–263 (as amended from time to time). In addition to Part 8, a number of other provisions in IA 1986, especially in the second group of parts (dealing with individual insolvency) are likely to be of direct or indirect relevance. Of particular relevance are the general provisions in Part 10 of IA 1986. These include the provisions governing the expanded creditors' decision procedures and the requirements in relation to office holders' notices that were introduced by SBEEA 2015.[9] Also included within Part 10 are specific provisions dealing with the supply of utilities, including some that are concerned exclusively with circumstances

---

8   SI 2016/1024: see below [1.11].

9   SBEEA 2015, s 123, inserting ss 379ZA–379ZC into IA 1986, replacing the more limited remote meetings provisions in s 379A with effect from 6 April 2017; s 379B, governing the use of websites by office-holders (which, like the now defunct s 379A, was introduced in 2010), remains in force; a new s 379C, providing creditor opt-out with regard to notices, must be read together with s 383A, both of which were inserted by SBEEA 2015, s 125.

that may arise upon the approval of an IVA.[10] Part 10 of IA 1986 also contains provisions dealing with jurisdiction and insolvency districts.[11]

Most importantly, Part 10 of IA 1986 also includes section 375, which governs **1.08** both the court's ability to review, rescind or vary earlier orders and also appeals.[12] The former is a form of discretionary relief unique to insolvency law,[13] which requires there to have been a material change of circumstances since the original order was made and in relation to which it is possible to adduce further evidence not before the court at the initial hearing under review.[14] The latter function much like appeals in any other context: they apply where the decision below was wrong for reasons that should have been apparent to the court below and fresh evidence is generally excluded; the procedure is essentially governed by Part 52 of the Civil Procedure Rules 1998 (as amended) (CPR),[15] supplemented by the Practice Direction on Insolvency Proceedings (IPD),[16] although there are also specific rules included within IR 2016.[17]

In relation to other parts of IA 1986, the definitions supplied in sections **1.09** 382–385 and 436 of IA 1986 are highly relevant;[18] other provisions in Parts 11 and 18 also have some bearing in certain circumstances – likewise, those of Part 12 (sections 386 and 387(5), read together with Schedule 6), dealing with preferential debts. Part 13, dealing with the authorisation and regulation of IPs generally, applies in the context of IVAs and in particular section 388 (as amended);[19] section 389A, which related specifically to IVAs, has been repealed.[20] Section 389B allows the Official Receiver (OR) to perform the functions of nominee and supervisor in relation to the IVA of an undischarged bankrupt.[21] In addition to this, sections 399–401 in Part 14, in relation to the OR generally may sometimes be relevant. The provisions of Part 16 of IA 1986, comprising sections 423–425 (applications relating to transactions intended to defraud creditors) apply in the context of IVAs and IVA super-

---

10   See below [11.07].
11   IA 1986, ss 373 and 374, respectively.
12   IA 1986, s 375(1) and (2), respectively.
13   For the equivalent jurisdiction in corporate insolvency, see IR 2016, r 12.59(1). Cases decided under the latter provision may be of assistance in determining the ambit of s 375(1) of IA 1986.
14   See generally the guidance offered in *Papanicola v Humphreys* [2005] EWHC 335 (Ch); [2005] 2 All ER 418, and in *Raguz v Scottish & Newcastle Ltd* [2010] EWHC 1384 (Ch), [2010] BPIR 945.
15   IR 2016, r 12.58. On the CPR generally, see below [1.15].
16   IPD 2020, para 17.
17   IR 2016, r 12.61 (on permission and time limits).
18   Although the application of IA 1986, s 382 is qualified: see Chapter 2 below.
19   IA 1986, s 388 was modified by IA 2000 with effect from 1 January 2003.
20   S 389A, inserted by IA 2000, was repealed by DA 2015, with effect from 1 October 2015.
21   IA 1986, s 389B was inserted by EA 2002: see below [11.02].

visors are specifically mentioned as being among those who have standing to make an application under section 423.[22]

1.10 Some of the provisions of Part 9 of IA 1986, concerned with bankruptcy, are directly relevant to IVAs: see especially sections 264(1)(c), 276 and 291A(2)–(4), in relation to bankruptcy petitions in the context of an IVA.[23] Until 6 April 2016 there were also provisions allowing a more circuitous route to an IVA, though this was abolished by the Enterprise and Regulatory Reform Act 2013 (ERRA 2013).[24] Other provisions in Part 9 potentially have an indirect relevance, not least in order to determine the appropriateness of an IVA in the first place. When formulating the terms of the proposal, it will often be helpful to bear in mind the provisions of Part 9, even though strictly speaking they do not apply to IVAs.

(ii) The Insolvency Rules

1.11 The provisions of IA 1986 are supplemented and qualified by the Insolvency Rules. Originally these were contained in the Insolvency Rules 1986 (IR 1986),[25] Part 5 of which was dedicated to the IVA procedure. Alongside the significant overhaul of the IVA regime implemented by IA 2000, the original Part 5 of IR 1986 was replaced with effect from 1 January 2003 by a new Part 5 which substantially recast the relevant rules.[26] These changes were not retrospective and only affected arrangements entered into after that date. Similarly, there were further amendments made following the changes brought in by EA 2002.[27] Further modifications were also introduced by the Insolvency (Amendment) Rules 2010.[28] The entirety of IR 1986 was subsequently repealed and replaced by IR 2016, with effect from 6 April 2017. The principal rules governing the IVA procedure are now to be found in Part 8 of IR 2016.

1.12 Beyond the specific rules in Part 8 of IR 2016, a number of other rules are likely to be relevant to some extent. The general provisions, located in Part 1 and Part 12 of IR 2016, apply to all forms of insolvency under Parts 1 to 11 of IA 1986, including IVAs. Beyond these, the most directly relevant rules are those governing decision making in Part 15 of IR 2016. Also relevant are the provisions of Part 11 dealing with the insolvency register, in particular rules

---

22   IA 1986, s 424(1)(b). See below [9.37]–[9.38].
23   See Chapter 12 below.
24   IA 1986, ss 273 and 274.
25   SI 1986/1925.
26   Introduced by the Insolvency (Amendment) (No.2) Rules 2002, SI 2002/2712.
27   By the Insolvency (Amendment) Rules 2003, SI 2003/1730.
28   SI 2010/686 (as amended).

11.14–11.15 and 11.22–11.23. Although not strictly applicable to IVAs, the provisions of IR 2016, r 14.2, governing debts provable in a bankruptcy, are likely to be at least indirectly relevant.[29] Part 17 also does not apply to IVAs, but where it is decided that a creditors' committee will be set up for the purposes of the IVA, these provisions will usually be at least indirectly relevant. Part 20 (in relation to non-disclosure of addresses in cases where there is a risk of violence), in particular rules 20.2 and 20.3, can apply in specific circumstances.

(b) Other UK legislation

Numerous other enactments will, from time to time, become relevant in the specific circumstances of any particular IVA to a greater or lesser extent. An obvious example of secondary legislation affecting IVAs is the Insolvency Practitioners Regulations 2005 (IPR 2005),[30] dealing with various aspects of the requirements and practicalities of how nominees and supervisors conduct themselves.[31] Other statutory instruments will apply only to a minority of IVAs, including the Administration of Insolvent Estates of Deceased Persons Order 1986 (DPO 1986).[32]   **1.13**

(c) European legislation

Insolvency law in England and Wales has been affected by the UK's membership of the European Union. In particular, the provisions of IA 1986 and its accompanying rules have had to accommodate the provisions of the EC Regulation on Insolvency Proceedings 2000 (the EC Regulation),[33] and its successor, the EU Regulation on Insolvency Proceedings 2015 (EU Regulation).[34] As a result of the UK's withdrawal from the EU and the effects of the European Union (Withdrawal Agreement) Act 2020 (EUWAA 2020) and the Insolvency (Amendment) (EU Exit) Regulations 2019 (IAEUER 2019),[35] the legislative framework has once again been amended so as to reflect the fact that the UK is no longer bound by the EU Regulation as of 11pm on 31 December 2020. Other than in relation to jurisdiction,[36] however, these   **1.14**

---

29   See further Chapter 2 below.
30   SI 2005/524.
31   Particularly in relation to the requirement to be bonded and also record-keeping (on which see below [11.17]–[11.19]).
32   SI 1986/1999: see Chapter 3 below.
33   Council Regulation (EC) on Insolvency Proceedings No. 1346/2000 (OJ L 160), which came into force on 31 May 2002: see below [1.23].
34   EU Regulation 2015/848, OJ L141/19 (also known as the 'Recast Regulation'), which came into force on 26 June 2017: see below [1.23].
35   SI 2019/146 (as amended).
36   See below [1.24].

changes have had less impact on IVAs than on other areas of insolvency law, such as bankruptcy or liquidation.

(d) Other rules, directions and guidance

(i) The CPR

1.15 Notwithstanding that insolvency proceedings, including IVAs, are governed primarily by their own dedicated rules, currently IR 2016, the general civil court procedures as laid down in the CPR remain substantially relevant in many respects.[37] IR 2016 specifically applies the provisions of the CPR to insolvency proceedings (including IVAs), with any necessary modifications, except so far as disapplied by or inconsistent with the provisions of IR 2016.[38]

1.16 All insolvency proceedings are automatically allocated to the multi-track for the purposes of the CPR, rendering the CPR provisions in relation to directions questionnaires and allocation to track inapplicable.[39] The CPR provisions on statements of truth and the consequences of making false statements in documents so verified apply equally to any documents for which such verification is required under IR 2016.[40] Part 57A of the CPR, relating to the Business and Property Courts of England and Wales (BPC), applies to any court proceedings in connection with IVAs brought in those courts; in particular, it should be noted that Practice Direction 57AC, which governs the preparation of witness statements for use at trial in the BPC, only applies to such proceedings if the court at any stage in those proceedings orders that it should.[41] Regarding the calculation of time, IR 2016 largely incorporates the provisions of CPR 2.8 in relation to periods expressed in days, adding some further stipulations of its own in relation to periods expressed in months.[42] Subject to time limits expressly stated in IA 1986 and to any specific powers under IA 1986 or IR 2016 in relation to extending or shortening time, the provisions of CPR 3.1(2)(a) are specifically incorporated.[43]

---

37 IR 2016, made pursuant to ss 411 and 412 of IA 1986, only covers insolvency proceedings under Parts 1–11 of IA 1986 (IR 2016, r 1.1); in consequence, proceedings under other parts of IA 1986 (including Part 16) are governed solely by the CPR: *Manolete Partners Plc v Hayward and Barrett Holdings Ltd* [2021] EWHC 1481 (Ch).

38 IR 2016, r 12.1(1); note also r 12.58 (see above [1.08]).

39 IR 2016, r 12.1(2).

40 IR 2016, r 12.1(3).

41 CPR, PD57AC, para 1.3(3).

42 See IR 2016, Sch 5, paras 1–2 (but, curiously, CPR 2.8(4), which excludes weekends and bank holidays from calculations of time of less than five days, is expressly excluded by IR 2016, Sch 5, paras 1, possibly on the basis that IA 1986 and IR 2016 tend to express time limits in terms of 'business days').

43 IR 2016, Sch 5, paras 3–4. See, in addition, IA 1986, s 376 (which deals exclusively with extending time).

(ii) The Insolvency Practice Direction

Insolvency proceedings are also governed by the Insolvency Practice Direction **1.17** (IPD), which is updated from time to time. The IPD became significantly out of step with the rules for a period following the introduction of IR 2016 in April 2017, a problem that was further compounded by the introduction of the Business and Property Courts of England and Wales in 2018. The IPD was substantially recast in July 2018, bringing it much more into line with IR 2016, since when a slightly amended version was issued in July 2020.[44] Other than directions in connection with interim orders and associated orders and guidance as to when such orders may be made on paper, there is little in the IPD that has any direct bearing on IVAs, but the practitioner will need to be aware of its terms.[45]

(iii) Professional guidance

IPs are members of and are regulated by a number of recognised professional **1.18** bodies (RPBs) that license them and provide them with professional guidance.[46] Prominent among these are the Insolvency Practitioners Association (IPA) and the Institute of Chartered Accountants of England and Wales (ICAEW). The Joint Insolvency Committee, which collectively represents the RPBs, has published a series of professional guidance notes, entitled 'Statement of Insolvency Practice' (SIP), which are updated from time to time.[47] These deal with a range of issues, including remuneration and reporting, but there are two SIPs specifically aimed at guidance in connection with voluntary arrangements: SIP 3 (Voluntary Arrangements) and SIP 3.1 (Individual Voluntary Arrangements).[48] SIPs do not carry the force of law; rather, they amount to statements of best practice, representing the standards of professional conduct expected of IPs, and are recognised by the courts as such.[49] Another source of guidance for IPs is the Code of Ethics published by the IPA.[50] This includes a number of overarching 'Fundamental Principles' by which the professional standards of IPs should be judged: integrity, objectivity (including avoiding bias, conflicts of interest and undue influence), professional competence and

---

44 [2020] BPIR 1211. References in this work are to the July 2020 version.

45 See Chapter 6 below. In response to the Covid-19 pandemic, a Temporary Insolvency Practice Direction (TIPD) was issued in April 2020 (and subsequently updated), but its only relevance to IVAs was in connection with the listing of applications.

46 IA 1986, ss 390A and 391.

47 Available, for example, on the ICAEW website.

48 SIP 3 was more or less superseded, with regard to IVAs, by SIP 3.1, but it remains relevant.

49 See *Brewer v Iqbal* [2019] EWHC 182 (Ch), at [80].

50 Last updated in 2014. See *Re One Blackfriars Ltd* [2021] EWHC 684 (Ch), at [252], for judicial recognition of the importance of the Code.

due care, confidentiality (in particular, preserving the confidentiality of any information acquired in the course of the IP's office) and professional behaviour (ensuring their conduct is lawful and does not discredit the profession and also treating others with courtesy and consideration).[51] Further relevant guidance is also offered by the Association of Business Recovery Professionals (R3) and by the Insolvency Service.[52]

2. Judicial interpretation

1.19   The IVA is a creature of statute, but the interpretation of the underlying statutory framework has been developed over the decades by the courts, and in order to understand how the legislative infrastructure is to be applied it is necessary to take account of the jurisprudence in relation to voluntary arrangements.[53] The IVA, as it was originally set out in Part 8 of IA 1986 and the supporting rules (IR 1986), represented a new departure for debt relief regimes,[54] but the courts have, where appropriate, been prepared to draw on earlier jurisprudence to assist in the statutory construction of the new regime.[55] That said, it is also important to bear in mind that the courts were at pains to stress in the years following the enactment of IA 1986 that it was not a consolidating Act and its provisions and those of the rules that support it must be interpreted in a way that is unfettered by the law as it existed beforehand.[56]

1.20   There has been some debate, both in judicial pronouncements and elsewhere, as to the correct approach the court should adopt in construing the terms of any particular IVA, its meaning and effect and the validity of the arrangement itself. In the first decade of this century a technical approach prevailed.[57] More recently, this has come to be viewed as overly rigid and the current orthodoxy favours a more liberal approach, adopting a purposive construction of the statutory framework.[58] There is perhaps a danger, if this more liberal approach is pressed too far, of ending up imposing upon debtors an arrangement that

---

51   Code of Ethics, para 4(a)–(e).
52   See further below at [1.32] and [1.50].
53   Including CVAs (see above [1.03]).
54   See [1.26] below.
55   See, for example, the judgment of Zacaroli J in *Lazari Properties 2 Ltd v New Look Retailers Ltd* [2021] EWHC 1209 (Ch), [2021] BPIR 920.
56   See *Re a Debtor (No.1 of 1987)* [1989] 1 WLR 271; and specifically in the context of IVAs, *Johnson v Davis* [1999] Ch 117, at 137F–G, *per* Chadwick LJ.
57   Typified by *Re Plumber* [2004] BPIR 767.
58   See *Smith-Evans v Smailes* [2013] EWHC 3199 (Ch); *Davis v Price* [2014] EWCA Civ 26; both relied on at first instance in *Narandas-Girdhar v Bradstock* [2014] EWHC 1321 (Ch); [2014] BPIR 1014, which was subsequently affirmed on appeal: *Narandas-Girdhar v Bradstock* [2016] EWCA Civ 88, [2016] 1 WLR 2366. For a fuller discussion of this last and where it leaves *Re Plumber* (above), see below [9.10]–[9.12].

might not be what they had actually agreed to, in extreme cases resulting in what has been described as an 'involuntary arrangement'.[59] Nevertheless, despite such criticism, the prevailing approach does at least have the advantage of avoiding the invalidation of IVAs on what many would regard as technical grounds.

3. Eligibility and jurisdiction

To be eligible to enter into an IVA, the debtor must be an individual who is **1.21** either an undischarged bankrupt or is able to make an application for their own bankruptcy.[60] The former condition is strict, so that even if the debtor is an undischarged bankrupt at the start of the process, if they subsequently receive their discharge prior to the approval of their proposal, they cease to be eligible to enter into an IVA in relation to their bankruptcy debts, since these will have been released on discharge.[61] The timescale is tight: unless discharge has been suspended, it will automatically take place after one year following the making of the bankruptcy order.[62]

These conditions ensure that the IVA regime is not available to solvent debtors **1.22** as a means of restructuring their debts. They also effectively require the debtor to satisfy the jurisdictional tests that apply in bankruptcy, since the individual must already be bankrupt or must be eligible to apply for their own bankruptcy.[63] Essentially, these jurisdictional tests are concerned with whether the debtor has sufficient connection with England and Wales. Those tests have changed as a result of the UK's withdrawal from the EU. To understand this properly, it is necessary to review the history of amendments to these jurisdictional provisions.

Originally, the bankruptcy jurisdiction test was satisfied if the debtor was **1.23** domiciled in England and Wales, or at any time in the three years preceding the presentation of the petition or the issue of the application (as the case may be) had been ordinarily resident or had a place of residence in England and Wales, or had carried on a business in England and Wales (the Domestic

---

59   See S Barber in [2014] 27 Insolv. Int. 133.
60   IA 1986, ss 255(1) and 256A(3).
61   IA 1986, s 281(1): see *Wright v Official Receiver* [2001] BPIR 196; *Re Ravichandran* [2004] BPIR 814. See also *Demarco v Perkins and Bulley Davey* [2006] EWCA Civ 188, [2006] BPIR 645 (but cf. below [10.06]). For the correct procedure to work around this, see below at [7.24]; in relation to the duty owed to the debtor by the nominee in this regard, see also below at [10.21].
62   IA 1986, s 279.
63   Currently, IA 1986, s 263I, inserted by ERRA 2013 with effect from 6 April 2016. Prior to that, the condition referred to debtor petitions under s 265 (as then in force).

Tests).[64] Following the adoption of the EC Regulation, these provisions became subject to Article 3 of that Regulation, which introduced the concept of the debtor's centre of main interests (COMI) into UK law.[65] With effect from 6 April 2016, the reforms introduced by ERRA 2013 recast the test so as to prioritise the location of the debtor's COMI: if the debtor's COMI was in England and Wales, the test was satisfied;[66] otherwise, if the debtor's COMI was not within an EU member state (other than Denmark), jurisdiction could be satisfied via the Domestic Tests.[67] When the EU Regulation superseded the EC Regulation, with effect from 26 June 2017, the test was amended to refer instead to the EU Regulation.[68]

1.24 As a result of Brexit and the EUWAA 2020, the UK ceased to be a member state of the European Union and the EU Regulation no longer had direct application in the UK as from 11pm on 31 December 2020 (the end of the Transition Period). Instead, in relation to any proceedings opened thereafter, a unilaterally modified version of the EU Regulation was incorporated into UK law and now applies to insolvency proceedings in England and Wales.[69] Simultaneously, amendments to reflect the UK's withdrawal from the EU and the EU Regulation were made to IA 1986 and to IR 2016, including some specifically relating to IVAs.[70] Among these statutory amendments were changes to sections 263I and 265 of IA 1986.[71] These amendments have the effect of subtly altering the jurisdictional test to be applied to bankruptcies commenced or 'opened' after the end of the Transition Period, so as to provide three alternatives: either the debtor's COMI is in England and Wales, or their COMI is in a member state of the EU (other than Denmark) and they have

---

64   IA 1986, s 265(1)(a) and (c), as enacted; 'carrying on a business' was glossed in s 265(2). In addition, jurisdiction was satisfied if the debtor was personally present in England and Wales on the day on which the petition was presented (s 265(1)(b)), but this test was removed by ERRA 2013 (as of 6 April 2016) and is no longer relevant.

65   IA 1986, s 265(3), as inserted by the Insolvency Act 1986 (Amendment) (No.2) Regulations 2002 (SI 2002/1240), with effect from 31 May 2002, which thereby also introduced the concepts of 'main' and 'territorial' proceedings into UK law (as defined in Art 3 of the EC Regulation).

66   IA 1986, s 265(1)(a), as substituted, and s 263I(1)(a), as inserted by ERRA 2013. 'COMI' was defined by reference to Art 3 of the EC Regulation (s 265(4), as then inserted).

67   IA 1986, s 265(1)(b), as substituted, and (2), as renumbered, as well as s 263I(1)(b) and (2), as inserted by ERRA 2013. The gloss on 'carrying on a business' in what had been s 265(2) was now renumbered as s 265(3) and reproduced in s 263I(3). Denmark was exempted because it never signed up to the EC Regulation (nor, later, the EU Regulation).

68   IA 1986, s 265(1)(b) and (4) and s 263I(1)(b) and (4) amended by the Insolvency Amendment (EU 2015/848) Regulations 2017 (SI 2017/ 702).

69   By IAEUER 2019, Sch 1, Part 1.

70   IR 2016, rr 8.3 and 8.19, as amended by IAEUER 2019, Sch 1, Part 4, paras 84–85; but cf. IR 2016, r 8.24 (below at [8.48]).

71   IAEUER 2019, Sch 1, Part 2, paras 31 and 33, respectively.

an establishment (as defined by Art 2(10) of the EU Regulation) in England and Wales or the Domestic Tests apply. This affects any IVA approved after that date.

C. VOLUNTARY ARRANGEMENTS IN CONTEXT

1. An historical perspective

Until the overhaul of insolvency legislation in the mid-1980s, there were few **1.25** mechanisms available to debtors who wished to try to avoid bankruptcy and these alternatives were scarcely attractive. Besides informal arrangements, that by their nature have always been precarious, there were county court administration orders, which only related to minor debts, formal schemes of composition or arrangement under the Bankruptcy Act 1914 (BA 1914)[72] and deeds of arrangement entered into under the Deeds of Arrangement Act 1914 (DAA 1914). These all had very limited application and even more limited appeal. Schemes of composition or arrangement under the BA 1914 only came into play once a receiving order had been made and were rarely successful. Deeds of arrangement tended to be both cumbersome and of insufficient benefit to either debtors or their creditors; they afforded the debtor almost no protection, since any creditor minded to do so could still petition for the debtor's bankruptcy, which was made all the more likely by the fact that entering into such a deed in itself constituted an act of bankruptcy. In one form or another these statutory regimes had existed even before the codification in the 1914 legislation.[73] By the mid-1980s, however, these alternatives had largely fallen into disuse.

The Cork Report[74] recommended a new voluntary arrangement regime as part **1.26** of a radical reshaping of insolvency law. Within a raft of measures intended to promote what later came to be known as the rescue culture, the Report set out proposals for a new personal insolvency regime that was both more efficient and more effective than those enshrined in the 1914 legislation. The main thrust of those proposals, although not in precisely the form originally envisaged, eventually became Part 8 of IA 1986. Following the enactment of IA 1986, schemes of composition or arrangement under the BA 1914 disappeared with the repeal of that Act. For many years thereafter, however, it

---

72 BA 1914, ss 16, 17 and 21.
73 On the historical development of these antecedents to the IVA, see the comments of Zacaroli J in *Lazari Properties 2 Ltd v New Look Retailers Ltd* [2021] EWHC 1209 (Ch), [2021] BPIR 920, at [68]–[72].
74 *Report of the Review Committee on Insolvency Law and Practice* (1982) Cmnd 8558.

still remained possible, at least in theory, to enter into a deed of arrangement under the DAA 1914 as an alternative statutory mechanism to the new IVA. In practice, however, the DAA 1914 regime was almost totally ignored and the deed of arrangement scheme effectively fell by the wayside. Finally, after many years of neglect, the DAA 1914 was formally repealed in 2015.[75]

1.27   When the IVA was first introduced in 1986, it was a necessary prerequisite of any IVA for the debtor first to obtain an interim order from the court. It was held in *Fletcher v Vooght*[76] that not only was this step mandatory but that its omission could not be cured by a retrospective order. As originally conceived in the 1986 legislation, the interim order had the dual purpose of providing both a moratorium, to protect the debtor's position while the proposal could be put to creditors, and also formal court sanction. The court was required to review the nominee's report on the proposal and be satisfied as to the viability of the proposal and the utility of putting it to the creditors before it would allow the matter to proceed to a creditors' decision.

1.28   The IVA regime proved much more popular than its predecessors, but it was felt that the interim order procedure was unnecessarily cumbersome. As a result, an alternative mechanism was proposed whereby the debtor need not apply to the court for an interim order but, as long as the nominee's report was positive, could proceed instead directly to laying the proposal before the creditors for their approval. This alternative mechanism was brought into existence by IA 2000, which inserted section 256A into IA 1986 with effect from 1 January 2003.[77] IA 2000 did not abolish the old interim order mechanism, and in certain circumstances it remained, and still remains, the preferable option, but the new mechanism quickly established itself as the more favoured route. Whilst this reform has made the entire process more accessible to and more efficient for debtors, it does also have the disadvantage of removing from the process an initial level of court scrutiny.[78]

1.29   Further reforms were introduced by EA 2002. One of the more innovative of these was a variant 'Fast Track' scheme, brought into play by the insertion of sections 263A to 263G into IA 1986 with effect from April 2004. This regime proved to be highly unsatisfactory and quickly fell into disuse; it was finally abolished by SBEEA 2015.

---

75   By DA 2015.
76   [2000] BPIR 435.
77   For the two mechanisms and how they work, see Part III of this work below.
78   See below [6.25] and [7.25].

In its original conception, as envisaged in the Cork Report, the IVA regime **1.30** presupposed that each arrangement would be tailored to the particular needs of the individual debtor and once approved would remain under the individual care of a dedicated, suitably qualified IP, who, as supervisor, would closely monitor the progress of the arrangement and the conduct of the debtor. In practice this rarely happens. In the first decade of the twenty-first century, following the relaxation of the system introduced by the IA 2000 reforms, an entire industry grew up solely for the purpose of providing the service of setting up and running of IVAs. Since 2007, IVAs have increasingly become handled by volume providers that process these arrangements on something like an industrial scale (indeed they are sometimes referred to as IVA 'factories'), with little or no recognition of the particular requirements of each case. Typically, such establishments are headed by an IP who in effect simply delegates the task of supervising the numerous IVAs to a large body of unqualified staff who operate with no, or scarcely any, supervision from the IP. Almost by their very nature, these providers have fostered bad practices, which, in turn, have led to a very significant failure rate.[79]

In the early part of this century the relatively high failure rate of IVAs gave rise **1.31** to some concerns that IVAs were either being put forward in circumstances where they were not suitable or that they were being poorly administered or that the costs of most IVAs were unnecessarily high. These concerns prompted three developments that were intended to address aspects of these perceived ills.

First, the Insolvency Service proposed a set of proposals for simplified and **1.32** streamlined versions of the IVA known as 'SIVA'. The proposals first saw light of day in 2005, but were abandoned in 2008 without ever being implemented, in part because the need for these reforms had somewhat abated due to the apparent success of the second initiative, the introduction of the IVA Protocol. The IVA Protocol is in essence a guide to best practice for the industry in relation to straightforward consumer IVAs. It was initially launched at the beginning of 2008 and has been amended from time to time since.[80] This must be viewed against the context that, in recent years, growth in consumer credit borrowing has significantly outstripped growth in gross domestic product (GDP) as a whole and this margin has persisted even while both figures fell

---

79   See *Insolvency Service Report on Monitoring and Regulation of IPs* (September 2018).
80   The IVA Protocol is available on the Insolvency Service website. See also below [1.39] and more fully at [4.08]–[4.10].

during the 2020 pandemic.[81] The third initiative was the introduction by R3 of a template, usually referred to as the Standard Conditions, that provides a set of model terms that can be adapted to form a basis for virtually any proposal.[82]

1.33 The latter two initiatives did help to improve the position. It is, however, clear that the ills that were identified in the first decade of this century have not gone away. Although the courts rarely get the opportunity to scrutinise such activities, such cases as do come before the courts show that these problems continue to plague the system.[83] This is undoubtedly in part due to the increasing prevalence of volume providers and may also owe something to the multiplicity of RPBs providing advice and regulation in relation to IVAs.[84]

2. A statistical analysis

1.34 IVAs are one of a number of debt relief mechanisms that are available to individual debtors. These range from bankruptcy at one end of the spectrum to informal arrangements reached between a debtor and their creditors at the other. In 2009, a new form of formal debt relief procedure was introduced (in what became Part 7A of IA 1986) in the form of the Debt Relief Order (DRO).[85] The DRO was introduced as a relatively low-cost alternative to bankruptcy for individuals with low levels of debt and only modest income and assets.[86] By 2013 the number of DROs surpassed the number of bankruptcy orders made for the first time and the margin by which the number of DROs has exceeded the number of bankruptcies has continued to widen ever since. Both bankruptcies and DROs are, however, dwarfed by the number of IVAs.

1.35 Since their introduction in the mid-1980s, IVAs have become increasingly popular as an alternative to bankruptcy. The number of IVAs varies from one year to the next, both in absolute and in relative terms, but the trend in recent years has been markedly, although not consistently, upward. According to the

---

81   See The Woolard Review – A Review of Change and Innovation in the Unsecured Credit Market, published by the Financial Conduct Authority (FCA) in February 2021 (the Woolard Review), para 1.5. The Woolard Review is available on the FCA website: www.fca.org.uk.

82   Available at www.r3.org.uk. See Chapter 4 below.

83   See *Varden Nuttall Ltd v Nuttall* [2018] EWHC 3868 (Ch), [2019] BPIR 738 (a case largely concerned with inadequate record keeping and accounting systems and lack of supervision: see below [11.29]); and *Royal Bank of Scotland plc v Munikwa* [2020] EWHC 786 (Ch), on which see below [8.39].

84   See Woolard Review, para 2.31 and the Executive Summary at p 7; see further at [1.38] below.

85   Inserted by the Tribunals, Courts and Enforcement Act 2007 with effect from 6 April 2009. The provisions of Part 7A of IA 1986 are supported by what is now Part 9 of IR 2016.

86   The limits in relation to debts, surplus income and assets (since October 2015 set at £20,000, £50 per month and £1,000, respectively), are subject to periodic review and there is currently consultation regarding their being raised further.

official figures published on the Insolvency Service website, IVAs overtook bankruptcies as the most widely used mode of formal individual insolvency in 2011 and have retained that supremacy ever since. In Q3 of 2018 there was a temporary drop in the number of IVAs, but nevertheless the number of IVAs in 2018 as a whole surpassed 70,000, setting a new record, which amounted to more than half again as many as bankruptcies and DROs combined. This upward trend continued in 2019, which saw yet another new record number of IVAs for the year as a whole of almost 78,000, while the number of bankruptcies and DROs remained more or less the same as the previous year. The figures for 2020 are even more striking: while the numbers of DROs and, in particular, bankruptcies fell appreciably in that year, the total number of IVAs continued to increase, albeit modestly, so that the statistical margin grew appreciably, with IVAs becoming more than twice as popular as bankruptcies and DROs combined.

Naturally, it must be borne in mind that 2020 was a very unusual year, due to   **1.36**
the Coronavirus pandemic, and part of the explanation for the steep decline in bankruptcies in that year is that Government policies effectively reigned in HMRC, which in other years represented statistically the most prolific petitioner. While the overall number of formal personal insolvencies has continued to decline somewhat during the pandemic, the figures for Q1 and Q2 of 2021 show that the 'market share' for IVAs has continued to increase, so that there were over three times as many IVAs as DROs and bankruptcies combined during the first half of 2021. In absolute terms, the numbers of IVAs fell back very slightly in Q2 of 2021, but the overall trend does not appear to have been affected. There is no reason to suppose that the proportion of IVAs, compared to bankruptcies and DROs, will change dramatically in the near future.

The IVA statistics can also be broken down by geographical region and the age   **1.37**
and gender of the debtor. On the whole, and unsurprisingly, the more affluent the region, the fewer IVAs per capita: London and the South East have the lowest density of IVAs, while the North West and most especially the North East have the highest. In 2019 this regional variation was quite marked, but the North East consistently tops the list, while London has always been at the opposite end of the spectrum since such statistics began to be compiled in 2000. The majority of IVAs are entered into by the young and middle aged, with those aged between 25 and 34 and those aged between 35 and 44 being significantly the largest groups; moreover, these are the fastest growing groups, so that the dominance of this age-demographic is increasing. Historically, men were more likely to enter into IVAs, but the proportion of women entering an IVA has been steadily growing: by 2015 they had reached parity and in each

year since the number of female debtors entering into an IVA has exceeded the number of men.[87]

1.38 Concomitant with the increasing popularity of the IVA as the solution of choice to the debt crisis is the rise of the volume providers, as referred to above. In recent years this prevalence has grown to a disturbingly high proportion: the overwhelming majority of IVAs are now administered by such providers.[88] It is likely this is connected to the high proportion of IVA failure.

1.39 Statistics provided by the Insolvency Service show that the failure rate (measured by the percentage of IVAs that are terminated prematurely within the first year, the first two years and the first three years following approval) varies both geographically and according to the age of the debtor: those in the north and south of the country tend to be more likely to reach a successful conclusion than those located in between; on the whole, the older the debtor, the more likely the IVA is to succeed. Failure rates improved significantly after the introduction of the IVA Protocol in 2008. That trend, however, later went into reverse: IVAs registered between 2014 and 2017 were appreciably more likely to suffer early termination than those registered in the half decade before. That said, figures published by the Insolvency Service in 2021 suggest that the failure rate has begun to improve. This may in part be due to an updated version of the IVA Protocol, first published in April 2020 (and updated thereafter), intended to provide some relief in response to the Coronavirus pandemic by allowing a reduction in payments due from the debtor.[89] The overall prognosis, however, does not suggest robust health.[90]

1.40 IVAs are entered into by the debtor either in order to avoid bankruptcy or, following the making of a bankruptcy order, by the undischarged bankrupt with a view to annulling the bankruptcy.[91] The vast majority of IVAs fall into the former category: post-bankruptcy IVAs typically account for less than 5 per cent of the total number of all IVAs in any one year.

---

87   When further broken down by age group, the only group in which the number of men still exceeds that of women is in the over-65s.

88   The statistics published by the Insolvency Service (in February 2021) reveal that just 16 IVA providers accounted for over 90 per cent of the new IVAs registered in England and Wales in 2020.

89   Coronavirus (Covid-19) Guidance for the Straightforward Consumer IVA Protocol: see https://www .gov.uk/government/publications/covid-19-individual-voluntary-arrangement-iva-protocol-guidance/ coronavirus-covid-19-guidance-for-the-straightforward-consumer-iva-protocol.

90   See the somewhat pessimistic view expressed in the Woolard Review.

91   See above [1.21].

D. SUITABILITY

1. Weighing up the pros and cons

In many cases, there are likely to be advantages to the debtor in entering into **1.41** an IVA rather than becoming bankrupt. This is due to a number of factors. In part, the attraction of IVAs lies in their flexibility and the fact that the debtor has (within certain limits and subject to the creditors' approval) control over the terms of the IVA itself. For example, subject to principles of openness and fairness, the debtor can opt to deal with different classes of creditors in different ways.[92]

Another significant consideration for some debtors is that IVAs are likely to **1.42** have a less serious impact on their lives and especially their professional careers. Bankruptcy can result in the suspension of professional licences for solicitors and accountants. The Company Directors Disqualification Act 1986 (CDDA 1986) prohibits a bankrupt from acting as a company director, or being directly or even indirectly involved in the promotion, formation or management of a company, without the permission of the court.[93] Although entering an IVA can have consequences for professionals, its effect is likely to be appreciably less catastrophic.

A further distinction lies in the fact that, upon the making of a bankruptcy **1.43** order, the debtor's property (with minor exceptions) vests in the trustee in bankruptcy, whereas, under an IVA (unless the terms specify otherwise) the debtor's property rights are not interfered with. One way in which this makes a material difference is in relation to any claim the debtor may have made against another, or cause of action to bring such a claim.[94] A debtor who is subject to an IVA is entitled to pursue such claims in their own name and will often be required to do so for the benefit of the IVA creditors under the terms of the IVA. Moreover, a court would be very slow to accept, without a good deal more, that in pursuing such a claim the debtor is acting as a nominal debtor, for the purposes of ordering security for costs against them under CPR 25.13(2)(f).[95]

It is also easy to see why IVAs often present an attractive proposition for cred- **1.44** itors. On the whole, IVAs usually provide a tangibly better return for creditors

---

92   See below [2.01]–[2.11].
93   CDDA 1986, s 11.
94   See *Heath v Tang; Stevens v Peacock* [1993] 1 WLR 1421 (CA); *Ord v Upton* [2000] Ch 352.
95   *Envis v Thakkar* [1997] BPIR 189 (CA).

than would be the case were the debtor to be made bankrupt. Through the approval mechanism and the right to call for modifications to the proposal, creditors also potentially get the opportunity to have some say in relation to the terms of the IVA. It can therefore be seen that, in many cases, an IVA will provide a more beneficial outcome for both debtor and creditors.

1.45   On the other hand, an IVA is not necessarily the best solution in every case. There are likely to be some disadvantages for the debtor as well as advantages. Save in the most straightforward cases, IVAs usually last much longer than bankruptcies (typically five years, as opposed to bankruptcies, where the debtor is usually discharged after one year). It is also worth bearing in mind that entering into an IVA can have a severe effect on the debtor's credit rating. An IVA may require the debtor to contribute considerable sums into the kitty to be distributed amongst the IVA creditors, but at the same time leaves the debtor vulnerable to being sued or even made bankrupt by a creditor whose debt is not caught by the IVA (for example, because it arises during the course of the IVA). As noted above, many IVAs fail.[96] IVAs can be expensive and, especially if not carefully thought through at the outset, could easily end up making the debtor's financial position worse rather than providing a solution.

1.46   There may be circumstances, therefore, in which a debtor might be better advised to seek some other solution. Where the creditors are few in number, it might be possible to reach some form of more or less informal accommodation with them, including time-to-pay arrangements. In other cases, the debtor might actually be better off entering bankruptcy, either by making an application for their own bankruptcy or on the petition of a creditor. If the debts are small enough to qualify for a DRO, and if the debtor's means fall under the statutory threshold, it could be that a DRO would provide an acceptable alternative.[97]

1.47   It is therefore advisable for the debtor to weigh up all the pros and cons before deciding to pursue an IVA. Of course, time may not be on the debtor's side. Often circumstances have caught up with the debtor, such that the time needed to consider properly whether an IVA provides the right solution or to seek professional advice might be limited. As of 4 May 2021, a new statutory Debt Respite Scheme became available, whereby the debtor can avail themselves of a 'breathing space' in which to seek such advice and make the

---

96   See above [1.39].
97   It should be noted, however, that DROs are not available to a debtor who has entered into a transaction at an undervalue or given a preference: see IA 1986, Sch 4AZ.

right choices.[98] The details of these provisions and the procedures involved are beyond the scope of this work, but the Insolvency Service has published guidance that creditors and lenders may find useful.[99] How helpful these provisions will prove to be in terms of affording debtors the opportunity to reach the most appropriate solution to their debt problems and what impact (if any) that will have upon the failure rates of IVAs remain to be seen.

2. Professional advice

Given the desirability at the outset of seriously evaluating whether an IVA represents the best debt relief regime, and given the complexities and the bewildering variety of possible ways for an IVA proposal to be structured, it is highly recommended for anyone considering entering into an IVA with their creditors to obtain proper and informed professional advice from a qualified IP. In offering such advice, IPs are expected to adhere to the professional guidance set out in SIP 3 and SIP 3.1.[100] At this stage, the IP owes the debtor a duty of care.[101]   **1.48**

Logically, and in practice, it makes sense for the debtor to seek this advice from the IP who will act as nominee, although in theory there is nothing to preclude a debtor from seeking advice from one quarter and appointing a different IP (or IPs) as nominee. It follows that in most cases the first practical question for the debtor to resolve will be the choice of nominee. The choice of advisor/nominee will depend on a number of factors, including price and the experience or expertise of the advisor in dealing with the debtor's circumstances. Whether an IVA is suitable and, if so, what form the proposal should take will vary considerably depending on the debtor's circumstances. Many IVAs arise in the context of consumer debt; others may arise in other situations, such as that of a sole-trader with significant business debts. Together, the debtor and advisor will need to establish the complete picture of the debtor's financial position, the extent and nature of their liabilities and of the assets and potential income that could be made available to meet them and the extent of the shortfall. Only once this basic information is properly understood can the IP begin to advise the debtor as to whether an IVA might be suitable at all and, if   **1.49**

---

98   The Debt Respite Scheme (Breathing Space Moratorium and Mental Health Crisis Moratorium) (England and Wales) Regulations 2020 (SI 2020/1311), made under ss 6 and 7 of the Financial Guidance and Claims Act 2018.

99   Available at https://www.gov.uk/government/publications/debt-respite-scheme-breathing-space-guidance/debt-respite-scheme-breathing-space-guidance-for-creditors.

100   SIP 3, section 3; SIP 3.1, paras 1–11 and, especially, para 12. See also below [4.01].

101   See *Prosser v Castle Sanderson (a firm)* [2002] EWCA Civ 1140; [2002] BPIR 1163 (albeit that here the duty was owed by the IP at a later stage: see below [8.35]).

so, what form it might take and how to structure the proposal so as to make it viable. At an early stage it will also be necessary to decide whether or not it is necessary or advisable for the debtor to apply for an interim order.[102]

1.50 Following the reforms introduced by IA 2000,[103] from June 2003 it became a requirement for any IP offering such advice or assisting a debtor in putting together a proposal for an IVA to provide the debtor with a copy of the leaflet entitled 'Is a Voluntary Arrangement right for me?' published by R3. This leaflet, which provides a useful overview of the main considerations, must be signed by the debtor and returned to the IP before the IP will be entitled to charge a fee for any work carried out on behalf of the debtor. Once this has been signed, the IP is obliged to provide a copy to the debtor for future reference.

---

102 See Chapters 6 and 7 below.
103 See above at [1.28].

2

NATURE AND EFFECT

A. THE ESSENTIAL NATURE

1. The core principles

There are certain core principles that underlie the individual voluntary **2.01** arrangement (IVA) regime that have helped to shape much of the legislative framework and the case law that interprets it. Many of these principles can be traced back to a period well before the IVA itself was introduced by the Insolvency Act 1986 (IA 1986).[1] They are essentially concerned with ensuring that the creditors are dealt with fairly. The two most pervasive of these principles may be characterised broadly as equality and good faith. Equality demands that every creditor should, broadly speaking, be treated on an equal footing; good faith demands that the debtor must treat their creditors fairly, honestly and openly. These two guiding principles are interlinked, but distinct. The overarching principle of fairness extends beyond both.

---

1   See the historical overview by Anthony Boswood QC in *Cadbury Schweppes plc v Somji* [2000] BPIR 950, at [1], [15]–[23], [27]–[29] (upheld on appeal: see below [2.05]), and more recently and more succinctly that by Zacaroli J in *Lazari Properties 2 Ltd v New Look Retail Ltd* [2021] EWHC 1209 (Ch), [2021] BPIR 920, at [68]–[105], especially at [68]–[75].

(a) Good faith

2.02 The principle of good faith is not a self-standing rule, but rather an aspect of the court's statutory powers to police the approval of an IVA (either under section 262 or under section 276 of IA 1986); its primary focus is on the conduct of the debtor and on practical consequences of the debtor's dealings with any particular creditor (or creditors).[2] Good faith is of paramount importance in the formation of an IVA, as has been emphasised by the courts on numerous occasions. Three seminal Court of Appeal decisions (considered below) are of particular importance to our understanding of this principle and how it is to be applied: *Somji v Cadbury Schweppes plc*;[3] *Kapoor v National Westminster Bank plc*;[4] and *Gertner v CFL Finance Ltd*.[5]

2.03 The principle of good faith has been characterised as 'in essence a principle of fair and open dealing'.[6] As this implies, it incorporates the need for transparency. The obligation of transparency extends to the requirement to provide complete and accurate information, an obligation which persists right up to the moment when the creditors approve the proposal and extends beyond the proposal itself to the statement of affairs and to any other documentation and information supplied (or omitted) by the debtor to convince the creditors to approve the arrangement.[7]

2.04 This aspect of the requirement of good faith is supported by a number of statutory provisions. A creditor is entitled to challenge the approval of the IVA on grounds of material irregularity where the information is sufficiently misleading, or to present a bankruptcy petition on the same basis.[8] In addition there are criminal sanctions that can apply to a debtor who has attempted fraudulently to induce the creditors to approve a proposal by deliberately providing false information or omitting material information.[9]

---

2   *Gertner v CFL Finance Ltd* [2020] EWHC 1241 (Ch), [2020] BPIR 752, at [94], *per* Marcus Smith J (containing a useful summary of the principle).

3   [2001] 1 WLR 615, [2001] BPIR 172.

4   [2011] EWCA Civ 1083, [2011] BPIR 1680.

5   [2018] EWCA Civ 1781, [2018] BPIR 1605.

6   *CFL Finance Ltd v Bass* [2019] EWHC 1839 (Ch), [2019] BPIR 1327, at [74] (citing from the judgment of Bingham LJ in *Interfoto Picture Libraries Ltd v Stiletto Visual Programmes Ltd* [1989] QB 433, a case concerned with good faith in a quite different context). Although the application of the principle in relation to the discretion under s 266(3) of IA 1986 was overturned on appeal (see *Gertner v CFL Finance Ltd* [2020] EWHC 1241 (Ch), [2020], BPIR 752), the analysis of the principle itself remains sound.

7   *Somji v Cadbury Schweppes plc* [2001] 1 WLR 615, [2001] BPIR 172 (CA); *CFL Finance Ltd v Bass* [2019] EWHC 1839 (Ch), [2019] BPIR 1327, at [77]–[78].

8   See below [9.09]–[9.14] and [12.17], respectively.

9   See below [9.34].

In *Somji v Cadbury Schweppes plc*,[10] the debtor had proposed an IVA that **2.05** was not acceptable to some of his creditors; a friend of his (with the debtor's knowledge) reached a side-deal with certain creditors to persuade them to vote in favour of the proposal at the adjourned meeting. This secret side-deal was not disclosed to the other creditors, one of whom presented a bankruptcy petition on the basis of the debtor's incomplete and misleading disclosure. At first instance the IVA was declared void and the petition granted. On appeal it was held that, although the judge had been wrong to declare the IVA void,[11] he had been right to make the bankruptcy order because the information given had been misleading and the existence of the side-deal suppressed; the requirement of good faith between competing unsecured creditors was strict, so that any secret inducement to one (or a select few) of the creditors was prohibited, even where that inducement did not come out of the debtor's own estate.

The principle of good faith is not solely concerned with obligations of transparency and full disclosure: merely supplying all the relevant documentation **2.06** does not equate to good faith.[12] Nor is it simply a matter of prohibiting secret deals. The second case referred to above, *Kapoor v National Westminster Bank plc*,[13] concerned an assignment by a creditor connected to the debtor to a third party who had no such connection, carried out for the purpose of getting round the rule that requires an IVA to be approved by a majority of the unconnected creditors.[14] The assignment was not concealed (on its face, it was legitimate and it was hoped that this would suffice). The court concluded that the assignment had been a cynical ploy intended to subvert the statutory safeguards that ensured fair play, largely if not wholly with the intention of precluding the greater scrutiny that a trustee in bankruptcy would be able to bring to bear on the information that the debtor had supplied about his assets: in short, it was an 'uncommercial arrangement inconsistent with any notion of good faith' as between debtor and creditors.[15] The principle of good faith thus includes notions of public policy.

In the third case, *Gertner v CFL Finance Ltd*, the Court of Appeal reviewed the **2.07** previous two authorities, with which it had a certain amount in common, to

---

10   [2001] 1 WLR 615, [2001] BPIR 172 (CA).
11   See below [9.11].
12   *Kapoor v National Westminster Bank plc* [2011] EWCA Civ 1083; [2011] BPIR 1680, at [65]; cf. more generally [47]–[69].
13   See above.
14   See below [8.46].
15   *Kapoor v National Westminster Bank plc* (above), at [67]–[69].

distil the essential ingredients of the principle.[16] As in the previous two cases, there had been a side-deal – here one that provided benefits to the majority creditor, Kaupthing Bank hf, as an inducement to vote in favour of approving the IVA while still allowing Kaupthing to remain a creditor for the purposes of casting that vote. Although, like *Somji* (above), there was an allegation of inadequate disclosure, the thrust of the application relied on the fact that the side-deal had placed Kaupthing on a different footing from the rest of the creditors in terms of the benefits of entering the IVA and that this amounted to a breach of the good faith principle.[17] As in *Kapoor* (above), public policy considerations were in play, as the effect of the side-deal was to deny the other creditors the opportunity, through a trustee in bankruptcy, to have a thorough investigation conducted into the debtor's assets and his assertions about them. The side-deal provided a collateral advantage to Kaupthing that went beyond a mere infringement of the *pari passu* rule and engaged the good faith principle. The significance of that principle in the context of material irregularity is not confined to cases where there had been blatant vote-rigging (of the type exemplified in *Somji*) nor to cases where it could be shown that, had there been full and frank disclosure, this would have made a difference to the outcome. A creditor who has been unfairly placed in a position of collateral advantage in this way is, by virtue of the good faith principle, disqualified from taking part in the vote altogether.[18]

(b) Equality

2.08 The cases referred to above demonstrate that the principle of good faith is necessarily closely linked to the principle of equality.[19] The latter is, however, more nuanced. It does not entail equal treatment in the abstract, but rather in the context of insolvency procedures and the doctrine of *pari passu*. Although this essentially requires that creditors should expect to be able to share in the meagre spoils on offer equally amongst themselves, that is subject to a number of exceptions and limitations. Most obviously, secured creditors are not on the same footing as unsecured creditors; preferential creditors also enjoy special statutory treatment. There are, however, more subtle variations that can be justified on other grounds. One such example is the differential treatment of the so-called 'football creditors' in the voluntary arrangements implemented

---

16   [2018] EWCA Civ 1781, [2018], BPIR 1605 at [65]–[72].

17   Ibid., at [63].

18   Ibid., at [80]. See also (in the context of the same debtor) *CFL Finance Ltd v Bass* [2019] EWHC 1839 (Ch), [2019] BPIR 1327, at [65]–[78], *per* Chief ICC Judge Briggs; but note the criticisms of the result of this decision, on appeal, in *Gertner v CFL Finance Ltd* [2020] EWHC 1241 (Ch), [2020] BPIR 752.

19   *Gertner v CFL Finance Ltd* [2018] EWCA Civ 1781, [2018], BPIR 1605; see also *Lazari Properties 2 Ltd v New Look Retail Ltd* [2021] EWHC 1209 (Ch), [2021] BPIR 920, at [103].

for various football clubs.[20] The differential treatment here was justified on the basis that the policy to treat such creditors more favourably in the event of the club's insolvency predated the insolvency of the club and had not been implemented as an inducement to them to rig the vote.[21]

Absent any of the vitiating factors that infringe the principle of good faith discussed above, differential treatment of creditors *per se* is not necessarily unfair – rather it merely gives cause for inquiry as to the justification (or otherwise) of the differential treatment.[22] Subject to the principles of openness and fairness, the debtor can opt to deal with different classes of creditors in different ways. In certain cases, it may even be necessary to do so specifically in order to avoid unfairness.[23] Differential treatment may also be justified where it can be shown that this is necessary for the proper survival of the business upon which the voluntary arrangement depends.[24] **2.09**

In relation to this last point, a particular situation that has come under careful scrutiny by the courts arises in the context of voluntary arrangements entered into by businesses in the struggling retail sector, involving the differential treatment of certain landlords. Although the courts have prohibited any interference with landlords' proprietary rights, the differential treatment of landlord creditors in this context can sometimes be justified and arrangements involving such differential treatments have been allowed to stand.[25] This does not mean that *any* such differentiation can be justified, and where there has been unfairness, the courts have stepped in.[26] For obvious reasons, this situation has arisen in the context of a company voluntary arrangement (CVA) rather than in relation to IVAs, but it is clear from the authorities that the principles operate in exactly the same way in both contexts. Although the differential treatment of landlords is much less likely in the context of an IVA, the departure from strict equal treatment of other kinds of creditor may be justified by analogy. **2.10**

---

20   *IRC v Wimbledon Football Club Ltd* [2004] EWCA Civ 635; *HMRC v Portsmouth City Football Club Ltd* [2010] EWHC 2013 (Ch).

21   See *Gertner v CFL Finance Ltd* [2018] EWCA Civ 1781, [2018], BPIR 1605, at [79].

22   *Re A Debtor (No. 101 of 1999)* [2000] BPIR 998, at 1006.

23   See below [2.11].

24   The above points were noted by Lightman J in *IRC v Wimbledon Football Club Ltd* [2004] EWHC 1020 (Ch) at [18]; cf. also *Lazari Properties 2 Ltd v New Look Retail Ltd* [2021] EWHC 1209 (Ch), [2021] BPIR 920, at [112]–[113].

25   See *Discovery (Northampton) Ltd v Debenhams Retail Ltd* [2019] EWHC 2441 (Ch), [2020] BCC 9; *Lazari Properties 2 Ltd v New Look Retailers Ltd* (above), especially at [203]–[214]; cf. *Nero Holdings Ltd v Young* [2021] EWHC 1453 (Ch), although in this case the differential treatment in the proposal was not actually in issue.

26   *Carraway Guildford (Nominee A) Ltd v Regis UK Ltd* [2021] EWHC 1294 (Ch).

(c) Fairness

2.11 The principle of fairness extends beyond good faith and equal treatment. In *Sea Voyager Maritime Inc v Bielecki*,[27] the court had to consider an IVA where the terms of the proposal precluded any creditor from taking further action on any claim they might have against the debtor. The term applied equally to all creditors and thus did not offend the equality principle in the narrow sense. However, one of the creditors had a potential claim against the debtor's insurer under what was then the Third Parties (Rights Against Insurers) Act 1930. Under the provisions of that act, no claim against the insurer could be pursued without the claimant having secured judgment against the insured, so that the blanket terms of the IVA unfairly prejudiced this particular creditor.[28] In this particular instance, therefore, in the interests of fairness, exception should have been made for this particular creditor (or a suitable exception drafted into the prohibitive clause of the IVA). Although such circumstances will be rare, the overriding principle of fairness remains of crucial importance.

2. Composition or scheme of arrangement?

2.12 The legislation refers to the debtor making 'a proposal to his creditors for a composition in satisfaction of his debts or a scheme of arrangement of his affairs'.[29] For the first decade or so following the initial enactment of this statutory scheme little attention was paid to alternatives suggested by this phrase. In *March Estates plc v Gunmark Ltd*[30] it was pointed out that not all voluntary arrangements involved a composition whereby the creditors agreed to give up their rights: the arrangement could instead involve a form of moratorium whereby creditors agreed to postpone their rights to provide a breathing space for the debtor. The latter would amount to a scheme of arrangement but not a composition and if the intention of the arrangement was for all debts to be extinguished by the arrangement, the proposal would have to make that very clear.

2.13 The distinction between the two forms of arrangement has assumed a particular importance in cases where a challenge has been mounted against the arrangement on the footing that the proposal did not constitute a proposal for a voluntary arrangement within the meaning of IA 1986 at all. Thus, in *IRC v*

---

27 [1999] 1 BCLC 133.

28 This particular problem has been mitigated by the enactment of the Third Party (Rights Against Insurers) Act 2010 (and see also Standard Conditions, para 4(5)(c)); but analogous issues could arise.

29 IA 1986, s 253(1); the equivalent wording appears in s 1(1) in relation to CVAs.

30 [1996] BPIR 439, *per* Lightman J (a CVA case, but the reasoning applies equally to IVAs).

Adam & Partners Ltd,[31] the Court of Appeal accepted that the proposal had not offered a compromise but held that it had proposed a scheme of arrangement wherein the creditors had postponed their debts and that this was capable of being a valid voluntary arrangement.[32] Moreover, there is nothing in principle against an arrangement being both a composition with regard to a certain class of creditors and a scheme for a different class or group of creditors. What it cannot be, however, is neither.[33]

B. EFFECT

1. Effect on debtors and their creditors

(a) A hypothetical statutory contract

The overall effect of the approval of an IVA by the requisite majority is **2.14** to bind the debtor and their creditors, both those entitled to vote in the decision-making process at which the approval is reached and those who would have been so entitled if they had had notice of it, as if all such creditors had been a party to the arrangement proposed by the debtor.[34] Because the arrangement is binding on creditors, whether or not they were present at the decision-making process and, if they were, whether they voted for or against, the legislative framework effectively imposes a 'statutory hypothesis' whereby the creditors are treated as if they had consented to the arrangement even when this is not necessarily the case for all the creditors that find themselves bound.[35] The voluntary arrangement has thus been characterised as having 'contractual effect';[36] it has even been described as 'a species of statutory contract',[37] or a 'form of statutory contract' or, more succinctly, a 'statutory contract'.[38] The effect is a binding arrangement that precludes the creditors so bound from subsequently asserting their rights against the debtor in respect of a debt that was provable in the IVA. In *El Ajou v Stern*,[39] Kitchen J referred to the process

---

31 [2000] BPIR 986 (CA).

32 This was a CVA case, but similar reasoning applied in *Pitt v Mond* [2001] BPIR 624, an IVA case that examined the extent of the duties owed by an IP when advising on the terms of a proposal.

33 In *IRC v Bland and Sargent* [2003] BPIR 1274, an arrangement was struck down as being, on proper analysis, neither a composition nor a scheme.

34 IA 1986, s 260(2).

35 *Johnson v Davies* [1999] Ch 117 (CA) at 138C, subsequently endorsed in *Raja v Rubin* [2000] Ch 274.

36 *Re MF Global UK Ltd (In Special Administration); Heis v Financial Services Compensation Scheme Ltd* [2018] EWCA Civ 1327, at [22] (a CVA case). The essential contractual nature of the IVA was stressed again in *Raja v Rubin* (above).

37 *Davis v Martin-Sklan* [1995] BCC 1122 (at 1125B–C).

38 *Re NT Gallagher & Sons Ltd* [2002] EWCA Civ 404; [2002] 1WLR 2380, at [4] and [48], respectively.

39 [2006] EWHC 3067 (Ch); [2007] BPIR 693, at [64].

as one whereby the creditors 'must be taken to have agreed that they will have no further claims' against the debtor in respect of such a debt and determined that it applied to interest as well as the principal sum.

2.15 The 'contractual' nature of an IVA means that, when interpreting and giving effect to the terms of the arrangement, the courts will generally be concerned with ordinary contractual principles of interpretation.[40] These include establishing the true intentions of the parties, and where the terms of the arrangement are clear, those intentions will be paramount. It follows that, within the usual limits of public policy and legality and subject to the core principles outlined above, debtors and their creditors are entitled to choose how to structure the IVA, even if the result might on occasion seem somewhat counterintuitive. Where more than one interpretation is possible, the court is entitled to opt for a construction that conforms with business sense.[41]

2.16 Its contractual nature does not preclude assets within the IVA being held on trust by the supervisor for the purposes of the IVA: whether they are so held will be a matter of construction of the terms of the proposal.[42] Similarly, it is a matter of construction as to whether the intention of the parties was that any such trust would survive the conclusion of the IVA. Where the IVA is terminated for default, any such trust is likely to persist until the funds held have been dealt with.[43] Where the IVA concludes successfully in accordance with its terms, the IVA would generally be understood to have come to an end upon the supervisor issuing a certificate of completion, and, in consequence, any trusts under which the assets accumulated during the course of the IVA are held would cease to be operative; however, this is not necessarily the position in every case and the IVA trusts may survive even the issue of a certificate of completion where the wording of the arrangement shows this to be the intension of the parties.[44]

2.17 It is possible for the courts to imply terms into the arrangement in much the same way as they would into any other form of contract and applying the usual common law principles. Thus, for example, unless the contrary intention is clear from the wording of the arrangement, there will be an implied term

---

40   *Re MF Global UK Ltd* (above); *Franses v Hay* [2015] EWHC 3468 (Ch), [2016] BPIR 355.
41   *Franses v Hay* (above).
42   *Welburn v Dibb Lupton Broomhead* [2002] EWCA Civ 1601; [2003] BPIR 768, at [14]–[16]; see also *Re Bradley-Hole* [1995] 1 WLR 1097 and *Re Leisure Study Group Ltd* [1994] 2 BCLC 65 (a CVA case).
43   *Re NT Gallagher & Sons Ltd* [2002] EWCA Civ 404, [2002] 1 WLR 2380.
44   *Green v Wright* [2017] EWCA Civ 111, on which see below [12.04].

that limitation will be suspended for the duration of the IVA.[45] The Standard Conditions published by R3 include a provision that makes this explicit.[46] Generally, the terms of the IVA cannot interfere with the pre-existing rights of secured creditors, including those with the benefit of final charging orders over the debtor's assets, unless those rights are expressly voluntarily surrendered.[47]

Although the analogy of a hypothetical statutory contract is important, it does **2.18** have its limits: the fact that the voluntary arrangement has 'contractual effect' does not make it a contract for all purposes.[48] Thus, for example, it has been held that it is at least strongly arguable that a voluntary arrangement is not a contract for the purposes of the Contracts (Rights of Third Parties) Act 1999 (CRTPA 1999);[49] on the other hand, there is no reason why an IVA cannot be explicitly made subject to CRTPA 1999. Further, the law of penalties does not apply in exactly the same way as it would under a simple contract.[50] Similarly an IVA does not constitute an 'agreement' for the purposes of section 203(1) of the Employment Rights Act 1996, so that a term in an arrangement which sought to exclude or limit the statutory rights of an employee would not be rendered automatically void.[51] In addition a proposal for an IVA does not constitute an 'offer' within the meaning of section 271(3) of IA 1986, justifying dismissal of a bankruptcy petition, because a proposal cannot be 'accepted' or 'refused' by the petitioning creditor alone, but only by the creditors in accordance with Part 8 of IA 1986.[52]

(b) IVA debts

The contractual hypothesis begs the question of who is a 'creditor' and what **2.19** constitutes a 'debt' for the purposes of an IVA. This is not an entirely straightforward question.

The obvious starting point is the statutory definition of what constitutes **2.20** a bankruptcy debt, which is contained in section 382 of IA 1986.[53] This

---

45   *Co-operative Bank plc v Phillips* [2017] 1320 (Ch); [2017] BPIR 1156, applying the earlier decision of *Tanner v Everitt* [2004] EWHC 1130 (Ch), [2004] BPIR 1026 and clarifying that it was a general proposition.
46   Para 4(4) of the R3 Standard Conditions.
47   See below [4.20].
48   *Re SHB Realisations Ltd (formerly BHS Ltd)(In Liquidation)* [2018] EWHC 402 (Ch); [2018] BCC 712, at [28]–[29], a CVA case.
49   *Re Rhino Enterprises Properties Ltd* [2020] EWHC 2370 (Ch), [2021] BPIR 144, at [71] and [86] (a CVA case); cf. the extended consideration of the 'contractual' nature of a voluntary arrangement at [30]–[86].
50   *Re SHB Realisations Ltd* (above) at [29].
51   *Re Britannia Heat Transfer Ltd* [2007] BPIR 1038.
52   *Re A Debtor (No.2389 of 1989)* [1991] Ch 326.
53   IA 1986, s 382(1), on its face, applies solely to bankruptcies; s 382(2)–(4) applies equally to bankruptcies and IVAs. On s 382(5) see below.

definition is exceptionally wide and includes contingent debts. The breadth of the definition of contingent debts was not properly understood prior to the decision of the of the Supreme Court in *Re Nortel*,[54] which overturned a line of authorities that had established a doctrine that where a future or contingent liability rested on the exercise of a discretion, most particularly in relation to costs that had yet to be determined by the court as at the relevant date, such a liability could not be a bankruptcy debt.[55] The general rule in bankruptcy is that, subject to certain specific exceptions, all creditors who are owed bankruptcy debts may prove in the bankruptcy in respect of those debts.[56]

2.21 The position with regard to what constitutes an IVA debt, which creditors are bound by the IVA and which debts are provable, is much more nuanced. The statutory framework for IVAs provides a mechanism that, within certain constraints, allows the debtor to seek what arrangement they can get from their creditors; unlike in bankruptcy, therefore, each IVA is different. It may be for this reason that the rules are not as prescriptive. This in turn has provided greater scope for judicial interpretation. To complicate matters further, a large number of the authorities dealing with this area are now quite old and many of the statutory provisions under which they were determined have been amended (or reinterpreted). Extrapolating generalised propositions from these authorities can therefore be a hazardous endeavour.

2.22 The statutory provisions that deal with what constitutes a debt for the purposes of an IVA are both partial and ambiguous: in contrast to bankruptcy, there is no comprehensive statutory definition of what constitutes a 'debt' or a 'creditor' for the purposes of IVAs in general. The provisions of section 382(2)–(4) of IA 1986, which apply equally to bankruptcies and to IVAs, offer some guidance, but crucially there is no equivalent for IVAs to the statutory definition of bankruptcy debt that appears in section 382(1). Although the majority of authorities have assumed that the provisions of section 382(1) should be applied, *mutatis mutandis*, to IVAs, it is submitted that this is highly doubtful for a number of reasons. First, there is a specific provision in IA 1986 that defines creditors for the purposes of an IVA where the debtor is an undischarged bankrupt as being 'every person who is a creditor of the bankrupt in respect of a bankruptcy debt and every person who would be such

---

54   *Re Nortel Companies; Bloom v Pensions Regulator* [2013] UKSC 52, [2014] 1 AC 209.

55   The overruled cases included *Glenister v Rowe* [2000] Ch 76 and *R (Steele) v Birmingham CC* [2005] EWCA Civ 1824; [2006] 1 WLR 2380 (similarly in corporate insolvency, *Re Wisepark Ltd* [1994] BCC 221, now also impliedly overruled); but cf. *Day v Haine* [2008] EWCA Civ 626, [2008] BPIR 1343.

56   IR 2016, r 14.2(1), the exceptions being spelt out in r 14.2(2)–(5); prior to April 2017, the equivalent provisions were to be found in IR 1986, r 12.3.

a creditor if the bankruptcy had commenced on the day on which notice of the creditors' decision process is given'.[57] This means that section 382(1) does indirectly apply to IVAs as long as the debtor is an undischarged bankrupt; by implication, however, where that is not the case, the definition of bankruptcy debts does not carry over. This conclusion is strengthened by the structure and wording of section 382 as a whole: since subsections (2)–(4) expressly refer to both, the express restriction of subsection (1) to bankruptcy must be taken at face value; moreover, the insertion of what is now section 382(5), which relates solely to IVAs, underlines the fact that the section as a whole does not apply equally to both regimes.[58]

Similarly, there is no equivalent in relation to IVAs to the provisions dealing **2.23** with what is a provable debt for the purposes of bankruptcy: rule 14.2 of the Insolvency (England and Wales) Rules 2016 (IR 2016),[59] like its predecessor in the Insolvency Rules 1986 (IR 1986),[60] concerns only debts 'provable against the company or bankrupt'; while that wording might be wide enough to cover debts in a CVA, it does not, in terms, cover those in an IVA.[61] Whether Parliament intended that there should be a different test for which debts are provable in CVAs and IVAs is a moot point, but there are rational arguments available as to why this might be the case.

One such argument stems from a significant distinction that sets IVAs apart **2.24** from both bankruptcies on the one hand and CVAs on the other. Under the bankruptcy regime, the debtor is discharged from bankruptcy after a certain period (currently one year, unless suspended by the court).[62] Upon such discharge, the debtor is automatically released from most, but crucially not all, of their bankruptcy debts.[63] Among the debts that are exempted from such release are certain debts arising in family proceedings.[64] There are no equivalent provisions in relation to IVAs. A creditor who would still have been able to pursue such a debt against the debtor in full following the latter's discharge from bankruptcy might be severely prejudiced by being locked into accepting a much lesser sum in the debtor's IVA, so that such creditors have

---

57 IA 1986, s 257(3). See, for example, *Re Bradley-Hole* [1995] 1 WLR 1097, at 1103C–E.
58 IA 1986, s 382(5), inserted by the Welfare Reform Act 2012 (with effect from 8 May 2012), excludes liabilities under the Child Support Act 1991 from being a debt for the purposes of IVAs; see further below [2.28].
59 SI 2016/1024.
60 IR 1986 (SI 1986/1925), r 12.3.
61 See *Re Bradley-Hole* [1995] 1 WLR 1097, at pp 1103A–F; 1112F–G; 1118C–D.
62 IA 1986, s 279.
63 IA 1986, s 281.
64 IA 1986, s 281(5)(b) and (8).

been referred to as being in a 'special position'.[65] Clearly, debts arising in family proceedings will play no part in CVAs.

2.25 A number of authorities have proceeded (usually without argument) on the basis that the rules dealing with debts that are provable in bankruptcy apply equally to IVAs. Thus, in *R v Barnet Justices, ex p Phillippou*,[66] an enforcement of a compensation order made in criminal proceedings was held not to infringe an interim order as it was not a debt capable of being proved in bankruptcy – and therefore, by extension, the debtor's IVA. Similarly, in *Re Hargreaves (In IVA); Booth v Mond*,[67] the debtor's former trustee in bankruptcy was entitled to prove in the debtor's subsequent IVA for arrears under a pre-existing income payments order on the basis that it would have been provable in a subsequent bankruptcy. Both decisions are justifiable on other grounds, but the basis upon which the decisions were actually reached is revealing.

2.26 Conversely, however, the distinction between debts provable in bankruptcy and those provable in an IVA has been stressed in other authorities, in particular in the context of debts arising in matrimonial proceedings.[68] Although judicial opinion is mixed, it is submitted that the better view is that provability in IVAs is not simply to be equated to what would be the case in bankruptcy. It is clear that the terms 'debt' and 'creditor' in the context of IVAs and the issue of what is capable of being proved in any particular IVA must be governed by the terms of the IVA and there is no reason in principle why these terms cannot be wider than would necessarily be the case in bankruptcy. This was the reasoning applied in *Golstein v Bishop*,[69] which concerned whether a costs order made after the commencement of the IVA was provable within the IVA. The case was decided a month before the Supreme Court handed down its judgment in *Re Nortel*,[70] and so proceeded on the basis of the law as it then stood, which was that such a debt would not have been provable in the debtor's bankruptcy.[71] Nevertheless, the judge found that this was not determinative

---

65 *Re A Debtor; JP v A Debtor* [1999] BPIR 206; the situation might be different where the IVA creditors are receiving 100 pence in the pound. See further below [2.33].

66 [1997] BPIR 134. Note, however, that a fine imposed by the Joint Disciplinary Tribunal of the ICA is not, for these purposes a fine and was provable: *Marcus v Institute of Chartered Accountants* [2004] EWHC 3010 (Ch), [2005] BPIR 413.

67 [2010] EWHC 1576 (Ch); [2010] BPIR 1111.

68 See *Re Bradley-Hole* [1995] 1 WLR 1097, and *Re A Debtor; JP v A Debtor* [1999] BPIR 206; both were matrimonial cases, on which see below [2.32]–[2.36].

69 [2013] EWHC 1706 (Ch), [2013] BPIR 708.

70 *Re Nortel Companies; Bloom v Pensions Regulator* [2013] UKSC 52, [2014] 1 AC 209.

71 Relying on *Glenister v Rowe* [2000] Ch 76 (see above [2.20]).

and that, on a true construction of the terms of the IVA, this was a debt provable in the IVA.

Where a creditor, entitled under contract to recover the costs of enforcement, **2.27** had expended such costs prior to the approval of the debtor's IVA, such expenditure would be likely to be provable in the IVA (irrespective of whether those costs had been quantified in a court order).[72] Arguably this would be the case where the obligation to pay such costs existed at the commencement of the IVA, even if they had not yet been incurred by that date.[73] Although a creditor bound by the IVA whose debt is caught by the IVA cannot subsequently claim to have retained the right to enforce their debt otherwise than by proving in the IVA, this does not apply to a new liability arising during the course of the IVA. In respect of the latter, the creditor may be entitled to payment, and thus enforcement (including by way of bankruptcy proceedings), outside the IVA.[74] This distinction was highlighted in *Jules v Robertson*,[75] where, on appeal, it was decided that a man who had provided funds to his son-in-law prior to the latter's IVA was not entitled to recover those sums other than by proving in the IVA (overturning the decision below), whereas he was entitled to recover the sums he had provided to his son-in-law to assist him during the course of the IVA itself. Similarly, a creditor was entitled to a final charging order with respect to a debt in relation to obligations that arose after the IVA had been approved.[76] As noted above, however, caution must be applied in relation to authorities dealing with contingent debts prior to 24 July 2013.[77]

There is another vital distinction that sets IVAs apart from bankruptcies. The **2.28** statutory regime for voluntary arrangements involves a (real or hypothetical) willingness on the part of the creditors to compromise their full rights, which is absent in bankruptcy. This in turn necessarily implies that, to participate in the IVA, the creditors must have the capacity to compromise the debt in question. A creditor who, for whatever reason, lacks the capacity to be in a position to do so cannot be bound by the IVA and their debt cannot be an IVA debt. This was the basis for the decision of the Court of Appeal in *Child Maintenance and*

---

72   *Coutts & Co v Passey* [2007] BPIR 323 (decided, correctly, pre-*Nortel*).
73   *Re Goldspan Ltd* [2003] BPIR 93, decided on the basis that, even though the costs were incurred after the commencement of the IVA, the creditor was bound by the IVA by virtue of having proved for this debt in the IVA (but post-*Nortel* it is likely that such a debt would be caught by the IVA in any event). Cf. *Cornelius v Casson* [2008] BPIR 504, which probably does not survive *Nortel*.
74   See below [12.30].
75   [2011] EWCA Civ 1322; [2012] BPIR 126.
76   *Peterkin v London Borough of Merton* [2011] EWHC 376 (Ch); [2012] BPIR 388.
77   The date of the judgment in *Re Nortel* (see above [2.20]).

Enforcement Commission v Beesley & Whyman,[78] a case that concerned arrears of child maintenance at a time before the insertion into IA 1986 of section 382(5).[79] Although the relationship between child maintenance and IVAs is now governed by statute, the reasoning of the decision in this case is still relevant to the analysis of which debts are provable in IVAs.[80]

2. Effect on third parties: co-obligors and guarantors

2.29 As a general principle, the fact that a debtor has entered into an IVA with a creditor in relation to a debt where a third party is a co-obligor jointly liable for the same debt will not, without more, affect the creditor's rights as against the third party. The IVA does not, *ipso facto*, constitute a new agreement between the debtor and the creditor whereby the original debt is extinguished and replaced, amounting to accord and satisfaction of the original debt and thereby having the effect of releasing any co-obligors of the original debt. This remains the case whether or not the creditor voted in favour of accepting the proposal.[81] In every case, it will be a matter of construction of the intentions of the parties. The Standard Conditions include a provision that expressly reserves the creditors' position in this regard (subject to any contrary indication in the proposal).[82] The courts will not readily imply that an IVA will compromise a creditor's rights against non-party co-obligors, in particular where the debts are joint and several. It is not necessarily the case, therefore, that a creditor must expressly reserve his position against any co-obligor to preserve its rights against the third parties; rather, as a general rule, for the IVA to bind the creditor with respect to its rights against third party co-obligors, the wording of the proposal must provide for this explicitly or by necessary implication. This is best illustrated by cases concerned with sureties and guarantors.[83]

78　[2010] EWCA Civ 1344, [2011] BPIR 608, which, at [60]–[61], approved the analysis of Rimer J in *Re Bradley-Hole* [1995] 1 WLR 1097, at pp 1118–1119, in relation to periodic maintenance payments that had yet to fall due at the operative date (said to have been the date of the debtor's first bankruptcy).

79　At the date of that decision no compromise or write off was possible, although this was due to a change with the introduction of statutory provisions that were not yet in force (which subsequently became ss 41D and 41E of the Child Support Act 1991, inserted by Child Maintenance and Other Payments Act 2008 with effect from Oct and Dec 2012); as noted above, by this later date s 382(5) had already been inserted into IA 1986.

80　This probably provides a more satisfactory basis for the result in *ex p Phillippou* (see above [2.25]).

81　*Johnson v Davies* [1997] 1 WLR 1511, in particular at 1514E–1519A. The result was upheld on appeal (*Johnson v Davies* [1999] Ch 117), albeit the Court of Appeal did not accept the notion, expressed by Jacob J below, that this was because IVAs were not by nature 'contractual'; but cf. *Re Rhino Enterprises Properties Ltd* (above).

82　Standard Conditions, para 4(2); the IVA Protocol adopts a similar position.

83　Ibid. See also *Green King plc v Stanley* [2001] EWCA Civ1966; [2002] BPIR 491 (a case that did include an express reservation of rights against the co-obligors); *Lombard NatWest Factors Ltd v Koutrouzas* [2002]

The above situation is likely to be different where a third party has merely **2.30**
guaranteed the performance of the principal debtor to comply with their
obligations to the creditor, rather than imposing an obligation to pay directly
on the guarantor as co-obligor. In these circumstances the debtor's IVA would
at least be likely to provide grounds for setting aside a statutory demand
against the guarantor, by analogy with the decision of the Court of Appeal in
Remblance v Octagon Assets Ltd.[84] It should be noted that there is a requirement
under the rules for the debtor to identify in the proposal any person who has
guaranteed any debts covered by the proposal and specify in each case whether
the guarantor is an associate of the debtor.[85]

The position in relation to other co-debtors is comparable.[86] In *Jones v The* **2.31**
Financial Conduct Authority,[87] the Financial Conduct Authority (FCA) had
imposed a penalty for misconduct on a firm that subsequently dissolved and
two of the three former partners entered IVAs; the FCA served a statutory
demand on the third, who sought to argue that it should be set aside on the
basis that the other partners' IVAs amounted to accord and satisfaction of the
debt to the FCA. The judge disagreed: nothing in the IVAs of either of the
other partners supported the argument that they had the effect of relieving
the applicant of his indebtedness to the FCA. The judge's reasoning does,
however, suggest that careful wording in an IVA proposal could, if this was
the ascertainable intention of parties to the IVA, be capable of extinguishing
the indebtedness of a co-obligor. Similarly, in *March Estates plc v Gunmark
Ltd*,[88] it was held that, while the terms of the arrangement bound both the
claimant and the defendant, in relation to the respective debts owed to each by
the debtor, it did not affect the right of the claimant landlord to claim arrears
of rent from the defendant former tenant pursuant to the latter's covenants.

EWHC 1084 (QB); [2003] BPIR 444; *Lloyds Bank v Ellicott* [2002] EWCA Civ 1333; [2003] BPIR 632
(where the creditor's claim against the co-obligor was only defeated on other grounds).

84   [2009] EWCA Civ 581; [2009] BPIR 1129, in which the Court of Appeal overturned by a majority the deci-
     sion of Mann J (on appeal from the county court) under what was then IR 1986, r 6.5(4)(d), the equivalent to
     IR 2016, r 10.5(5)(d), on the basis that it would be unfair to allow the statutory demand to stand even though
     the guarantor could avail himself of the principal debtor's cross-claim.

85   IR 2016, r 8.3(m).

86   *Re Goldspan Ltd* [2003] BPIR 93.

87   [2013] EWHC 2731 (Ch) [2013] BPIR 1033.

88   [1996] BPIR 439 (a CVA case).

3. IVAs in the context of matrimonial proceedings

(a) A problematic interrelationship

2.32 There has always been a tension between insolvency law and matrimonial law and there are a great many authorities dealing with many different aspects of the relationship between matrimonial law and bankruptcy.[89] The principles that apply in bankruptcy, which in themselves are not always consistently articulated, are not however transferable into the context of IVAs in an entirely straightforward way: this is due in part to the particularities of matrimonial law and in part to the distinctions between bankruptcy and IVAs, not least in relation to the provability of debts.[90]

2.33 Initially, the 1986 legislation excluded liabilities arising in family proceedings altogether from debts provable in bankruptcy,[91] but in 2005, following judicial criticism, lump sum orders and orders for costs in family proceedings were exempted from the exclusion and these remain provable under IR 2016.[92] As noted above, however, the fact that (all or some) liabilities arising in family proceedings are not provable in bankruptcy does not mean that they are not provable in an IVA.[93] In addition, such debts are exempted from the effect of discharge in the context of bankruptcy; again, there is no equivalent in the context of IVAs. The combination of these distinctions places spouses with the benefit of orders made in family proceedings in a 'special position' in relation to IVAs.[94] As a result, particular care needs to be taken when drafting a proposal in cases where family proceedings have been instituted so as not to create a situation where the non-debtor party to the marriage could be unfairly prejudiced by the IVA; in particular this may mean providing within the proposal for the debts arising in family proceedings not to be extinguished by the IVA, to mirror the effect of bankruptcy.[95] It is also the case that the existence of divorce

---

89 Notably such cases as: *Re Holliday* [1981] Ch 405; *Mountney v Treharne* [2002] EWCA Civ 1174; [2002] BPIR 1126; *Hill v Haines* [2007] EWCA Civ 1284; [2008] Ch 412.

90 See above [2.22]–[2.26].

91 IR 1986, r 12.3(2)(a). For the definition of 'family proceedings' see IA 1986, s 281(8); see also *Weymeher v Weymeher* [2001] BPIR 548; *Cadwell v Jackson* [2001] BPIR 966; *Cartwright v Cartwright* [2002] EWCA Civ 931; [2002] BPIR 895. Regarding costs in matrimonial proceedings (prior to 2005), see *Levy v Legal Services Commission* [2000] BPIR 1065.

92 IR 1986, r 12.3 was amended by Insolvency (Amendment) Rules 2005 (SI 2005/527), with effect from 1 April 2005. This is now carried over into IR 2016, r 14.2(3)–(4). For the judicial criticism, see in particular *Woodley v Woodley (No 2)* [1994] 1 WLR 1167; *Ram v Ram* [2004] EWCA Civ 1452; [2005] BPIR 616.

93 *Re Bradley-Hole* [1995] 1 WLR 1097, at 1103A–F.

94 *Re A Debtor; JP v A Debtor* [1999] BPIR 206. This was a case dealing with a lump sum order at a time when such orders were still not provable in bankruptcy.

95 As explained in *JP v A Debtor* (above).

proceedings can produce unwelcome problems for the smooth implementation of the IVA, which may even cause the IVA to fail.[96]

All of this means that the nominee must be alive to the possibility of family **2.34** proceedings and must be sure that any orders made in such proceedings are appropriately addressed in the proposal so that the position is not unfairly prejudicial to the spouse or former spouse. They must ensure that the (former) spouse has notice of the decision-making process and is allowed to vote. In such circumstances, the nominee's report should always clarify the position of the spouse in the IVA as compared to bankruptcy (where many such liabilities would not be provable), so as to allow the creditors an opportunity to reach an informed decision as to whether the IVA is, nevertheless, preferable to bankruptcy.[97] Where a decree absolute has been made in the divorce proceedings by the date of the decision, the former spouse's vote will rank with that of any other creditor; but where the final divorce is still pending, the divorcing spouse will still remain an associate for the purposes of calculating the requisite majority.[98]

(b) Relative timing

The relative timing of the family proceedings and the IVA procedure is likely **2.35** to be of considerable significance. Where an order has been made in matrimonial proceedings prior to the debtor's proposal, the IVA would have to take full account of this, as stated above. Were a debtor to propose an IVA having failed to comply with an existing property adjustment order, the proposal would have to treat the order as having been carried out.[99] Where orders have not yet been made in family proceedings in favour of the non-debtor spouse, those proceedings would be caught by any interim order the debtor obtained; whether permission would be granted for them to continue notwithstanding the interim order might depend on the orders being sought and the terms of the proposal.[100] In the limbo period before any orders are made in the family proceedings, the non-debtor spouse may still rank as a contingent creditor

---

96   See, for example, *Bonney v Mirpuri* [2013] BPIR 412.
97   Cf. *JP v A Debtor* (above).
98   IR 2016, r 15.34(6)–(7) and (for the meaning of 'associate') s 435(2)(a) of IA 1986.
99   Just as the spouse with the benefit of such an order would have an equitable interest in the property to be transferred that would bind even a trustee in bankruptcy: *Mountney v Treharne* [2002] EWCA Civ 1174; [2002] BPIR 1126.
100 See below [6.09].

and care must be taken when considering some older cases in relation to what might constitute a contingent debt for these purposes.[101]

2.36 Where the divorce proceedings are commenced after the debtor has entered an IVA, any financial provision orders made in favour of the non-debtor spouse in the subsequent family proceedings will not fall within the IVA (and may of course derail it). However, the family court's discretion would be likely to be cut down by the terms of the IVA: in particular no property adjustment order could be made in respect of property that was included within the IVA and where the supervisor of the IVA held the IVA assets on trust for the IVA creditors, the position would be entirely analogous to that which would pertain had the debtor been declared bankrupt. In the context of bankruptcy, where it is clear that there will be surplus, the court has considered it may be appropriate to order the bankrupt to pay a lump sum.[102] There is no reason to suppose the position would be any different in the context of an IVA where it could be ascertained that the assets in the IVA exceeded the requirements of the IVA. Conversely, the fact that one party to matrimonial proceedings is a debtor who has entered into an IVA will not necessarily impact on the exercise of the court's discretion when deciding whether to make financial adjustment orders *in favour* of the debtor spouse.[103]

---

101 Following *Re Nortel Companies; Bloom v Pensions Regulator* [2013] UKSC 52, [2014] 1 AC 209 (see above [2.20]). In *Re Jones* [2008] BPIR 1051 (in the context of a preference claim), the court rejected the argument that the spouse had been a creditor prior to the order made in the family proceedings, but this reasoning must now be questioned in light of *Nortel*; cf. *Re Rich* [2008] BPIR 485.

102 *Hellyer v Hellyer* [1997] BPIR 85; *Young v Young* [2013] EWHC 3637 (Fam); [2014] 2 FLR 786.

103 See *R v R* [2012] EWHC 2390 (Fam); [2013] 1 FLR 106.

3

DEATH AND TAXES

A. THE DEATH OF THE DEBTOR

1. Introduction

The death of the debtor who is seeking to enter or has entered an individual **3.01** voluntary arrangement (IVA) will effectively bring the procedure to a close, but exactly how this operates will depend on the circumstances. To some extent the issues are governed by the Administration of Insolvent Estates of Deceased Persons Order 1986 (DPO 1986).[1] DPO 1986 operates in the main by modifying the Insolvency Act 1986 (IA 1986) in the event of the debtor's death. This is, however, a highly problematic piece of legislation and nowhere more so than with regard to IVAs. The effect of the debtor's death will partly depend on the stage that the procedure has reached at the time of death and also, where the death occurs during the course of the IVA, on the terms of the particular arrangement. Due to a quirk of drafting of DPO 1986, it will also make a difference (at least in theory, if not in practice) whether the debtor has obtained an interim order.

2. Death prior to initiation

Where a debtor who intends to make a proposal to his creditors dies prior **3.02** to the formal initiation of the procedure, the procedure cannot be pursued

---

1 SI 1986/1999, as amended.

by their personal representative. The personal representative of a debtor who had died prior to issuing an application for an interim order, or after issue but before the court had granted the order, would not be eligible to make or continue such an application on behalf of the deceased.[2] Where the debtor's application for an interim order was still pending at the date of death, the personal representative should notify the court immediately and upon such notification the court would dismiss the application. Any interim order made by the court in ignorance of the circumstances would be a nullity and would subsequently be set aside as such.

3.03 Similarly, where a debtor who intends to make a proposal to their creditors without seeking an interim order dies prior to submitting the proposal to the nominee, the personal representative would not be eligible to submit the proposal on behalf of the deceased debtor.[3] If the death occurred after the debtor had formally submitted the proposal to the nominee but prior to the nominee making their report to the creditors, the nominee could take no further steps for the same reasons and should down tools.

3.04 In any of the above circumstances, the personal representative of the deceased would have no alternative but to apply to the court for an insolvency administration order pursuant to DPO 1986.

3. Death following an interim order

(a) Death occurring between the interim order and the creditors' decision

3.05 Where a debtor dies after an interim order has been made, the situation is governed by Part 3 of Schedule 1 to DPO 1986.[4] These provisions are not well drafted, even though the situation was improved somewhat by amendments that came into effect in 2017.[5]

3.06 Where the death occurs after an interim order has been granted but prior to submitting the proposal and statement of affairs to the nominee, the nominee is required to notify the court of the death as soon as they are aware of it and upon receiving such notice the court must discharge the interim order.[6] DPO

---

2   The debtor would no longer fall within IA 1986, s 253(1) and the personal representative could not bring themselves within s 253(3).

3   As the conditions in section 256A(1) of IA 1986 would no longer be satisfied.

4   Part 3 of Sch 1 to DPO 1986, which applies exclusively where the court has made an interim order pursuant to s 252 of IA 1986.

5   The Deregulation Act 2015 and Small Business, Enterprise and Employment Act 2015 (Consequential Amendments) (Savings) Regulations 2017 (SI 2017/540), with effect from 6 April 2017.

6   DPO 1986, Sch 1, Part 3, para 1.

1986 is silent as to what should happen if the debtor dies between the date on which the nominee receives the documents referred to in section 256(2) of IA 1986 and the date on which the report is filed at court pursuant to section 256(1), or indeed at any time down to the court extending the interim order to allow the creditors the opportunity to consider the proposal, but the nominee would be well advised to follow the same procedure and the court would inevitably discharge the interim order in the same way.[7]

Where the debtor dies after the nominee has filed the report but prior to the creditors formally approving the IVA, no such approval may take place; in addition, where the debtor was (at the time of their death) an undischarged bankrupt, the personal representative must also notify the deceased's creditors, the Official Receiver (OR) and the trustee in bankruptcy (if different).[8] The legislation makes no provision for how the personal representative is supposed to obtain the relevant information to be able to notify the debtor's creditors, nor does it explain why this is necessary only in the event of the debtor having been an undischarged bankrupt.[9]   **3.07**

As long as the debtor is still living at the date of the creditors' decision, the procedure under section 258 will proceed as normal and any approval of the IVA will be valid, even if the debtor subsequently dies.[10] Rather curiously, however, DPO 1986 (as amended) then goes on to apply a modified version of section 259 of IA 1986, whereby a new provision is inserted as subsection (1A), dealing with the situation where the debtor has died *before* the creditors have decided whether to approve the proposed voluntary arrangement.[11] This is infelicitous, to say the least, for a number of reasons: **3.08**

- section 259 of IA 1986 is solely concerned with 'when the creditors have decided',[12] so that it makes no sense to add in a subsection dealing with a different premise: the new subsection (1A) prohibits the creditors from approving the arrangement, when (*ex hypothesi*) the entire section only applies where that decision would already have taken place; it may be that subsection (1A) was intended to apply where the creditors had reached a decision *in ignorance of the fact that the debtor had died*, but, if so, it is ineptly drafted;

---

7   On these procedural steps, see below [6.35]–[6.40].
8   DPO 1986, Sch 1, Part 3, para 2, as substituted, which modifies s 257 of IA 1986. The procedural picture was less clear if the death occurred prior to 6 April 2017, but the general effect would have been much the same.
9   See below [3.09].
10   DPO 1986, Sch 1, Part 3, para 3, as amended.
11   DPO 1986, Sch 1, Part 3, para 3A, as inserted.
12   IA 1986, s 259(1).

- the different scenario addressed in subsection (1A) is covered elsewhere in DPO 1986 in almost identical terms,[13] which renders this provision largely otiose;
- the only significant difference is that the personal representative is also obliged to notify the court 'that the proposal has not been approved', which is somewhat ambiguous.[14]

3.09 It is submitted that the following practical guidance can be extracted from these poorly drafted provisions:

- If the debtor dies during the decision-making process, the creditors cannot validly approve the IVA;[15]
- Upon the debtor's death, the personal representative should identify the nominee and notify them of the debtor's demise at the earliest opportunity (this is not a statutory obligation, merely common sense and the most practical way for the personal presentative to carry out their express obligations);
- Assuming this occurs prior to the creditors' decision, the nominee should inform the creditors, stop the decision-making procedure and (together with the personal representative) notify the court that approval is now impossible;[16]
- If this information was not communicated to the nominee in time to halt the procedure and the creditors (in ignorance of the death) voted to approve the IVA, the personal representative is obliged to notify the creditors of the fact (and date) of the debtor's death and, since the death occurred prior to the decision, of the fact that any purported approval would therefore have been a nullity;[17] as it is unlikely the personal representative would know the identity and contact details of all the deceased's creditors, it would be more sensible, and more practical, for this to be carried out by, or with the assistance of, the nominee;

---

13   DPO 1986, Sch 1, Part 3, para 2 (see above), which more appropriately deals with this within s 257 of IA 1986.

14   IA 1986, s 259(1A)(b), as inserted by DPO 1986, Sch 1, Part 3, para 3A.

15   This is the effect of both para 2 and para 3A of DPO 1986, Sch 1, Part 3.

16   DPO 1986, Sch 1, Part 3, para 3A appears to place the obligation to notify the court solely on the personal representative, but for practical reasons it would make more sense for this to come from the nominee, and reading paras 1, 2 and 3A together, it is reasonable to infer that the nominee does in fact have such an obligation.

17   Although, strictly speaking, s 259(1A)(c), as inserted by para 3A of DPO 1986, Sch 1, Part 3, only applies where the debtor was an undischarged bankrupt at the date of death, it should be followed in every case as a matter of practicality.

- Any purported approval by the creditors made in ignorance of the debtor's death would be a nullity and the personal representative and/or the nominee should notify the court of the fact of that nullity (or non-approval);[18]
- Upon receiving such notice (in either form) the court would discharge the interim order (if it had not lapsed by the time the court was notified);[19]
- Where the debtor was an undischarged bankrupt, the personal representative should also notify the OR and the trustee.[20]

(b) Death during the course of the IVA

Where the debtor dies after the IVA has been approved, the impact of the death would depend at least to some extent on the terms of the IVA and what had taken place within the IVA in the period between the creditors' approval and the debtor's death. As soon as practicable after becoming aware of the debtor's death the supervisor should notify the creditors and, if the IVA has already been registered on the insolvency register, must also provide notice to the Secretary of State, which must include the date of death. Upon receiving notice of the date of the debtor's death, the Secretary of State must cause the fact and date of the death to be entered onto the register.[21]   **3.10**

The terms of the IVA may expressly stipulate that the arrangement will automatically terminate upon the death of the debtor.[22] Even where this is the case, however, it is conceivable that if the debtor had effectively completed all that was required of them under the terms of the IVA prior to their death, so that full implementation was achievable, the intervening death might not necessarily result in failure. Depending on the terms of the IVA, even if the debtor had not fully complied with all the obligations, but had substantially complied, such that the supervisor was in a position to certify substantial compliance, the debtor's death might not result in the complete failure of the IVA.[23] It may also be the case that any IVA trust would survive the debtor's death and continue to be administered for the benefit of the participating creditors. In addition, other rights and duties would continue to apply, notwithstanding the death of the debtor. There may be outstanding issues in relation to the IVA that would   **3.11**

---

18   This may well be the intended meaning of s 259(1A)(b), as inserted by para 3A of DPO 1986, Sch 1, Part 3. On the nominee's obligations, see above.

19   By analogy with DPO 1986, Sch 1, Part 3, para 1 (see above).

20   This is the effect of both para 2 and para 3A of DPO 1986, Sch 1, Part 3.

21   Insolvency (England and Wales) Rules 2016, SI 2016/1024 (IR 2016), r 11.23. This rule was originally inserted into Insolvency Rules 1986 (IR 1986), as r 6A.8(2), by the Insolvency (Amendment) Rules 2009 (SI 2009/642), with effect from 6 April 2009.

22   See Standard Conditions, para 11(1)(c).

23   See below [12.05].

need to be resolved by the court and it is clear that the right of supervisor to apply to the court for directions under section 263 of IA 1986 would survive the debtor's death and in many cases would have a vital role to play.

3.12 In addition to the general observations set out above, which would apply in every case, other specific issues arise where the IVA had been secured with the benefit of an interim order. The supervisor is expressly required to give notice to the court that the debtor has died.[24] In addition, section 263 of IA 1986 continues to apply, modified so as to allow the debtor's personal representative, in addition to the debtor's creditors, to apply to the court where they are dissatisfied with any act, omission or decision of the supervisor.[25] By implication, where the debtor had already made such an application prior to their death, the personal representative would be entitled to pursue that application to its conclusion.

3.13 A number of other sections of IA 1986, namely sections 260 (the effect of approval), 261 (annulment) and 262 (challenge to the IVA) cease to apply on or after the debtor's death.[26] In the case of any annulment application pursuant to section 261 or any challenge pursuant to section 262 that was pending as at the death of the debtor, this would mean that the application could no longer be pursued. On the other hand, the position is slightly different where the debtor, being an undischarged bankrupt at the commencement of the IVA, has already succeeded in having the bankruptcy order annulled pursuant to section 261 of IA 1986. As will be discussed more fully in a later chapter, such a debtor is entitled to insist that the OR advertise the fact of the annulment.[27] If, however, the debtor dies after the annulment has been granted but before being able to require the OR to advertise the fact, the rules expressly empower the debtor's personal representative to stand in the debtor's place for this purpose.[28]

3.14 The modification to section 260 of IA 1986 is more wide-reaching. In effect this means that, upon the death of the debtor, the IVA would cease to bind the creditors. This is likely to imply the immediate or imminent failure of the IVA. In the event of the debtor's death occurring during the course of the IVA, therefore, the supervisor or any creditor bound by the IVA (or, by implication, would have been so bound, but for the modification of section 260 by DPO

---

24   DPO 1986, Sch 1, Part 3, para 5(b).
25   DPO 1986, Sch 1, Part 3, para 5(a).
26   DPO 1986, Sch 1, Part 3, para 4.
27   See below [10.16].
28   IR 2016, r 8.36(4).

1986) may petition to have the insolvent estate of the deceased debtor wound up, under a modified version of s 264(1)(c) of IA 1986.[29] They must do so using Form 2, as annexed to DPO 1986.[30] The respondent would be the executor who has proved the will or the personal representative to whom letters of administration had been granted. Form 2 itself effectively sets the grounds of the petition as being the death of the debtor (without the need for more) and it is to be noted that section 276(1) of IA 1986 (the grounds that generally apply in the case of a section 264(1)(c) petition against a living debtor) does not apply to such a petition. Nevertheless, section 276(2) of IA 1986 (relating to the expenses of administering the insolvent estate) does still apply.[31]

4. Where there is no interim order

The general observations set out above regarding the effect of the death of the debtor prior to initiating the IVA procedure apply in every case.[32] Curiously, however, DPO 1986 is entirely silent as to what precisely should happen if the debtor elects not to obtain an interim order but instead chooses to follow the alternative procedure and then subsequently dies at any stage during the process, whether before or after the creditors have approved the proposal.[33] The position must be approached by analogy with the position under the DPO 1986, using a combination of common sense and the common law.   **3.15**

Where a debtor is pursuing an IVA without an interim order, the stage the procedure has reached at the date of death will be significant, just as it was in an interim order case. If the debtor should die prior to the creditors approving the IVA, the process cannot continue (with or without the support of the deceased debtor's personal representative).[34] It follows that, in such circumstances, the nominee should not proceed with the decision procedure and that, in any event, the creditors cannot validly approve the proposal. Although the modifications to sections 257 and 259 of IA 1986 required by the DPO 1986, discussed above, do not technically apply where the debtor has not obtained an interim order, it is submitted that the same procedures, *mutatis mutandis*, should be followed.   **3.16**

---

29   DPO, Sch 1, Part 2, para 1.
30   DPO, Sch 1, Part 2, para 1(d) and Sch 3, Form 2. This form appears to have survived the general abolition of prescribed court forms that was introduced by IR 2016.
31   DPO, Sch 1, Part 2, para 8. See below [12.21].
32   See above [3.03].
33   It appears this is because it was never amended to take account of the insertion of s 256A into IA 1986 by Insolvency Act 2000 and this oversight was not picked up in the amendments introduced in 2017.
34   As neither the deceased debtor nor their personal representative would be within s 256A(1); cf. [3.06]–[3.09] above in the context of an interim order.

3.17 Equally, the modifications to sections 260–263 of IA 1986 discussed above in the context of an interim order case do not, technically, apply where there is no such order. Nevertheless, it would be absurd if the modification to section 263(3), allowing the personal representative to stand in the debtor's shoes, were held not to apply in such a case. The fate of any outstanding applications under sections 261 or 262 of IA 1986 is more debatable, but it would surely be anomalous for the court to permit them to continue. Although the supervisor may not be obliged formally to notify the court of the death of the debtor where no applications are pending,[35] it is obvious that they would be obliged to inform the court where such applications are on foot.

3.18 Since the modification disapplying section 260 in the event of the debtor's death does not technically apply in non-interim order cases, it is conceivable that the creditors would find themselves still bound. It is clear in such circumstances, however, that the situation would be unsustainable. In the short term, the supervisor might need to apply to the court for directions,[36] but in most cases the simple solution would be for the supervisor (or any creditor bound by the IVA) to petition pursuant to section 264(1)(c), using Form 2, as discussed above.[37]

B. INCAPACITY

3.19 Where it becomes apparent that a debtor had lacked mental capacity at the date of the creditors' approval of the proposal, or at the date the proposal was made, this would not automatically have the effect of rendering the IVA void (unless there was clear evidence not only that the debtor lacked the requisite capacity at the time but also that the creditors were aware of that fact). By analogy with the principles that would obtain in the context of a simple contract, the question for the court would be whether, on the basis of expert medical evidence, the debtor lacked the ability to obtain, receive, understand and retain information relevant to the decisions that needed to be made and weigh that information in reaching those decisions. The question would be whether that debtor had the ability to understand the matters relevant to the key features of the proposed transaction, rather than every detail of it, not

---

35 Since DPO Sch 1, Part 3 (and in particular para 5) does not technically apply, and there being no interim order, there may be no pressing reason for the court to be informed.

36 Upon such an application, where necessary, the court would doubtless give suitable directions having regard, by analogy, to the provisions of Part 3 of Sch 1 to DPO 1986.

37 See [3.14] above. The modifications in DPO 1986, Sch 1, Part 2 are not confined to interim order cases.

whether they had actually understood it.[38] Where this is shown to be the case, the court may decide to set the IVA aside.

Separately, there are rules governing the situation where it becomes apparent **3.20** to the court at any stage that the debtor lacks mental capacity or is suffering from a mental or physical disability or affliction that renders the debtor unable to manage and administer their own property and affairs.[39] In such circumstances, the court has power to appoint a suitable person, either generally over the affairs of the debtor or in respect of a more limited aspect, such as for the purposes of a particular application or function.[40]

The court may make such an order upon the application of an appropriate **3.21** person, which includes the nominee or supervisor of the IVA and also the OR, but also any other person who appears to the court to be a suitable person to make such an application, which would include any person who has been appointed by any court in any jurisdiction to manage the affairs of or represent the debtor.[41] Unless the debtor lacked mental capacity, this could also include the debtor. Where such an application is made it must be supported by evidence in the form of a witness statement made by a medical practitioner as to the mental or (as the case may be) physical condition of the debtor.[42] Such an application may also be made without notice to any other party; however, the court can, as it thinks fit, insist on notice being given to the incapacitated debtor and/or to any other person (which in these circumstances would include the office-holder in respect of the particular IVA) and may adjourn the application to allow this to be done.[43] The order can also be made on the court's own initiative, without the need for any formal application.[44] In terms of the court's powers with respect to mental capacity, it is also important to bear in mind the provisions of the Civil Procedure Rules 1998 (CPR).[45]

---

38 *Fehily v Atkinson* [2016] EWHC 3069; [2017] Bus LR 695, especially at paragraphs [117]–[121], [126].
39 IR 2016, rr 12.23–12.26; the wording of these provisions (and how the words are arranged within the rules) is subtly different than under their predecessors (IR 1986, rr 7.43–7.44), which had themselves been subject to slight amendments introduced by the Insolvency (Amendment) Rules 2010 (SI 2010/686). It is not yet clear what difference, if any, these minor changes make.
40 IR 2016, r 12.24(1)–(2). In the context of bankruptcy, see for example *Marquis de Toucy v Bonhams 1793 Ltd* [2011] EWHC 3809 (Ch); [2012] BPIR 793; *Levy v Ellis-Carr* [2012] EWHC 63 (Ch); [2012] BPIR 347.
41 IR 2016, r 12.24(3)(a)–(d).
42 IR 2016, r 12.25.
43 IR 2016, r 12.24(4)–(5).
44 This is now explicit in IR 2016, r 12.24(3), but it was implicitly the case under IR 1986 also, see *Hunt v Fylde BC* [2008] BPIR 1368, at [13].
45 CPR, Part 21. On the interrelationship between CPR Part 21 and the provisions of what are now IR 2016, rr 12.23–12.26, see *Marquis de Toucy v Bonhams 1793 Ltd* (above).

3.22 As already referred to above, a debtor who succeeds in having their bankruptcy annulled pursuant to section 261 of IA 1986 is entitled to insist on having the fact of that annulment advertised by the OR. Where a debtor in that position lacks the capacity to do so, the rules specifically empower the person appointed by the court to represent the debtor, in accordance with the procedure set out above, to stand in the debtor's shoes for the very limited purpose of insisting that the OR advertise the fact of the annulment of the debtor's bankruptcy.[46]

C. TAXATION

3.23 Taxation in relation to IVAs is a complex topic and it is not proposed to give more than a very brief outline here. It is important, however, for any debtor and any professional advising them to appreciate the broad outlines.

3.24 In the first place it must be emphasised, as should be clear from the analysis above, that any liability to tax that has accrued prior to the approval of the debtor's proposal will be included within the IVA. Similarly, if any repayment is due to the debtor from HMRC at the outset, this will usually be off-set against any liability due to HMRC.[47] With regard to income tax, although any liability that accrues within the fiscal year in which the IVA commenced (i.e., down to 5 April following the approval) would likewise be included, any income tax referable to subsequent years, including during the course of the IVA, would be a separate liability for which the debtor would be solely liable outside the IVA.[48] With regard to VAT, any VAT due on realisations in the IVA must be accounted for to HMRC by the supervisor, and if the debtor is registered for VAT and has proposed a trading IVA, the VAT must be accounted for in the usual way. Capital gains tax arising on realisations of IVA assets during the course of the IVA will normally be an expense of the IVA, although the tax can only be computed at the end of the fiscal year in which the realisation took place.

3.25 The IP's remuneration, both in relation to initial advice and acting as nominee and also in supervising the IVA, in most cases will be exempt from VAT.[49]

---

46 IR 2016, r 8.36(4); cf. above [3.13] and below [10.16].

47 On set-off, see below [4.45]. Such set-off may have unintended consequences, of which the debtor should be made aware at the outset.

48 See *Rowland v Revenue and Customs Commissioners* [2019] UKFTT 544 (TC), at [28]–[33], although the point was ultimately conceded by the taxpayer without much argument (and the case was particularly chaotic).

49 *Paymex Ltd v Commissioners for HM Revenue and Customs* [2011] UKFTT 350 (TC); Value Added Tax 1994, s 31 and Sch 9, Group 5, item 5.

However, HMRC regards the fees of the nominee and of the supervisor as a single supply for VAT purposes,[50] so that if for any reason (contrary to the norm) the nominee does not go on to become the supervisor, then although the nominee's fees would be exempt, the remuneration of the supervisor (which is likely to be far greater) would not be.

---

50   A point made in *Paymex Ltd v HMRC* (above). See also HMRC's VAT Financial Guidance (VATFIN) 3260.

PART II

THE PRIMARY DOCUMENTS

4

THE PROPOSAL

A. BROAD OUTLINES AND PRECEDENTS

1. Initial considerations

At the heart of the Individual Voluntary Arrangement (IVA) procedure stands **4.01** the proposal, which is often, though not invariably, put together with the assistance of the proposed nominee. Where the debtor seeks advice from an insolvency practitioner (IP) at this preliminary stage, they will be expected to follow the guidance set out in the relevant Statement of Insolvency Practice (SIP).[1] While every proposal will necessarily be unique and tailored to the debtor's needs and circumstances, there are strict rules about what the proposal

---

1   SIP 3, sections 3 and 4 and the Appendix; SIP 3.1, at paras 8–14, especially 12–14.

must, at a minimum, contain, which are set out in the Insolvency (England and Wales) Rules 2016 (IR 2016).[2] Before sorting out the details of the proposal and ensuring it complies fully with the rules, the debtor will need to determine its basic structure. From the outset it must be borne in mind that the proposal must provide an attractive proposition for the creditors for the requisite majority (75 per cent by value) to approve it, and it must also be realistically capable of being fully implemented. This is not merely a matter of practicality: the debtor is specifically required to make out the case on both likelihood of acceptance and viability within the proposal itself.[3] Where an IP assists the debtor in putting together the proposal, the IP should 'try to structure an arrangement that will be capable of achieving the necessary statutory majorities and will not be unfairly prejudicial to any creditor'.[4]

4.02   Exactly how the IVA will be structured to meet these needs will depend very much on the debtor's individual circumstances, the nature of the debts involved and the means by which these are to be satisfied. The proposal will need to spell out in precise detail all the liabilities caught by the IVA, and the assets (and potentially the income) that will be made available within the IVA to meet them. Alongside the proposal, the debtor will also need to prepare a statement of affairs, setting out his financial position in relation to liabilities and assets in accordance with the rules.[5] The debtor will have to consider carefully how to structure the proposal so as to meet their liabilities in a way that is sufficiently attractive to a sufficient number of their creditors. This will include giving careful thought to the length of time the IVA will need to be in place in order to achieve its aims.

4.03   In some cases, the debtor will have to bring all their assets into the IVA, but by no means all IVAs are advanced on this 'all-assets' basis. In the alternative, known as a 'defined assets' IVA, the debtor will exclude certain assets from the IVA and only provide for specified assets to be included. The nature of the assets included will need to be carefully considered. Where these include real property, there is an important distinction between freehold and leasehold properties, the latter often giving rise to a greater number of problems. Valuations will have to be provided and justified. It is important to consider at the outset that subsequent changes in values can sometimes lead to unintended

---

2   In particular those set out in IR 2016, r 8.3.

3   See below [4.12].

4   *SISU Capital Fund Ltd v Tucker* [2005] EWHC 2170 (Ch), [2006] BPIR 154, at [118] (in the context of the duties imposed on a liquidator when assisting to formulate a proposal for a CVA).

5   See Chapter 5 below.

consequences, of which the debtor should be forewarned.[6] In some cases, the proposal may include third party assets, including assets that are jointly owned by the debtor and another. If the proposed nominee is assisting the debtor in putting together the proposal, it is essential that they satisfy themselves that any such third party has given informed consent.

Where the debtor is a sole-trader it will be necessary to consider whether **4.04** the business should continue, possibly becoming an integral support for the IVA, or whether actually the creditors might be better off if the business did not continue to trade but rather was sold off. If the intention is to implement a trading IVA, a host of considerations are likely to arise that will need to be factored into the planning of the proposal. It will be essential to establish at the outset whether the business is, or could be made to become, profitable and whether existing resources will be sufficient to sustain it or, if not, what alternative resources could be sourced. Would the existence of the IVA jeopardise the business, for example by reason of breaching dealership or franchise or licence agreements or breaching the rules of professional bodies that authorise and regulate the business? It will be necessary to ensure that supply chains are secure (and to establish whether such suppliers are among the significant creditors), and if they are not, what alternative suppliers might be found. It will be essential to establish whether the business operates from rented premises and if so what the position of the landlord might be; similarly, the attitude of secured creditors (if any) must be ascertained. If there are employees, to what extent are they creditors, are they generally likely to be supportive and is the business overstaffed, so that decisions about redundancies might be necessary?

If the debtor is an undischarged bankrupt intending to apply for the annulment **4.05** of their bankruptcy upon the approval of the IVA, this fact should be made clear in the proposal, since the annulment process will incur costs, which may affect the debtor's obligations under the IVA. Where the debtor is an undischarged bankrupt or has a bankruptcy petition pending against them, allowance should be made for the petitioning creditor's costs, which would normally rank as an expense of the IVA, ranking above the supervisor's costs.[7]

2. The Standard Conditions

IVAs come in myriad shapes and sizes, but the vast majority have many **4.06** characteristics in common. The problems to be addressed and the potential

---

6   See *Pitt v Mond* [2001] BPIR 624.
7   See para 5(4) of the Standard IVA Conditions (on which, see below [4.06]).

solutions for them tend to fall into well-established patterns, so that it is rarely necessary to create an entirely bespoke proposal from scratch. In recent years, it has become common practice to incorporate into the proposal the Standard IVA Conditions prepared by R3 (the Standard Conditions).[8]

4.07 The Standard Conditions provide a comprehensive set of model terms that can be easily adapted to fit almost any proposal. There is no requirement to include the Standard Conditions in any proposal, but in practice the overwhelming majority of modern proposals do so.[9] By their very nature, the Standard Conditions can only deal with the generic situation and must be supplemented by specific terms tailored to the needs and circumstances of the individual debtor. The usual practice is to annex the Standard Conditions to the individually drafted terms of the proposal, which in turn expressly incorporate them. This then allows the main body of the proposal to vary or exclude any terms in the Standard Conditions that do not fit the debtor's particular circumstances. To what extent the debtor wishes to adopt, adapt or reject the provisions of the Standard Conditions is ultimately a matter for the debtor acting on proper advice. The Standard Conditions provide that, in the event of any conflict between the Standard Conditions and the specific terms of the proposal (as modified by the creditors or otherwise), the proposal will prevail, thereby ensuring that the individually drafted terms of the proposal (as modified) take precedence.[10]

3. The IVA Protocol

4.08 A common scenario giving rise to the need for an IVA is the consumer credit trap, usually connected with credit card debt. Many such cases conform to a fairly similar pattern and to cater for this kind of relatively straightforward consumer IVA, the Insolvency Service publishes a template, known as the IVA Protocol.[11] In effect, the IVA Protocol is a kind of voluntary code designed to assist consumer debtors to formulate a proposal for paying off creditors within a specified time (usually five years). Where the IVA Protocol is adopted, the Standard Conditions would not be incorporated. The IVA Protocol is likely to be appropriate where the debtor is in receipt of a regular sustainable income, usually but not exclusively from regular employment or from a regular pension, and have three or more lines of credit from two or more creditors.[12] It is suita-

---

8   Available at www.r3.org.uk. References are to Version 4 (January 2018).
9   Other than those governed by the IVA Protocol: see below [4.08].
10   Standard Conditions, para 2.
11   See above [1.32].
12   IVA Protocol, para 3.1.

ble whether or not the debtor is a home-owner, but in the former case it should be made clear to the debtor that there is no expectation that their home should be sold as a part of the IVA.[13] The IVA Protocol may also have application in the case of the self-employed debtor, provided the source of income is sufficiently regular and predictable.[14] It is however unlikely that it would be suitable in cases where the debts are substantially disputed or where the debtor holds investment properties; nor in cases where full settlement of debts is likely to be possible within one year.[15]

The IVA Protocol is designed to facilitate the efficient handling of relatively **4.09** straightforward consumer IVAs. It is intended to supplement and clarify the regulatory framework that governs the activities of, on the one hand, IPs and the firms that employ them and, on the other, creditors who are members of Finance UK (formerly the British Bankers' Association), which has signed up to the IVA Protocol.[16] The IVA Protocol has the effect of ensuring in advance the cooperation and reasonable attitude of the creditors who are Finance UK members and is thereby intended to help implement the statutory procedure in such a way as to improve the likelihood of a successful outcome.[17] By reason of the standardisation in the IVA Protocol, creditors are more likely to be content with the proposal without the need for over-extensive scrutiny. It also minimises the likelihood that last-minute modifications will be required.[18] In this way, the IVA Protocol is intended to streamline the process, saving time and costs.

The IVA Protocol also provides guidance to assist the consumer debtor on **4.10** dealing with issues such as income and expenditure within the IVA and suggests mechanisms for equity release from the debtor's home, where necessary.[19] Special care needs to be applied when dealing with consumer debtors who are 'vulnerable', within the meaning applied by the Financial Conduct Authority.[20] It is a requirement of the IVA Protocol that the debtor in every case should receive appropriate advice and information in light of their individual circumstances, including non-financial considerations, so as to enable them to assess properly the advantages and disadvantages of all available debt resolution

---

13   IVA Protocol, para 3.3.
14   IVA Protocol, para 3.2.
15   IVA Protocol, para 3.4.
16   See IVA Protocol paras 2.1–2.3.
17   See IVA Protocol paras 12.1–12.3.
18   See IVA Protocol, paras 13.1–13.5.
19   See IVA Protocol, paras 7.3–7.10; 9.1–9.9.
20   See IVA Protocol, paras 2.8–2.10.

processes.[21] Even where it is not strictly appropriate for the individual debtor, the IVA Protocol may also provide some useful guidance.[22]

B. THE STATUTORY REQUIREMENTS

1. Overarching formalities

4.11 Whatever the details of the proposal, there are certain formalities that must be adhered to and various matters that must be included. These are set out in the relevant provisions of the Insolvency Act 1986 (IA 1986) and IR 2016. In addition to the specific requirements set out in Part 8 of IR 2016, which are dealt with below, reference must also be had to the general rules in Part 1 of IR 2016 dealing with the preparation of documents when complying with those requirements.[23]

4.12 There are some fundamental formalities that must be met: the proposal must be in writing;[24] it must be authenticated, in accordance with the rules, and dated by the debtor.[25] The proposal must identify the debtor and set out both why the debtor considers the IVA that is being proposed is desirable and why the debtor expects the creditors to agree to an IVA and to the terms of this proposal in particular.[26] This is usually achieved with the aid of a comparative outcome statement, showing how it would be likely that the creditors would fare better under the IVA as proposed as opposed to what would be likely to be the case in the event of the debtor being made bankrupt.

2. Assets

(a) The debtor's assets

4.13 The proposal must provide details of all the debtor's assets together with an estimate of their values.[27] All assets must be addressed and the debtor will need to bear in mind the wide definition of 'property' in IA 1986.[28] There is

---

21 IVA Protocol, paras 6.1 to 6.3.
22 See IVA Protocol, para 3.4. On the court's approach to the IVA Protocol, see *Mond v MBNA Europe Bank Ltd* [2010] EWHC 1710 (Ch), [2010] BPIR 1167.
23 Particularly IR 2016, r 1.6–1.9.
24 The requirement that it must be in writing, which is fundamental to the statutory provisions, is made explicit in IA 1986, ss 256(2)(a) and 256A(2)(a).
25 IR 2016, r 8.2(1)(d); for what amounts to authentication, see IR 2016, r 1.5.
26 IR 2016, r 8.2(1)(a)–(c).
27 IR 2016, r 8.3(a).
28 IA 1986, s 436(1).

no set rule in relation to the provision of estimates, but clearly if the assets are of substantial value, for example in the case of real property, it will almost inevitably be necessary to have relatively recent professional valuation. If any of the assets are charged, the proposal must set out the details and extent of the charge in each case.[29] This applies equally to equitable charges and charging orders under the Charging Orders Act 1979 (COA 1979) as it does to legal charges and mortgages.

It is often the case that the debtor will propose only including certain assets in the IVA and will exclude others that the debtor considers are not necessary for the success of the IVA. Where certain assets are to be excluded in this way, the debtor must set this out clearly in the proposal.[30] It is usually a good idea for the debtor to explain why any such assets are being excluded. Of course, the creditors may not accept this interpretation of what is needed to furnish the IVA, and it is not uncommon for the creditors, when considering the proposal, to insist on modifications to include one or more such excluded assets (or, more correctly, to insist on the removal of their exclusion).[31] **4.14**

(b) Third party assets

The debtor may also wish to include within the IVA property that they co-own with another person. In such a case, generally the debtor may only propose to include their own beneficial interest in the property. Even in such circumstances the co-owner would have to be consulted beforehand. It is also possible, however, for assets owned jointly by the debtor and a third party (often a relative of the debtor) to be brought wholly into the IVA for the benefit of the debtor's creditors. This is, of course, only possible in practice with the informed consent of the third-party co-owner of the asset in question. There are also circumstances in which a third party (again usually a relative) may be willing to allow an asset belonging solely to that party, in which the debtor has no interest, to be brought into the IVA, either by way of increasing the available assets from the outset or by way of a contingency in the event of a shortfall arising at a subsequent date (due to some other asset in the IVA not achieving its estimated value on realisation, for example). The use of third-party assets in this way (whether co-owned by the debtor or in which the debtor has no interest), is one of the ways in which an IVA can be made to be a more attractive proposition to creditors than would be the case if the debtor were made bankrupt. **4.15**

---

29   IR 2016, r 8.3(b).
30   IR 2016, r 8.3(c).
31   On modifications, see below [8.37]–[8.38].

4.16 Where the debtor does intend to include any asset belonging partly or wholly to a third party within the IVA for the benefit of the creditors, the proposal must give full particulars of any such asset, including the proper identification of who owns the asset in question and the precise terms on which it will be made available for inclusion within the IVA.[32] If those terms include that assets are to be held on trust for the third party in the event of failure of the IVA, this must also be made explicit.[33] The nominee will also need to see evidence from the third party (or parties) in question in relation to their agreement to the inclusion of the asset on those terms, so as to be sure that the necessary consent has been freely given. It is good practice for any third party who has agreed to make assets available for the purposes of the IVA to be required to sign the proposal, as provided for in the Standard Conditions.[34] Some thought will also need to be given to the mechanisms to be made available to the supervisor, or to the debtor, to enforce any obligation on the part of such a third party with regard to any such assets.[35]

3. Liabilities

(a) General liabilities

4.17 The proposal must provide full details of the nature and amount of all the debtor's liabilities.[36] It must also set out how it is proposed that these liabilities will be met, modified, postponed or otherwise dealt with by means of the IVA.[37] In deciding these issues, the debtor will have to be careful not to structure the IVA in such a way as to unfairly prejudice the interests of any one creditor or class of creditors. The proposal should deal with all matters in connection with how such debts will be processed in the IVA, including proofs of debt, the assessment and determination of such debts upon the submission of proofs and how any disputes will be handled. These matters are dealt with on a generic level at some length in the Standard Conditions, but even where the Standard Conditions are applied there are likely to be specific details that will need to be considered and spelt out in the proposal.[38] There are, in addition, certain matters that must be specifically addressed in the proposal regarding certain types of liability.

---

32   IR 2016, r 8.3(d); see also *Re Hussein* [1996] BPIR 160 (Blackburne J).
33   *Cooper v OR* [2002] EWHC 1970 (Ch), [2003] BPIR 55.
34   Standard Conditions, para 80(2).
35   See Standard Conditions, para 80.
36   IR 2016, r 8.3(e).
37   IR 2016, r 8.3(f).
38   See Standard Conditions, paras 31–48. Note that Part 14 of IR 2016 does not apply to IVAs (unless specifically incorporated in some way).

(b) Preferential and associated creditors

The debtor is specifically required to give details of how any preferential **4.18**
creditors will be dealt with.[39] The treatment of preferential creditors is exhaus-
tively prescribed by statute, and in general, except with the concurrence of the
creditor concerned, the creditors are not permitted to approve any proposal or
any modification to a proposal that purports to interfere with the priorities of
preferential debts as dictated by these provisions.[40] What constitutes 'preferential debts' for these purposes is defined in IA 1986.[41] The 'relevant date' for calculating such debts in the context of IVAs will depend upon the circumstances
of the debtor and the type of procedure followed to inaugurate the IVA: save
where the debtor is an undischarged bankrupt, the relevant date is the date
of the interim order made under section 252 of IA 1986, where there is such
an order, or otherwise the date on which the IVA takes effect.[42] Although IA
1986 does not explicitly define the relevant date in cases where the debtor is an
undischarged bankrupt, the most satisfactory view is that the relevant date for
the purposes of preferential debts within the IVA is to be understood as the
date of the bankruptcy order with respect to any debt within the bankruptcy
and the date of the creditors' decision with respect to any other debt.[43]

The proposal must also make specific provision for dealing with creditors who **4.19**
are associates of the debtor.[44] In terms of the voting rights of such creditors and
whether their vote can be counted in respect of reaching the required majority
for the purposes of approval of the proposal, this is governed elsewhere in
the rules.[45] What is required here is any proposed differential treatment of
associated creditors, for example the postponement or discount for dividend
purposes of a particular debt. Again, it would be necessary for any such creditor
to agree to any such terms of the proposal.

(c) Secured creditors

The proposal must also expressly cover the arrangements for dealing with the **4.20**
debts due to creditors who are, or claim to be, secured.[46] The rights of secured
creditors will, up to a point, be governed by the terms of the proposal (with
any modifications); but, except with the agreement of the secured creditor con-

---

39   IR 2016, r 8.3(f)(i).
40   IA 1986, s 258(5). See also Standard Conditions, para 58(1)–(2).
41   IA 1986, s 258(7), referring to s 386, which in turn refers to Sch 6 to IA 1986.
42   IA 1986, s 387(5).
43   This derives from reading s 387(5) and s 387(6) alongside s 257(3)(a) and (b).
44   IR 2016, r 8.3(f)(ii); for the meaning of 'associate' in this context, see IA 1986, s 435 and especially s 435(2).
45   IR 2016, r 15.34(6)–(7); cf. r 15.28(5) and r 15.31(3).
46   IR 2016, r 8.3(f)(i).

cerned, those terms could not legitimately interfere with the rights of secured creditors to enforce their security.[47] There is, however, nothing in principle to prevent a secured creditor from voluntarily surrendering their security for the benefit of the IVA creditors generally, and if this happens it usually means that the creditor in question can prove for the entirety of their debt (as if no security had ever been granted).[48]

4.21   The proposal should also deal with the position where such security is realised during the course of the IVA.[49] Whether, as a matter of practicality, it is prudent or reasonable for a creditor holding security to attempt to enforce their security may depend on the facts: where there is no value in the security (because, for example, the creditor holds a second charge over the property and there will be no moneys available to meet that charge after the first charge has been satisfied), it may serve no valid purpose for the creditor to pursue realisation.[50] Generally speaking, therefore, it is prudent for the debtor (and any IP advising them) to ascertain in advance the attitude of the secured creditors to what is being proposed.[51]

4.22   For these purposes, an execution creditor with the benefit of a walking possession agreement, even where goods have not been sold, would be counted as a secured creditor.[52] The same applies equally to any creditor who has perfected execution against the goods or land of the debtor by obtaining a charging order under COA 1979 prior to the commencement of the IVA. Where such execution was incomplete, in that any charging order had not been made absolute as at the date of the approval of the proposal, the terms of the proposal would normally preclude any such execution being perfected.[53]

4.23   Where a creditor holds security, but the security is insufficient to cover the entirety of the debt, the creditor in question would be entitled to prove for and receive a dividend in the IVA in relation to the unsecured portion of the debt.[54] With regard to voting rights, these are governed by other rules that broadly

---

47   See s 258(4); notwithstanding the heading of this subsection, it applies to proposals and not just modifications. See Standard Conditions, para 4(5)(a), and also *Rey v FNCB Ltd* [2006] EWHC 1386 (Ch); [2006] BPIR 1260.
48   See Standard Conditions, para 40(2).
49   See Standard Conditions, para 40(6).
50   *Co-operative Bank plc v Phillips* [2014] 2862 (Ch); [2014] BPIR 1430, on which see further below [4.46].
51   See SIP 3 and paras 4.3(a)(x)–(xi), 6.4(e).
52   *Re A Debtor (No. 10 of 1992)* [1995] BCC 525.
53   See the Standard Conditions, para 6.
54   See the Standard Conditions, para 40(1).

reflect the same principle.[55] A creditor holding insufficient security to cover the entire debt and who participates in the IVA for the unsecured element is not necessarily precluded thereby from later enforcing its security.[56] Conversely, where the creditor values the security at nil for the purpose of participating in the IVA, this can have the effect of extinguishing the security.[57] Ideally the proposal should also make provision for the situation where the value of the security in question changes.[58]

(d) Antecedent transactions

In addition, the proposal must set out matters relating to liabilities arising **4.24** or potentially arising under certain specified provisions of IA 1986: namely, sections 339 (transactions at an undervalue), 340 (preferences) and 343 (extortionate credit transactions). Such claims could only arise in the event that the debtor is made bankrupt. Where the debtor is an undischarged bankrupt at the date of the proposal, the proposal must state whether any claim has been made under any of these statutory provisions and, if so, whether any and if so what provision is being made to indemnify the bankrupt's estate in respect of any such claim or claims.[59] Where the debtor is not an undischarged bankrupt, the proposal must set out whether there are circumstances which might give rise to such a claim in the event that the debtor were made bankrupt and, if such circumstances do exist, then it must also set out whether and if so what provision will be made to indemnify the bankruptcy estate in the event of a bankruptcy order subsequently being made against the debtor.[60]

(e) Excluded liabilities

Certain debts are not capable of being brought within an IVA (or at least not **4.25** without the express consent of the creditor). These include in particular any liability arising under the Child Support Act 1991.[61] In most cases, liabilities consisting of arrears under orders made in family proceedings (other than lump sum orders and orders for costs) will remain outside the IVA.[62] An IVA cannot include liabilities in the nature of fines. In *R v Barnet Justices, ex p Phillippou*,[63] this was held to include a compensation order (as being within the wider

---

55   IR 2016, 15.31(4)–(4); cf. the Standard Conditions, para 64(3).
56   *Whitehead v Household Mortgage Corporation plc* [2002] EWCA Civ. 1657; [2003] BPIR 1482; see also *Rey v FNCB Ltd* [2006] EWHC 1386 (Ch); [2006] BPIR 1260.
57   *Kahn v Permayer* [2001] BPIR 95 (CA).
58   See Standard Conditions, para 40(3)–(5).
59   IR 2016, r 8.3(f)(iii). Note also SIP 3, para 4.3(c), where an IP is assisting with the proposal.
60   IR 2016, r 8.3(f)(iv).
61   IA 1986, s 382(5).
62   But this is a complex area: see above [2.33].
63   [1997] BPIR 134.

definition of 'fine' in section 281(8) of IA 1986). In addition, student loans (or postgraduate degree loans) received or eligible to be received by the debtor student, whether before or after approval of the proposal, cannot be included within the IVA.[64]

4. Information relating to office-holders

(a) Identification of the proposed nominee/supervisor

4.26 The proposal must identify the person who is to act as nominee in relation to the proposal and who will become the supervisor of the IVA in the event that it is approved; such a person must be qualified to act as an IP or authorised to act as nominee in relation to the IVA.[65] The proposal must state the name of the proposed nominee, the fact that it is proposed that they should hold that office, their postal address and either an email address or a telephone number through which they may be contacted.[66] It must also confirm that the proposed nominee is a qualified IP or other person authorised to act as supervisor of the proposed IVA and specify the relevant professional body that is the source of the proposed supervisor's authorisation.[67]

4.27 For the IVA to function efficiently, it is necessary for the debtor, the creditors and the supervisor to understand clearly the nature and extent of the supervisor's functions and powers, which must therefore be set out in the proposal.[68] These matters will need to be discussed and agreed with the proposed supervisor in advance. Sometimes is it necessary or desirable for the supervisor to take a more hands-on approach to the supervision of the IVA; sometimes the 'touch' will be fairly light. Although the rules are not prescriptive in this regard, there are a number of issues that will need to be covered in the proposal and the Standard Conditions provide a sensible template that can be modified or augmented as the debtor's circumstances require.[69]

4.28 Two or more persons can be joint nominees and/or joint supervisors. In circumstances where joint supervisors are to be appointed, it will be necessary for the proposal to set out how the functions and powers will be exercised by them,

---

64 Education (Student Loans) (Repayment) Regulations 2009, reg. 80(2)(c)–(d) (as amended).
65 IA 1986, s 253(2); there is no precise equivalent in s 256A, but it is implicit in s 256A(2)–(3).
66 IR 2016, r 8.3(h) in conjunction with r 1.6(1)–(2) and paragraphs (o)–(r) of the subsequent table.
67 IR 2016, r 8.3(i). On the qualification and authorisation of IPs, see ss 390 and 390A of IA 1986.
68 IR 2016, r 8.3(k).
69 Standard Conditions, paras 12–16, discussed more fully in section C of this chapter below.

in particular whether acts in connection with the IVA may be done by one or more of them or whether they must be done by all acting together.[70]

(b) The fees and expenses of the nominee and the supervisor

The proposal must set out clearly the fees and expenses that the nominee **4.29** will be able to claim.[71] Self-evidently this should be agreed with the proposed nominee in advance. The prospective nominee will have to bear in mind the guidance in the relevant SIP.[72] The fees must, in any event, be within the realms of reasonableness, as unjustifiably high nominee fees could undermine the viability of the proposal.[73]

In addition, the proposal must also set out how the fees and expenses of the **4.30** supervisor will be determined and paid.[74] The rules do not dictate how the supervisor's fees are to be calculated; rather this is a matter that is left to the debtor and the creditors to decide between them. In essence there are three alternative bases: it could be a fixed sum, a percentage of funds brought into the IVA or calculated with reference to the time spent by the supervisor and the supervisor's staff. Where the choice is for time-costs, provision should also be made for the supervisor to keep the creditors informed of any fees and expenses incurred; it may also be prudent to provide a mechanism by which any decision of the creditors in relation to the supervisor's fees or expenses can be referred by the supervisor to the court for the court to give a definitive view binding on both the creditors and the supervisor.[75]

In deciding these issues, the debtor will need to bear in mind the likely views **4.31** of the creditors as well as of the proposed supervisor.[76] The fees need to be reasonable: they cannot be too low, or this would hamper proper supervision; equally, they should not be unrealistically high.[77] In many cases a fixed fee or at least a cap is agreed, but this can be problematic unless carefully drafted.[78] Wherever possible, precise limitations are best avoided, so as to allow the

---

70   IR 2016, r 8.3(l).

71   IR 2016, r 8.3(g).

72   SIP 9 Payments to Office Holders and their Associates (Dec 2015).

73   See *Re Julie O'Sullivan* [2001] BPIR 534, where an application for an interim order was dismissed on the basis that the level of nominee's fees could not be justified.

74   IR 2016, r 8.3(j).

75   See Standard Conditions, para 17; see also paras 14(2) and 57. For the need to keep the creditors informed, see also IR 2016, r 8.38 and below at [11.15].

76   As well as SIP 9 (see above).

77   Note the cautionary tale of *Royal Bank of Scotland plc v Munikwa* [2020] EWHC 786 (Ch), on which see below [8.39].

78   See, for example, *Re a Block Transfer by Kaye and Morgan; Re Paul Murphy* [2010] BPIR 602, on which see below [11.14].

supervisor to deal with the IVA in a flexible manner without leading to difficulties in the event of unforeseen contingencies arising.

5. Guarantees

4.32 The rules require the proposal to state whether any guarantees have been given in respect of any of the debtor's debts by third parties, and in each case whether the guarantor is an associate of the debtor.[79] The proposal must also state whether any guarantees are proposed to be offered by third parties for the purposes of the IVA and, if so, to provide full details of the proposed guarantor and whether security is to be given or sought.[80] Guarantees offered by third parties should be expressed to be for the benefit of the supervisor of the IVA and their successors in title.[81]

6. Timing

(a) Duration

4.33 The proposal must specify the proposed duration of the IVA.[82] This would typically be three to five years, although this will depend on the type of IVA and the specific circumstances of the debtor and it could be shorter or longer than this. The duration must be expressed in clear and definite terms. Care should be exercised not to choose a longer period than is needed (particularly in a trading IVAs). Conversely the debtor may wish to include terms to allow for some flexibility in case of unforeseen delays.[83]

(b) Distributions

4.34 The rules also require that the proposal must specify the dates of proposed distributions to creditors and estimate the amounts that will be included in such distributions.[84] In many cases precision may not be possible, but some estimation should be provided.[85]

---

79   IR 2016, r 8.3(m).
80   IR 2016, r 8.3(n).
81   *Cooper v OR* [2002] EWHC 1970 (Ch), [2003] BPIR 55.
82   IR 2016, r 8.3(o).
83   See below [4.47]–[4.48].
84   IR 2016, r 8.3(p).
85   On dividends, see also Standard Conditions, paras 49–58.

7. Type of proceedings

Until the end of 2020, the proposal had to specify whether the IVA would **4.35** be governed by the EU Regulation on Insolvency Proceedings (the EU Regulation),[86] and, if so, whether the proceedings would be 'main' or 'territorial' within the meaning of Article 3 of the EU Regulation, providing reasons in support of these assertions.[87] As a result of Brexit, however, this requirement has been amended with effect from 11pm on 31 December 2020 to require the proposal to state whether the resulting IVA would be 'COMI proceedings, establishment proceedings or proceedings to which the EU Regulation as it has effect in the law of the United Kingdom does not apply'.[88]

8. Financial matters during the IVA

(a) Conduct of debtor's business

If the debtor owns and runs a business and it is proposed that this business **4.36** should continue during the course of the IVA and should provide funds for the IVA, this will need to be taken into account at the earliest stage of planning the IVA, as this will colour the kind of proposal that will be required. Thought will have to be given to the extent of the supervisor's powers to intervene in the debtor's conduct of the business. In any event it will be necessary to work out in detail how the business will be conducted during the IVA and to set this out in the proposal.[89]

(b) Further credit facilities

Where it is proposed that the debtor will seek further credit facilities during **4.37** the course of and for the benefit of the IVA, the proposal must provide the details of any such proposed facility and how the debts so arising will be paid.[90]

(c) Funds arising in the IVA

The proposal is required to set out the precise manner in which funds held **4.38** for the purposes of the IVA are to be banked, invested or otherwise dealt with pending distribution to creditors and also how funds held for the purpose of payment to creditors that remain undistributed at the date of termination of

---

86   Reg. 2015/848, OJ L141/19.
87   IR 2016, r 8.3(q); see also IR 2016, r 1.7.
88   IR 2016, r 8.3(q) as substituted by the Insolvency (Amendment)(EU Exit) Regulations 2019 (SI 2019/146), Sch 1, Part 4, para 84.
89   IR 2016, r 8.3(r).
90   IR 2016, r 8.3(s).

the IVA will be dealt with.[91] This requires careful consideration. One important issue the debtor will need to decide is whether the assets included within the IVA, and any funds representing the realisation of such assets, that are in the possession, custody or control of the supervisor should be held by the supervisor on trust for the purposes of the IVA. The wording of section 253(2) of IA 1986 makes it clear that the nominee, once acting as supervisor of the IVA, may or may not act as trustee; whether the supervisor does in fact act as trustee will be determined by the terms of the proposal, as a matter of construction.[92] These issues are dealt with in the Standard Conditions, which provide for a trust and deal with the position post-termination,[93] but even where the Standard Conditions are adopted these provisions can be modified or replaced by the specific terms in the main body of the proposal.

4.39 A further matter the proposal must deal with is how it is proposed that creditors who do not have notice of the IVA, but are nevertheless bound by it by virtue of section 260(2)(b)(ii) of IA 1986, should be dealt with.[94] This is not entirely straightforward but the Standard Conditions provide a workable solution.[95]

9. Other matters

(a) Previous proposals

4.40 The rules also require that the proposal provides details of any previous attempts by the debtor to put forward a proposal for an IVA within the 24 months prior to the date of the submission of the current proposal to the nominee, whether or not that attempt was successful. The proposal must state whether any such proposal was sent to creditors for their approval, and if so whether it was approved or rejected, if it was approved, whether it was completed or terminated and, if it was rejected, in what respects the previous proposal differs from the present one.[96] The proposal should also state if an application for an interim order was made in connection with any such previous proposal and, if so, whether the interim order was made.[97]

---

91   IR 2016, r 8.3(t)–(u).
92   See *Welburn v Dibb Lupton Broomhead* [2002] EWCA Civ 1601; [2003] BPIR 768, at [14]–[16]. See also above [2.16].
93   Standard Conditions, para 29.
94   IR 2016, r 8.3(v).
95   Standard Conditions, paras 44–48.
96   IR 2016, r 8.3(w).
97   IR 2016, r 8.3(w)(ii).

(b) Any other matters

The list of statutory requirements ends by requiring the debtor to provide **4.41** details of any other matters that the debtor considers appropriate to enable the creditors to reach an informed decision on the proposal. This is, in effect, a catch-all, intended to ensure that debtors provide full and frank information to the creditors.[98]

C. ADDITIONAL MATTERS FOR CONSIDERATION

1. Decisions, committees and after-acquired assets

The statutory requirements must all be properly dealt with in the proposal, **4.42** but there are a number issues that these do not cover that are none the less desirable in most cases and should at least be considered. Some are of greater significance than others and not all will necessarily be relevant to every proposal, but any IP assisting the debtor in putting together the proposal would need to go through these additional issues with the debtor. Most, if not all, are addressed to a greater or lesser extent in the Standard Conditions. Those discussed below are only some of the more important additional issues that should be considered.

One area where the proposal could usefully expand on the minimum required **4.43** under the rules is the general powers of the supervisor.[99] The Standard Conditions incorporate the provisions in IA 1986 and IR 2016 relating to the powers of the trustee in bankruptcy, modified as necessary, together with the power to seek the views of creditors (either directly by decision procedure or through a creditors' committee, if the proposal has provided for one), allowing the supervisor to deal with unforeseen eventualities.[100] Whether it is necessary or desirable to establish a creditors' committee will depend on the complexity of the IVA and the extent of the liabilities; in more complex arrangements, well-drafted provisions for such a committee may allow for greater efficiency in dealing with such eventualities.[101] Whether or not a creditors' committee is

---

98   IR 2016, r 8.3(x). On the need for transparency, see above [2.03]–[2.04].

99   See Standard Conditions, para 13.

100 Standard Conditions, para 15; these powers are expressly granted without prejudice to the supervisor's right to apply to the court for directions (under IA 1986, s 263(4)).

101 Standard Conditions, para 59; para 59(3) incorporates the general rules pertaining to creditors' committees under Part 17 of IR 2016.

established, provision should be made to govern the decision-making procedures whereby the supervisor can consult the creditors.[102]

4.44 Another matter beyond the statutory requirements that deserves consideration is the issue of how assets acquired by the debtor during the term of the IVA should be dealt with. The Standard Conditions provide a workable precedent.[103]

2. Set-off

4.45 One of the more significant matters not touched upon by the statutory requirements is the treatment of mutual debts and the issue of set-off. This is an important lacuna because the statutory provisions for automatic set-off in the case of mutual dealings in bankruptcy do not apply to IVAs.[104] It is therefore strongly recommended that some form of provision to deal with these issues be included in the proposal. For this reason, the issue is comprehensively addressed in the Standard Conditions, adapting the statutory provisions that apply in bankruptcy to the circumstances of an IVA.[105]

4.46 The set-off provisions in an earlier edition of the Standard Conditions were considered by Morgan J in *Co-operative Bank plc v Phillips*.[106] Here a creditor holding a second charge had to discontinue enforcement proceedings once it became clear that there was no equity in the property to satisfy the security. It was held that the proceedings were not an abuse or brought for a collateral purpose and that, because they had been started after the commencement of the debtor's IVA, there could be no 'mutual dealings' for the purposes of setting off the costs awarded to the debtor against the underlying debt. It is now likely that, had the proceedings been issued prior to the commencement of the IVA, set-off could apply.[107]

3. Variation, extension, full implementation and termination

4.47 Another significant lacuna in the statutory requirements that deserves careful attention is how and under what circumstances the IVA can be varied.[108] This is of importance because unforeseen circumstances frequently arise and the

---

102 See Standard Conditions, para 61–69.
103 Standard Conditions, para 28.
104 IA 1986, s 323.
105 Standard Conditions, para 7.
106 [2014] 2862 (Ch), [2014] BPIR 1430, at [79]–[81] (cf. above [4.21]).
107 See above [2.20].
108 See Standard Conditions, para 81.

court has no power to vary the IVA once approved.[109] Although, even absent such express power, the creditors and debtor can, in theory, agree to alter the way in which the arrangement applies to them (on contractual principles), this often leads to unsatisfactory results that can be avoided by a properly worded variation clause in the proposal.[110]

One especially important context for the exercise of the power to vary is in **4.48** relation to the duration of the arrangement. A provision dealing with the power to extend the IVA is highly desirable, because the court has no power to direct any extension to the duration of the IVA during the course of the IVA and, once the term of the IVA has expired, neither the court nor the creditors have any power to extend it further.[111] The suggested provision in the Standard Conditions dealing with extensions also permits the supervisor to exercise the power in certain circumstances and to a limited degree without the need expressly to seek creditor approval.[112]

There are a number of other issues surrounding the end of the IVA that should **4.49** be addressed in any well-drafted proposal. This is an area that the statutory provisions leave almost entirely open. One such issue concerns the precise definition of what constitutes full implementation of the IVA, to which may be added a term allowing the supervisor to certify substantial compliance in certain circumstances.[113] Equally, the proposal should address the precise circumstances in which, and the mechanisms by which, the IVA may or must be brought to an end prematurely by reason of default.[114] These should include provisions dealing with the presentation of a bankruptcy petition in relation to the debtor's default, including expenses in relation to such a petition (which may require a specific payment into the IVA at the outset, by the debtor or a third party, to be retained by the supervisor for this purpose).[115] Ideally, the proposal should also deal with the supervisor's powers in the context of the IVA coming to an end, and in particular with the terms on which the supervisor should continue to hold and deal with any remaining funds (especially funds held on trust).[116] Provisions should also be included in relation to

---

109   *Re Alpha Lighting Ltd* [1997] BPIR 341.
110   See below [11.23] and, on variation generally, [11.20]–[11.22].
111   *Strongmaster Ltd v Kaye* [2002] EWHC 444 (Ch), [2002] BPIR 1259; see below at [12.02].
112   Standard Conditions, para 8.
113   See Standard Conditions, paras 9–10; see below [12.05].
114   See Standard Conditions, paras 11, 70–71. See Chapter 12 below.
115   See Standard Conditions, paras 71–72.
116   See Standard Conditions, paras 14 and 56(2)–(3).

the supervisor's vacation of office, whether by resignation or otherwise, the removal and/or replacement of a supervisor and the supervisor's release.[117]

D. AMENDMENT OF THE PROPOSAL

4.50 After the proposal has been submitted to the nominee, it may be amended with the written approval of the nominee, but only up to the point where the nominee delivers the report to the court or, as the case may be, to the creditors.[118] This rarely arises in practice, since in most cases the nominee will have had considerable input in drafting the proposal in the first place. Once the nominee has formally considered the proposal and reported on it, the proposal cannot be amended without restarting the process. However, when considering the proposal, the creditors may insist upon certain modifications prior to approving it.[119] Once approved, the proposal as such may not be amended, although the terms of the IVA may be varied if such a power exists.[120]

---

117 See generally Standard Conditions, paras 18–22.
118 IR 2016, r 8.2(2).
119 See below [8.37]–[8.40].
120 See above [4.47].

5

STATEMENT OF AFFAIRS

A. INTRODUCTION

1. The requirement

5.01 In order to put a proposal for an individual voluntary arrangement (IVA) to the creditors under Part 8 of the Insolvency Act 1986 (IA 1986), the debtor is generally required to make a full statement, known as a statement of affairs, disclosing their financial position in detail and containing such information as may be prescribed. The procedural niceties and form of the statement of affairs, as discussed below, are largely dictated by IA 1986 and the Insolvency (England and Wales) Rules 2016 (IR 2016).[1]

5.02 Whether or not the debtor is applying for an interim order, the statement of affairs must be supplied to the nominee alongside the proposal.[2] The only exception to this is where the debtor is an undischarged bankrupt and has delivered a statement of affairs within the bankruptcy pursuant to section

---

1   SI 2016/1024.
2   IA 1986, s 256(2)(b) or s 256A(2)(b), depending on whether or not an interim order is being sought.

288 of IA 1986: where this is the case, unless the nominee requires a further statement of affairs to supplement the earlier one delivered in the bankruptcy, the debtor need not submit a new statement of affairs along with the proposal.[3]

2. Purpose

5.03 The proposal is the document that sets out in detail the terms on which the debtor is proposing to enter an arrangement with their creditors. The terms of the proposal must be comprehensive and will deal with which of the debtor's assets will be included in the arrangement and which (if any) will remain outside, as well as what other assets (if any) will be made available and what the debtor's liabilities are, all in accordance with the requirements discussed in the previous chapter. Over and above the detail contained in the proposal, however, the debtor is required to provide a good deal more in-depth information about their financial position, which information must be set out in the statement of affairs.[4] It is an essential part of the process for the debtor to provide such information against which the viability and appropriateness of the proposal may be judged, initially by the nominee for the purposes of compiling their initial report on the proposal and, subsequently, by the creditors. The statement of affairs, together with the supporting documentation that should be annexed to it, thus fulfils a vital role by going into a level of detail that the proposal would not generally be required to provide and to do so in such a way as to enable the creditors to reach an informed decision as to whether it is in their interests to accept the proposal, with or without modifications.

5.04 The debtor's duty of good faith and transparency applies every bit as strictly to the preparation of the statement of affairs and its supporting documents as it does to the proposal itself.[5] The debtor should be constantly aware throughout the process of compiling this statement that any misstatement it contains or any significant inaccuracies in or omissions from the information so provided could amount to a 'material irregularity' (within the meaning of section 262 of IA 1986), rendering the IVA open to challenge by an aggrieved creditor.[6] Where the debtor deliberately makes a false statement this may even render them criminally liable.[7] Where an insolvency practitioner (IP) is assisting the

---

3   IR 2016, r 8.5(6).
4   On the prescribed contents, see section B of this chapter, below.
5   On the obligations of good faith and transparency, see Chapter 2 above.
6   On which, see Chapter 9 below.
7   IA 1986, s 262A, on which see below [9.34]. See also below [5.06].

debtor in putting together the proposal and statement of affairs, it is imperative that they bring these points to the debtor's attention.[8]

B. FORMALITIES AND CONTENTS

1. Prescribed formalities

(a) The operative date

As a general rule, the statement of affairs must be made up to a date no earlier **5.05** than two weeks before the date of the proposal.[9] However, where circumstances make it more practical, the nominee may allow the statement of affairs to be made up to a date earlier than two weeks (but not earlier than two months); where this is the case the nominee's report must include an explanation of why the earlier date was allowed.[10]

(b) Statement of truth

The debtor must sign the statement of affairs with a statement of truth.[11] The **5.06** contents of the statement of truth are set out in Part 22 of the Civil Procedure Rules 1998 (CPR).[12] Proceedings for contempt of court may be brought against a debtor who signs a statement of affairs with a statement of truth without having an honest belief in the truth of the contents of the statement of affairs.[13] This is entirely separate from the criminal sanctions referred to above.[14]

2. Prescribed contents

The information that the debtor is required to include in the statement of **5.07** affairs is set out in IR 2016.[15] Essentially, this concerns the debtor's assets and liabilities and dictates the level of detail that is required in each respect.

(a) Assets

The statement must contain a list of all the debtor's assets, divided into catego- **5.08** ries so as to allow easy identification, with estimated values provided for each

---

8   Statement of Insolvency Practice (SIP) 3, para 4.1.
9   IR 2016, r 8.5(2).
10   IR 2016, r 8.5(3)–(4).
11   IR 2016, r 8.5(5).
12   As incorporated by IR 2016, r 12.1(1).
13   CPR 32.14, as specifically applied by IR 2016, r 12.1(3).
14   At [5.04].
15   IR 2016, r 8.5.

category.[16] Assets of any significant value may require formal valuations, copies of which should be annexed to the statement. The valuations should be recent enough to comply with the statutory requirements as to timing.[17]

5.09 Where any claim against the debtor is wholly or partially secured against any property of the debtor's, the statement must provide full particulars of the claim that is secured in this way and how and when that security was created.[18] Again, it will usually be necessary to obtain up-to-date information on the current redemption value of the security as part of the information relating to the value of the asset in question.

(b) Liabilities and creditors

5.10 The statement must also contain a list of the debtor's unsecured creditors. The first part of this list needs to set out the names and addresses of every preferential creditor and the amounts of their respective claims.[19] The list should then proceed to set out the same information with respect to all the debtor's other unsecured creditors.[20]

(c) Dealings with associates

5.11 The statement must also, and separately, provide particulars of any debts which are owed to any associate of the debtor and of any debt owed to the debtor by any person who is an associate.[21] These details are required in this separate fashion, both to assist the nominee in compiling the necessary report and to assist the creditors in weighing up the proposition presented in the proposal. This information is also of assistance to the nominee/chair of the decision-making procedure that follows in calculating the votes in accordance with the rules.[22]

(d) Information required by the nominee

5.12 Where the intended nominee has been assisting the debtor in putting together the proposal, they may form the view that the bare essentials required to be set out in the statement of affairs by the rules are insufficient for the purposes

---

16 IR 2016, r 8.5(1)(a). See also SIP 3, paras 4.1 and 4.3(b).
17 See above [5.05].
18 IR 2016, r 8.5(1)(b).
19 IR 2016, r 8.5(1)(c); 'preferential debts' are defined in IA 1986, s 386 and Sch 6, although it should be noted that this definition is liable to change from time to time.
20 IR 2016, r 8.5(1)(d).
21 IR 2016, r 8.5(1)(e) and (f), respectively; for the meaning of 'associate' in this context, see IA 1986, s 435 and especially s 435(2).
22 On the calculation of votes and rules relating to associates, see below [8.46].

of compiling their initial report on the proposal to be sent to the court or (as the case may be) to the creditors. In such a case, especially where the nominated IP is also assisting the debtor with preparing the statement of affairs, generally they would be expected to inform the debtor, as part of that advice, what further information is needed to produce a fully compliant statement of affairs.[23] Where the nominee has had no involvement in preparing the statement of affairs, they may still become aware of circumstances in the debtor's affairs or in the proposal that may require further elucidation. Where the nominee forms the view that, for the purposes of making their initial report, it would be necessary for the debtor to provide certain additional particulars (over and above the statutory minimum requirements set out above), they may require the debtor in writing to provide such further particulars; where they do so the debtor must include these additional particulars within the statement of affairs.[24]

The nominee may also form the view that further information is required even **5.13** after having formally been provided with the proposal and statement of affairs. To the extent that this may require the debtor to amend the proposal, this is expressly permitted, subject to the nominee's approval.[25] There is, however, no such formal statutory power in relation to amending the statement of affairs. There is no difficulty in the debtor supplying further and better information,[26] but if significant corrections need to be made to the statement of affairs, the nominee would have to take a pragmatic view.

C. FURTHER INFORMATION AND DOCUMENTATION

1. Further information to be provided by the debtor

(a) General information on the debtor's affairs

The nominee has to be satisfied that the proposal and, in particular, the state- **5.14** ment of affairs that supports it, represent a true picture of the debtor's affairs and financial position. Among the matters to which the nominee's report must address itself is whether or not the debtor's financial position is materially different from that presented in the proposal.[27] To be in a position to make that assessment, and indeed the other matters that are required to be dealt with in

---

23 See SIP 3, para 4 generally and SIP 3.1, para 14(a), (b) and (e).
24 IR 2016, r 8.5(1)(g).
25 See above [4.50].
26 See IR 2016, r 8.7 (discussed below [5.15]–[5.16]).
27 See SIP 3.1, para 14(a)(i); on the contents of the report generally, see below [8.04]–[8.09].

the report, the nominee may need to have access to further information and documentation than is contained within the proposal and statement of affairs themselves.

5.15 Where it appears to the nominee that the report cannot properly be prepared on the basis of the information supplied in the proposal and statement of affairs, the nominee may require the debtor to provide such further information relating to the debtor's affairs as the nominee thinks necessary for the purpose of compiling the report.[28] The nominee is empowered to require the debtor to provide further information relating to specific matters that should, properly speaking, have been provided by the debtor in the proposal. Most obviously, this relates to the circumstances in which, and the reasons why, the debtor is proposing an IVA.[29] If the proposal has been prepared with the assistance of the IP who is the designated nominee, then, provided the IP has carried out their functions properly, the occasion for such requests should arise very rarely.

(b)   The debtor's previous brushes with insolvency

5.16 The nominee is also empowered, where they believe it is necessary for the purposes of compiling the report, to require the debtor to provide further and better information than was set out in the proposal in relation to any previous proposal the debtor has made for an IVA within the 24 months preceding the date of the proposal currently under consideration.[30] In addition, the nominee may also require to be provided with information concerning any other previous proposals for an IVA made by the debtor, whenever those were made.[31] This latter goes beyond what was strictly required to be included within the proposal.

5.17 In addition, the nominee may require information relating to the debtor's potential involvement in various other forms of insolvency event. The specific subjects on which the nominee may require information or further information in this regard relate to whether and in what circumstances the debtor has at any time:

- entered into any other sort of arrangement with their creditors (besides a formal IVA, dealt with above);[32]

---

28   IR 2016, r 8.7(1)(d).
29   IR 2016, r 8.7(1)(a).
30   IR 2016, r 8.7(1)(b); on the requirement, under IR 2016, r 8.3(w), to include particulars of previous proposals within the proposal, see above [4.40].
31   IR 2016, r 8.7(1)(b) and (c), respectively.
32   IR 2016, r 8.7(2)(d).

- been made bankrupt;[33]
- been the subject of a debt relief order;[34] or
- been concerned in the affairs of a company (wherever incorporated) or a limited liability partnership that has become the subject of insolvency proceedings.[35]

2. Access to the debtor's financial records

Quite separately, the debtor is in any event under an obligation to give the nominee access to such of the debtor's accounts and records as the nominee may require for the purposes of considering the proposal and compiling the report.[36] The purpose of this provision is to ensure that the nominee is well placed to assess the accuracy (or otherwise) of the financial information provided in the proposal and the statement of affairs. In practice, where (as is commonly the case) the proposal was put together with the assistance and advice of the IP who is the designated nominee, they should have insisted on reviewing any relevant documentation of this kind at an earlier stage, so that this provision will rarely be relied upon.[37] On the other hand, where the nominee has not previously seen such documentation and there is anything in the proposal to suggest that the debtor's finances are not necessarily as set out in the proposal and statement of affairs, the nominee is under a positive duty to consider what further investigation may be necessary;[38] in such circumstances, the nominee may insist on being able to inspect such documents. **5.18**

D. OMISSION OF PREJUDICIAL INFORMATION

Notwithstanding the requirement of transparency and full disclosure, indeed doubtless to some extent precisely because of it, there is in place a statutory safeguard designed to protect the IVA from sabotage or to provide protection to vulnerable people, should any information provided in the statement of affairs pose a threat to either if made public. Where the court is satisfied, upon an application made to it by a relevant person, that certain information contained in the statement of affairs would be likely to prejudice the conduct of the IVA or might reasonably be expected to lead to violence against any person, it **5.19**

---

33   IR 2016, r 8.7(2)(b).
34   IR 2016, r 8.7(2)(c).
35   IR 2016, r 8.7(2)(a).
36   IR 2016, r 8.7(3).
37   Note the guidance in SIP 3.1, in particular paras 12–14 and 15(a).
38   See *Greystoke v Hamilton-Smith* [1997] BPIR 24; see below [8.06].

may order that the specified information in question should be omitted from the statement of affairs when that document is delivered to the creditors. For these purposes, a relevant person who may bring such an application may be any of the following to whom it appears this threat exists: the debtor, the nominee or any other person who appears to the court to have an interest in the matter.[39] This category is intentionally broad.

5.20 The application should be made to the court in which the debtor has applied or is intending to apply for an interim order or, where no interim order is being sought, then the appropriate court or hearing centre in accordance with the rules.[40] The rules do not prescribe any timing for such an application, but obviously it needs to be made at the earliest possible opportunity and in any event prior to the statement of affairs being provided to the creditors.[41]

---

39 IR 2016, r 8.6. This provision was originally inserted (into the Insolvency Rules 1986, as r 5.68) by the Insolvency (Amendment) Rules 2010 (SI 2010/686).

40 IR 2016, r 8.9 and r 8.20, respectively.

41 Notwithstanding the wording of IR 2016, r 8.20(1), there is no reason to suppose that such an application could not be made prior to the nominee making his report and indeed it would be usual for that to be the case.

PART III

INITIATING PROCEDURES

6

INTERIM ORDERS

A. THE PURPOSE AND EFFECT OF INTERIM ORDERS

1. Overall purpose

6.01 As originally drafted, the Insolvency Act 1986 (IA 1986) was structured so that if a debtor wished to propose an individual voluntary arrangement (IVA), they would first have to obtain an interim order. The purpose of an interim order is to provide a breathing space, by imposing a moratorium, to enable the debtor to put their proposal to their creditors without fear that any of those creditors might proceed to make the debtor bankrupt or take any steps that might interfere with the efficacy and fairness of the IVA by pre-emptively securing an advantage over the other creditors (for example by perfecting execution over the debtor's property or goods).[1] The procedure also offers greater pro-

---

1   IA 1986, s 252.

tection where the debtor is an undischarged bankrupt or where a bankruptcy petition is pending.[2] Even prior to the court considering whether to make an interim order, the statute provides a level of protection that comes into play the moment an application for an interim order is made.[3] This ensures that the assets of the debtor are preserved for the benefit of the unsecured creditors as a whole.

2. Protection pending an application for an interim order

As soon as an application is made to the court for an interim order under **6.02** section 253 of IA 1986, a degree of protection for the debtor's property is imposed and remains in place for as long as the application remains pending.[4] There are four elements to this protection. First, any court in which proceedings are pending against the debtor may, on proof that an application for an interim order in respect of the debtor has been made, stay those proceedings or allow them to continue on such terms as it sees fit.[5] Secondly, the court to which such an application had been made may stay any action, execution or other legal process against the property or person of the debtor.[6] With effect from 1 January 2003, two further elements of protection were bolted onto the above provisions.[7] From that date, no landlord or other person to whom rent is payable may exercise the right of forfeiture by peaceable re-entry in relation to premises let to the debtor where the debtor has failed to comply with any term of the tenancy, except with the leave of the court.[8] Finally, since 1 January 2003, the court seized of the interim order application may also forbid the levying of any distress on the debtor's property and/or its subsequent sale.[9]

Pursuant to these provisions, a landlord wishing to forfeit the debtor's lease **6.03** would have to make an application to the court in which the interim order application was pending for permission. Whether to grant such permission or, in every other case, whether to forbid the levying of distress (or sale) or to impose the stay, is a matter of discretion for the court concerned. That discretion would only be exercised in favour of providing the protection to the debtor or his property to the extent that the action in question would or might jeopardise the outcome or viability of the proposal being put to creditors. If,

---

2   See below [6.05] and [6.29]; cf. [7.22]–[7.23].
3   IA 1986, s 254. See below [6.02]–[6.04].
4   IA 1986, s 254.
5   IA 1986, s 254(2).
6   IA 1986, s 254(1), as it was in force down to 31 December 2002, which is now preserved within s 254(1)(b).
7   As inserted by the Insolvency Act 2000 (IA 2000).
8   IA 1986, s 254(1)(a).
9   IA 1986, s 254(1)(b) (being additional words inserted into what was then s 254(1) by IA 2000).

for example, the asset or assets in question would in any event not be included within the IVA, it is most unlikely that the court would interfere with the rights of the creditor concerned.

6.04 Where the court makes an order pursuant to section 254(1)(b) granting a stay of any action, execution or other legal process pending the hearing of an application for an interim order, that order must contain certain information prescribed by the Insolvency (England and Wales) Rules 2016 (IR 2016).[10] It must state that it is made under section 254(1)(b) of IA 1986 and provide the details of the action, execution or other legal process that is being stayed, the date on which the application for an interim order will be heard and the date on which the order granting the stay is made.[11] There are no equivalent requirements for any order preventing distress or prohibiting sale following distress. Nor are there any specific requirements relating to orders for stay made in other courts before which proceedings against the debtor are pending, although clearly any such court would need to be informed of the date of the hearing of the application for an interim order and would no doubt make specific reference to it in any order.

3. The effect of an interim order

(a) General effect

6.05 Once an interim order has been granted, it imposes a moratorium on a range of actions against the debtor or the property of the debtor. First and foremost, it precludes any bankruptcy petition from being presented or proceeded with for as long as the interim order is in force.[12] Were a bankruptcy order to be made on such a petition in ignorance of the fact that an interim order had been granted, this would provide grounds for annulment of the bankruptcy order.[13] In addition, for as long as the interim order is in force, no other proceedings and no execution or other legal process may be commenced or continued against the debtor, except with the leave of the court.[14]

6.06 Just as with a pending application for an interim order, the protection afforded by section 252 of IA 1986 was widened, with effect from 1 January 2003, to include a curb on the rights of landlords. From that date, except with the leave

---

10   SI 2016/1024.

11   IR 2016, r 8.10.

12   IA 1986, s 252(2)(a).

13   Pursuant to s 282(1)(a) of IA 1986, although the court retains a discretion as to whether to grant any such annulment.

14   IA 1986, s 252(2)(b).

of the court, no landlord or other person to whom rent is payable may exercise any right of forfeiture by peaceable re-entry in relation to premises let to the debtor in respect of the debtor's failure to comply with any term of the tenancy and no distress against the debtor or their property may be levied.[15]

As noted above, part of the rationale for the moratorium imposed by an interim order is to prevent one creditor from stealing a march on others. An obvious example where this comes into play is where a judgment creditor seeks to obtain security through obtaining a charging order under the Charging Orders Act 1979, or, having started down that road, seeks to have an interim charging order made final. A party who presses ahead with an action or execution where an interim order has been made without getting leave of the court is likely to come unstuck. Where such action is taken in ignorance of the existence of the interim order, it may be possible to salvage the situation by applying for leave retrospectively; but where that is not done (or where it is not successful) the proceedings or execution or other legal process will be set aside.[16] **6.07**

(b) Application by a creditor for leave to continue

Section 252(2) provides the court with a discretion to permit a creditor to continue, notwithstanding the moratorium, where the circumstances justify this.[17] In this context 'the court' usually means the insolvency court which granted the interim order. It is not uncommon for a leave application to be made in anticipation of the interim order being granted and, in such circumstances, the two applications would be heard together. Where other proceedings against the debtor are pending in the High Court, the court seized of those proceedings may also entertain an application for leave to continue those particular proceedings.[18] **6.08**

The test usually applied is that leave to continue with any particular step in proceedings, execution or other legal process will generally be allowed where that step is unlikely materially to affect the creditors as a whole in the IVA. For example, where a party to a construction contract had obtained an adjudication award in its favour, the court was prepared to allow the claimant to enter summary judgment in the usual way, albeit without permission to enforce, as **6.09**

---

15 IA 1986, s 252(2)(aa) and (b), respectively; s 252(2)(aa) was inserted and additional wording added to s 252(2)(b) in relation to distress by IA 2000.

16 *Clarke v Coutts & Co* [2002] EWCA Civ 943; [2002] BPIR 916, where a final ('absolute') charging order obtained in ignorance of the interim order, was set aside in accordance with the principles laid down in *Roberts Petroleum Ltd v Bernard Kenny Ltd (In Liquidation)* [1983] 2 AC 192 (HL).

17 IA 1986, s 252(2)(b); similarly (for forfeiture), s 252(2)(aa).

18 *Hall and Shivers v Van der Heiden* [2010] EWHC 357 (TCC), [2010] BPIR 585.

this regularised the position between the parties without giving the creditor an unfair advantage over any other creditor in the event that the defendant's proposal for an IVA were accepted.[19] Equally, where the proposal excludes a property from the IVA, there can be little or no prejudice to other creditors in allowing a judgment creditor to obtain a final charging order over the excluded property. So, in *Dewji v Banwaitt*,[20] where two of the properties that were the subject of the charging order were excluded entirely and the third was only being used as collateral, final charging orders were granted notwithstanding the moratorium.

6.10 Where the court to which the application is made forms the view that the interim order was obtained in questionable circumstances and/or cynically for the purpose of thwarting the party seeking permission to continue from obtaining judgment, the court may grant permission to continue even where that might provide an advantage to the applicant over other creditors. In circumstances where the debtor waited until the eve of a 15-day trial to apply for and obtain an interim order, the trial judge was sufficiently unimpressed as to allow the trial to proceed notwithstanding the interim order.[21] Similar considerations obtained in *Dewji v Banwaitt*,[22] where the judge agreed with the master that there was more than a whiff of cynicism in the debtor's conduct. In *Stella v Harris*,[23] a creditor had been granted summary judgment on part of his claim but the debtor had been granted permission to defend the remainder on the proviso of making a payment into court (on an 'unless' basis); without making the payment into court by the required date, the debtor applied for and obtained an interim order, but in the circumstances the court permitted the creditor to enter judgment for the rest of his claim.

(c)   Matters unaffected by an interim order

6.11 Certain types of legal process, by their very nature, either do not concern the subject matter of an IVA or are considered outside the ambit of this protection for policy reasons. Such legal processes are, in consequence, unaffected by an interim order. Such exceptions include fines imposed on the debtor, restraint orders made in criminal proceedings, criminal compensation orders or any similar orders made under the Proceeds of Crime Act 2002.[24] Obligations to

---

19   *Premier Construction Services v Steene* [2018] EWHC 2597 (TCC).
20   [2013] EWHC 3746 (QB); [2014] BPIR 63. The facts in this case were highly unusual.
21   *Hall and Shivers v Van der Heiden* (above).
22   Above.
23   [2014] EWHC 4492 (Ch); [2015] BPIR 926.
24   *Re M (Restraint Order)* [1992] 2 WLR 340 (restraint order under the Drug Trafficking Offenses Act 1986); *R v Barnet Justices, ex p Phillippou* [1997] BPIR 134 (criminal compensation order).

repay student loans and postgraduate degree loans are specifically exempted,[25] as are orders made under the Child Support Act 1991.[26] The position with regard to liabilities arising out of family proceedings (other than for a lump sum or costs) is more nuanced.[27] A maintenance order or periodic payments order made against the debtor prior to the date of the proposal would not normally be capable of being caught by an IVA, so that there is no good reason why enforcement proceedings in relation to such orders should be affected by the moratorium.

Conversely, in contrast to the position in bankruptcy, there is nothing in the nature of an IVA to affect the debtor's ability to pursue or continue a claim against a third party (although often this will be expressly for the benefit of the IVA creditors). As a result, an interim order has no effect on such rights.[28] **6.12**

B. THE PROCEDURE

1. Application for an interim order

(a) Who may apply?

Where the debtor is an undischarged bankrupt, an application for an interim order can be made either by the debtor, or alternatively by the debtor's trustee in bankruptcy or the Official Receiver (OR).[29] Otherwise the application can only be made by the debtor.[30] **6.13**

(b) Conditions that must be satisfied

In order to make an interim order, the court must be satisfied that the debtor meets certain criteria, which are therefore threshold pre-conditions for any debtor to seek an interim order.[31] The first two are relatively self-evident. First, the debtor must be an individual who intends to make a proposal for an IVA under Part 8 of IA 1986;[32] a copy of the proposal must be annexed to the **6.14**

---

25 Education (Student Loans) (Repayment) Regulations 2009, reg. 80(2)(c)–(d), as amended.
26 IA 1986, s 382(5): see above [2.28].
27 See above [2.32]–[2.36].
28 See *Envis v Thakkar* [1997] BPIR 189 (CA): the case actually concerned the question of whether the defendant to such an action was entitled to the benefit of an order for security for costs against a debtor in an IVA, on the basis that the latter was acting in a nominal capacity.
29 IA 1986, s 253(3)(a).
30 IA 1986, s 253(3)(b).
31 IA 1986, s 255(1).
32 IA 1986, ss 252(1) and 255(1)(a).

evidence in support of the application.[33] The second criterion is that, on the day of making the application, the debtor is either an undischarged bankrupt or entitled to apply for their own bankruptcy.[34]

6.15 The third pre-condition is that the debtor may not apply for an interim order if they have previously made another such application within the period of 12 months ending on the day of making the new application.[35] This rule is absolute. Where a debtor has made an application for an interim order that fails, the debtor cannot get around this rule by applying for a review of that decision pursuant to IA 1986, s 375(1) in respect of what amounts to a different proposal, as this would in effect amount to a second application.[36] It follows that any debtor wishing to make a proposal within the period of 12 months from the date of a previous application for an interim order will not be entitled to make use of the interim order moratorium to do so.[37]

6.16 The final condition is that the court can only grant the interim order if it is satisfied that the nominee named in the proposal is willing to act as such in relation to the proposal.[38] The person so named must be a qualified insolvency practitioner (IP), who is willing to act as a nominee in relation to the IVA, and that willingness must be certified in writing in advance by the IP.[39]

6.17 The debtor must submit the proposal and the statement of affairs to the nominee to enable the nominee to compile their report on the proposal and it is implicit that they should do so as soon as the interim order has been made.[40] The rules then require that, as soon as reasonably practicable after receiving the proposal from the debtor, the nominee must deliver to the debtor a written notice of the nominee's consent to act in relation to the proposal and the notice must contain the date on which they received it.[41] For practical reasons, however, this does not reflect the true order of play. As the court can only grant the interim order once it is satisfied of the nominee's willingness to act, the rules reasonably require that the witness statement in support of the application must not only state as much in terms but must also annex a copy

---

33   IR 2016, r 8.8(2)(a).
34   IA 1986, s 255(1)(b).
35   IA 1986, s 255(1)(c).
36   *Hurst v Bennett (No.2)* [2001] EWCA Civ 1398, [2002] BPIR 102 (refusing permission to appeal the decision of Ferris J, which is reported in full under the BPIR citation).
37   They would have to use the alternative procedure: see Chapter 7 below.
38   IA 1986, s 255(1)(d).
39   For the mechanics, see below [6.17]; for the requirements of the proposal, see above [4.26].
40   This is the natural reading of IA 1986, s 256(1)–(2).
41   IR 2016, r 8.4(1)–(2).

of the nominee's notice of consent to act.[42] It follows that the nominee's notice certifying such willingness cannot post-date the making of the order. The correct order of play, therefore, is for the debtor to submit the proposal and statement of affairs to the nominee, for the nominee to certify willingness to act, noting the date on which the proposal was submitted, for this certificate to be annexed to the application and then for the application to be issued.

In addition to the above, where the debtor is an undischarged bankrupt, the **6.18** debtor must give notice of the proposal to the OR and also to the trustee in bankruptcy (if other than the OR).[43] Such notice must contain the name and address of the nominee.[44]

(c) The court to which the application is to be made

The application for an interim order must be made to the court specified in the **6.19** rules: where the debtor is an undischarged bankrupt, the application must be made to the court (and hearing centre if applicable), if any, that has conduct of the bankruptcy;[45] otherwise it must be made to the court (and hearing centre if applicable) to which the debtor would have to apply in order to appeal the adjudicator's refusal to make a bankruptcy order.[46] The latter court is to be ascertained in accordance with the rules applicable to such an application.[47] Moreover, the application must contain sufficient information to establish that it has been made to the correct court or hearing centre.[48]

Although the rule is couched in mandatory terms, if the application is not made **6.20** to the correct court in accordance with these provisions, it does not follow that the application would be a nullity merely for being sued in the wrong court: the court has a discretion as to whether to proceed with the application, transfer it to the correct court or dismiss it.[49] At the very least, however, issuing in the wrong court would be likely to cause delay and, given the nature of the relief sought, that is to be avoided if at all possible.

---

42   IR 2016, r 8.8(1)(e) and (2)(b), respectively.
43   IA 1986, s 253(4).
44   IR 2016, r 8.8(5). Again, this must refer to a nominee who has formally consented to act.
45   IR 2016, r 8.9(1)(a).
46   IR 2016, r 8.9(1)(b).
47   IR 2016, r 10.48 and Sch 6.
48   IR 2016, r 8.9(2).
49   IR 2016, r 12.31.

(d) Making the application

6.21 An application for an interim order must be made in accordance with the general provisions for making applications under IR 2016.[50] In addition to these general provisions, however, there are some specific requirements that must be adhered to in an application of this kind.

6.22 The application must be supported by evidence in the form of a witness statement and this statement must contain certain specified information.[51] First, it must state the reasons for making the application;[52] in so doing, it should refer to the proposal, a copy of which must (as already noted) be annexed to the statement.[53] The statement must then provide information about any action, execution, other legal process or the levying of any distress that, to the debtor's knowledge has been commenced against the debtor or the debtor's property.[54] It must confirm that on the day of making the application the debtor is either an undischarged bankrupt or entitled to apply for their own bankruptcy and that the debtor has not made any previous application for an interim order within the period of 12 months ending on the day of making the application.[55] As noted above, it must also confirm that the person named in the witness statement is willing to act as nominee in relation to the proposal and is qualified to act as an IP or is an authorised person in relation to the debtor and a copy of the nominee's notice of consent to act must be annexed to the statement.[56] Once the statement and supporting documents are in order, the application must be issued and the appropriate issue fee paid.

6.23 As soon as the application and the accompanying witness statement have been received by the court, the court will fix a venue and time for the hearing and provide a notice of the hearing to the applicant.[57] In practice, given the nature of the application, this generally happens promptly and the hearing is usually expedited. The applicant must then deliver a copy of the notice of hearing to the prescribed recipients at least two business days before the hearing.[58] The persons to whom the applicant must deliver the notice of the hearing are as follows: in every case, to the nominee;[59] in addition, where the debtor is an

---

50   In particular, IR 2016, rr 1.6–1.9 and 1.35.
51   IR 2016, r 8.8(1).
52   IR 2016, r 8.8(1)(a).
53   IR 2016, r 8.8(2)(a).
54   IR 2016, r 8.8(1)(b).
55   IR 2016, r 8.8(1)(c)–(d), respectively.
56   IR 2016, r 8.8(1)(e) and r 8.8(2)(b), respectively. On the certificate, see above [6.17].
57   IR 2016, r 8.8(3).
58   IR 2016, r 8.8(4).
59   IR 2016, r 8.8(4)(a).

undischarged bankrupt, to whichever is not the applicant out of the debtor, the OR and the trustee;[60] where the debtor is not an undischarged bankrupt, to any creditor who (to the debtor's knowledge) has presented a bankruptcy petition against the debtor.[61] Although the rule does not make this explicit, this obviously only relates to petitions that are still pending at the date of the application.

(e)   The hearing

Any person who was, or should have been, given notice of the hearing pursu- **6.24** ant to the rules has the right to attend or be represented at the hearing of the application.[62] In deciding what order to make, the court is required to take a number of matters into consideration, including any representations made by or on behalf of any such person who does attend or is represented at the hearing.[63] As long as it is satisfied that the threshold pre-conditions referred to above are met, the court has a discretion to make an interim order if it thinks this would be appropriate for the purpose of facilitating the consideration and implementation of the debtor's proposal.[64]

In practice this imposes a judicial filter, in that it requires the court to be **6.25** satisfied that the proposal is serious and viable and that it does indeed have a realistic prospect of being accepted by the creditors.[65] The proposal must have substance and be one which should seriously be considered by the cred- itors or at least be capable of serious consideration.[66] What it offers should not be derisory.[67] Nor should the assets upon which it is based be fanciful or illusory.[68] In arriving at its decision, the court has a wide discretion.[69] The court is entitled, in the exercise of that discretion, to refuse to make an interim order in circumstances where the proposal included nominee's fees at a figure that was unjustifiably high, such that it might affect the viability of the IVA.[70] The bar that the applicant needs to cross here is not, however, a high one.[71] Where

---

60   IR 2016, r 8.8(4)(b).
61   IR 2016, r 8.8(4)(c).
62   IR 2016, r 8.11(1).
63   IR 2016, r 8.11(2).
64   IA 1986, s 255(2); for the threshold pre-conditions, see above [6.14]–[6.16].
65   *Cooper v Fearnley, Re a Debtor (No.103 of 1994)* [1997] BPIR 20; *Hook v Jewson Ltd* [1997] BPIR 100; *Shah v Cooper* [2003] BPIR 1018. See further below [7.25].
66   *Cooper v Fearnley* (above).
67   *Knowles v Coutts & Co* [1998] BPIR 96.
68   *Davidson v Stanley* [2004] EWHC 2595 (Ch), [2005] BPIR 279.
69   *Hook v Jewson Ltd* [1997] BPIR 100.
70   *Re Julie O'Sullivan* [2001] BPIR 534. This was a 'plain case of overcharging', but the court will only interfere in this manner judiciously.
71   *Knowles v Coutts & Co* [1998] BPIR 96; *Tucker v Atkins* [2014] EWHC 2260 (Ch); [2014] BPIR 1569.

the prospects of success depended on the votes of opposing creditors that are disputed, the more prudent course is for the court to grant the order and allow the vote to proceed.[72]

6.26 In an appropriate case, where the papers are in order and the relevant conditions are satisfied, the Practice Direction on Insolvency Proceedings (IPD) permits the court to make the initial interim order on paper.[73] The conditions that must be met for the court to make the order on paper in this way are that the nominee's signed consent to act includes a waiver of notice of the application or the nominee has indicated consent to the making of an interim order without attendance and that the debtor is not an undischarged bankrupt, nor (as far as the court is aware) is there a bankruptcy petition pending against the debtor. Even where the above conditions are met, however, the court may still insist on attendance.[74]

(f)   The form of the order

6.27 Initially, the court can only make an interim order for a period of 14 days (beginning with the day after the order is made), and thereafter it will automatically cease to have effect.[75] As we shall see, however, the period for which the order takes effect may subsequently be extended by further order of the court or even, in the right circumstances, at the same time as the initial order.[76] The order in effect allows a breathing space in which to allow the nominee to report back to the court on the proposal, which must be done no later than two business days prior to the expiry of that primary time limit, in sufficient time to allow the court the opportunity to consider the report and make such further orders as may be necessary.[77] When making the order, the court must fix the venue for the consideration of the nominee's report, which must therefore be within the 14-day period.[78]

6.28 Both the 14-day period for the expiry of the order and the venue for the court to consider the report must be explicitly set out in the terms of the order.[79] In addition the order must contain certain other prescribed matters, namely: the identification details for the proceedings, the fact that the order is made

---

72   *Singh v Singh* [2013] EWHC 4783 (Ch); [2014] BPIR 1555.
73   IPD [2020] BPIR 1211, July 2020, para 14.1(1).
74   IPD, para 14.2.
75   IA 255(6).
76   See below [6.36] and [6.41]–[6.47] (extensions); [6.39] (concertina orders).
77   IA 1986, s 256(1); IR 2016, r 8.15(1); cf. also r 8.12(e).
78   IR 2016, r 8.11(3).
79   IR 2016, r 8.12(c) and (h), respectively.

pursuant to section 252 of IA 1986, the precise wording of section 252(2) as to the effect of the order, an order requiring the nominee to deliver the nominee's report to the court by no later than two business days before the date fixed for the court's consideration of that report and the date on which the order itself is made.[80]

In addition to the above, which apply in every case, there are additional **6.29** requirements that apply where the debtor is an undischarged bankrupt. In such cases the court should consider whether to make provisions as to the conduct of the bankruptcy and the administration of the bankrupt's estate during the period for which the order is in force.[81] In exercising this discretion, unless the court is satisfied that the provision it is contemplating would be unlikely to result in a significant diminution in, or in the value of, the debtor's estate for the purposes of the bankruptcy, the court must not make any provision in relation to the bankrupt to relax or remove any requirements imposed by the provisions of the group of parts dealing with personal insolvency (Parts 8–9).[82] With that proviso, however, the court has a wide discretion to make any provision it considers appropriate, including staying the bankruptcy or modifying any provision with Parts 8–9 of IA 1986 or any provision of the rules in their application to the debtor's bankruptcy.[83] Where the court does make any such order, this must be recorded within the interim order itself.[84] In addition, in every case where the debtor is an undischarged bankrupt, save where the OR is the applicant, the interim order must contain an order requiring the applicant to deliver a copy of the interim order to the OR as soon as reasonably practicable.[85]

Although the requirements as to the contents of the order are set out in **6.30** mandatory terms, a failure to follow these requirements would not render the interim order invalid. In any event, a court can depart from the strictures of these provisions if it sees fit.[86]

---

80   IR 2016, r 8.12(a), (b), (d), (e) and (i), respectively.
81   IA 1986, s 255(3).
82   IA 1986, s 255(5).
83   IA 1986, s 255(4). This could include an order suspending discharge: see below [7.24].
84   IR 2016, r 8.12(f).
85   IR 2016, r 8.12(g).
86   IR 2016, r 12.63.

(g) Service and notice of the interim order

6.31   Once the interim order is made the court will provide at least two sealed copies of the order to the applicant.[87] As soon as reasonably practical thereafter the applicant must deliver a copy of the interim order to the nominee and, where the debtor is an undischarged bankrupt, another copy to the OR, unless the OR was the applicant.[88] In addition the applicant must provide notice that the order has been made (though not necessarily deliver a copy of the order) to every person who was, or should have been, given notice of the hearing but was not actually in attendance or represented at it.[89] Where the court has made the interim order on paper, however, sealed copies of the order will be posted to the applicant (or their solicitors) and to the nominee.[90]

2.   The nominee's report and further order

(a) Preparing the report

6.32   The nominee's report to the court must state whether, in the opinion of the nominee, the IVA that the debtor is proposing has a reasonable prospect of being approved and implemented and whether the debtor's creditors should consider the proposal.[91] The detail of what the report needs to cover and the duties of the nominee in compiling the report will be considered in a later chapter,[92] but in essence the report must be based on a proper consideration of the information and documentation provided by the debtor and must provide an explanation for the opinions that it reaches.[93]

6.33   Until relatively recently, it was a statutory requirement that the report, if it was favourable, had to specify the precise date, time and place for the meeting at which it was proposed the creditor's decision should be made.[94] Major changes to the way creditor decision-making procedures are to be conducted, permitting a range of procedures, were introduced by the Small Business, Enterprise and Employment Act 2015 (SBEEA 2015) with effect from 6 April 2017.[95] As part of this overhaul in procedure, the above-mentioned express requirement

---

87   IR 2016, r 8.13(1).
88   IR 2016, r 8.13(2)(a).
89   IR 2016, r 8.13(2)(b), referring back to r 8.8(4): see above [6.23].
90   IPD, para 14.2.
91   IA 1986, s 256(1).
92   See below [8.03]–[8.09].
93   IR 2016, r 8.15(3); and see Statement of Insolvency Practice (SIP) 3, 6.1–6.7, especially 6.4, and SIP 3.1, para 15(b); see also *Greysotke v Hamilton-Smith* [1997] BPIR 24.
94   IA 1986, s 256(1)(b), as originally enacted; cf. also the original wording of s 257(1). This was also true where the report was being prepared under the alternative procedure.
95   On these reforms and the choice of decision procedures, see below [8.10]–[8.12].

for the report to specify the details of the creditors' meeting was abolished.[96] Notwithstanding these amendments, the removal of this requirement is not the whole story where the debtor has chosen to follow the interim order procedure. This is because, under this procedure, the rules still require the court, when making an order upon considering the nominee's report, to set out in the body of the order the details of the proposed decision procedure that the nominee has chosen.[97] It follows that, even though the express requirement to include any such details in the report were deliberately expunged, there remains an *implicit* requirement to provide the details of the decision-making procedure the nominee is proposing to use. This in turn means that the nominee must still make the choice and communicate the details of that decision to the court at the time of filing the report (and, in practice, will do so within the body of the report itself).[98]

(b) Further information from the debtor

As already discussed in the previous chapter, if the nominee considers that **6.34** further information is required from the debtor at this stage for the purposes of properly preparing this report, the nominee may require the debtor to supply further information relating to a range of matters and, if necessary, also to supply further documentation.[99] These powers are, however, rarely invoked as in most cases the IP who is named in the proposal as the nominee will have assisted the debtor in putting together the proposal and the statement of affairs in the first place and will usually have identified the gaps at a much earlier stage and insisted that the debtor provide the necessary information prior to finalising the primary documents.

(c) Filing the report

The nominee's report must be filed with the court two business days before the **6.35** date fixed for the court's consideration, in accordance with the timing set out in the interim order (or any extension), together with a copy of the report, a copy of the proposal (as amended, if amended) and a copy of the statement of affairs (or a summary of it).[100] At the same time as filing the report with the court, the nominee must deliver a copy of the report to the debtor.[101] Upon receipt by the court of the nominee's report, the court will endorse the report, and also the

---

96   IA 1986, s 256(1)(b) was omitted and s 257(1), (2), (2A) and (2B) substituted for the old s 257(1)–(2), by SBEEA 2015, Schedule 9.

97   IR 2016, r 8.16(e): see further below [6.37].

98   Cf. where the alternative procedure is followed: below [7.09].

99   IR 2016, r 8.7, on which see above [5.14]–[5.18].

100 IA 1986, s 256(1) and IR 2016, r 8.15(1).

101 IR 2016, r 8.15(2).

copy that was filed with it, with the date it was filed, and return the copy to the nominee.[102] Upon receipt of the endorsed copy the nominee must deliver a copy of the report, a copy of the proposal and a copy (or summary) of the statement of affairs to the relevant parties: where the debtor is an undischarged bankrupt, the relevant parties are the OR and (if other) the debtor's trustee in bankruptcy; where the debtor is not an undischarged bankrupt, but there is a bankruptcy petition pending against the debtor, the relevant party is the petitioning creditor on that petition.[103]

(d)   Consideration of the report and further order

6.36   The court will then consider the report in accordance with the venue fixed in the interim order (or any extension thereto).[104] Any person to whom notice of the initial interim order hearing was (or should have been) delivered is entitled to appear or be represented at the hearing to consider the nominee's report.[105] If the court is satisfied that the creditors should be given the opportunity to consider the proposal, it must direct that the period for which the interim order has effect be extended for such period as it specifies in the direction for that purpose.[106] There is no statutory guidance over how long such an extension should be for, but in essence it needs to be long enough to allow time for the decision process to take place, followed by enough time for the matter to be reported back to the court and to allow for the grace period for potential challenges: the standard order is to extend the interim order to a date seven weeks after the proposed decision date, to direct the implementation of the decision procedure and to adjourn the matter to a date approximately three weeks after the decision date for further consideration.[107]

6.37   As with an interim order, the contents of such an order are prescribed by the rules.[108] The order must contain the identification details for the proceedings, the fact that the order is made under section 256(5) of IA 1986 and the date that the nominee's report was filed.[109] It must then state that the period for which the interim order has effect is extended to a specified date, for the purposes of enabling the creditors to consider the proposal.[110] It must then also

---

102   IR 2016, r 8.15(4).

103   IR 2016, r 8.15(5) and (6), respectively.

104   On extensions to the interim order generally, see below [6.41].

105   IR 2016, r 8.18(1), referring back to r 8.8(4); see above [6.23].

106   IA 1986, s 256(5). On what it takes for the court to be 'satisfied', see *Greystoke v Hamilton-Smith* [1997] BPIR 24 (see below [7.25]).

107   This standard order is reflected in the wording of IPD, para 14.1(2), on which see below.

108   IR 2016, r 8.16.

109   IR 2016, r 8.16(a)–(c).

110   IR 2016, r 8.16(d).

state that the nominee will be inviting the creditors to consider the proposal and provide details of the decision procedure that the nominee intends to use.[111] As noted above, it is implicit in this that the nominee must therefore already have communicated this choice to the court.[112] In addition, where the debtor is an undischarged bankrupt (and the nominee is not the OR), the order must require the nominee to deliver a copy of the order to the OR as soon as reasonably practicable.[113] Finally, the order must note the date on which it was made.[114] The requirements for service and notice of the order are the same as applied to the original interim order.[115]

Providing the debtor is not an undischarged bankrupt and that there is no **6.38** bankruptcy petition pending against the debtor and that certain other conditions are met, the court may make such an order on paper, without the need for attendance.[116] The additional conditions are that the nominee's report complies with section 256(1) of IA 1986 and that it proposes a decision date that is not less than 14 days from the date the report was filed at court nor more than 28 days after the date on which the court is considering the report. Where all these conditions are met, the court will usually make a standard order (as referred to above) on paper.

(e) 'Concertina orders'

Where the court considers it appropriate to do so, it can combine the interim **6.39** order, pursuant to section 252 of IA 1986 (which can be for a maximum of 14 days), with an order extending the interim order to enable the creditors to consider the proposal, made pursuant to section 256(5). This is known as a 'concertina order'.[117] The purpose of such an order is to save time and costs in circumstances where, for whatever reason, time is particularly pressing. The court will only make such an order, however, where it is satisfied that the proposal is both viable and sufficiently serious that the creditors should be given a chance to consider it. If the debtor wishes the court to make a concertina order, they would have to ensure that the nominee's report was filed prior to the court considering the interim order application, and this almost invariably

---

111 IR 2016, r 8.16(e).
112 See above [6.33]; on the choices facing the nominee, see below at [8.10]–[8.12].
113 IR 2016, r 8.16(f). In theory the nominee could be the OR, pursuant to IA 1986, s 389B, but in practice this is very rare.
114 IR 2016, r 8.16(g).
115 IR 2016, r 8.18(2), referring back to r 8.13 (see above [6.31]).
116 IPD, para 14.1(2).
117 This was first recognised by Practice Direction (Bankruptcy: Voluntary Arrangements) [1992] 1 WLR 120 and is now reflected in IPD, para 14.1(3). For an example, see *Shah v Cooper* [2003] BPIR 1018.

means that it is filed along with the application. This is, therefore, something that would need to be discussed between the debtor and the nominee at an early stage. To be satisfied that it was appropriate to make the order in this way, the court would normally need to have had the benefit of hearing from the parties that would have had the right to address it at the consideration stage. Unless circumstances make it impracticable, the debtor should put any such party on notice that a concertina order is being sought and invite them to signify their position to the court in writing in advance if they do not intend to attend hearing.

6.40 In an appropriate case, a concertina order can be made by the court on paper without the need for attendance.[118] The court will only make a concertina order in this way where the conditions for making both the interim order and the further order under section 256(5) on paper are met and where the application is accompanied by the nominee's report.[119]

3. Extension, Variation, Discharge and Cessation

(a) Extensions and variations

6.41 Notwithstanding that the period of the interim order is strictly circumscribed by statute, the procedure does allow the court to grant extensions. As already noted above, once the report has been filed, the court will grant a (further) extension to allow the creditors the opportunity to consider the proposal, if it is satisfied that the creditors ought to have that opportunity and can do so at the same time as granting the original interim order by way of a concertina order.[120] In addition, in certain other circumstances the procedure permits the court to grant extensions to the interim order, or to vary or grant a renewal of the interim order.

6.42 Where the nominee has failed to file the report required under section 256 of IA 1986, or has died, the debtor may make an application to the court for a direction that the nominee be replaced by another person qualified to act as an IP or authorised to act as a nominee in relation to the IVA.[121] The rules require that the debtor give the nominee five business days' notice before filing any such application.[122] This would clearly not be possible where the nominee

---

118 IPD, para 14.1(3).
119 Ibid. For the relevant conditions for making each element of the order on paper, see above at [6.26] and [6.38], respectively.
120 See above [6.39].
121 IA 1986, s 256(3)(a).
122 IR 2016, r 8.17(1).

has died, but might be difficult even where the nominee failed to file the report in time for some other reason, unless it was obvious at a very early stage that this was going to be the case. Where the nominee has run into difficulties such as to preclude the timely delivery of the report, it is unlikely there would be sufficient time to comply with this requirement without risking the lapse of the interim order. Where the nominee has died, the court could and would dispense with the service requirement; where the nominee is running late, the court could overlook the defect or direct that time be abridged.[123] Where the court is considering replacing the nominee under these provisions, the proposed replacement must file at court a statement confirming that they are qualified to act as nominee and consent to do so in this case.[124]

Alternatively, where it has become impracticable for the nominee to file the **6.43** required report or for some reason it has become apparent that it would be inappropriate for the nominee to continue to act as such, either the debtor or the nominee can apply to the court for a direction that the nominee be replaced in like manner.[125] In such a case, the applicant, whether nominee or debtor, must give five business days' notice to the other, but again in an appropriate case the court can direct otherwise.[126] As with the procedure under section 256(3)(a), above, any proposed replacement must confirm their qualification and consent.

In addition, where the nominee has failed (or it is anticipated will fail) to file **6.44** the required report in time, but there is no need for a different nominee to be substituted, the debtor may apply for an extension of the interim order so as to allow further time for the nominee to finalise and file the report.[127] On such an application the court may direct that the interim order shall continue in force, or (if it has already lapsed) may order that it be renewed for such further period as the court may specify. There are no specific rules governing such an application nor any specific statutory guidance as to the length of time for which the court can order the extension or, as the case may be, the renewal; however, although the 14-day limit in section 255(6) of IA 1986 is expressed to be 'subject to the following provisions of this Part', the better view is that the court should not extend or renew for longer than a further 14 days at any one time.

---

123   IR 2016, r 12.64 and/or CPR 3.1(2)(a), by reference to IR 2016, r 12.1(1). Oddly, IA 1986, s 376 does not address the question of abridging time.
124   IR 2016, r 8.17(3).
125   IA 1986, s 256(3)(b).
126   IR 2016, r 8.17(2); on abridging time, see above [6.42].
127   IA 1986, s 256(3A), as inserted by IA 2000 with effect from 1 January 2003.

6.45 The court may also extend the period for which the interim order has effect upon the application of the nominee, so as to provide further time in which to enable the nominee to file the required report.[128] The need for such an extension may well arise, for example, where the nominee has had to go back to the debtor to request further information or inspect documents.[129] Where the court grants such an application, the order must contain certain specified matters (largely reflecting the requirements relating to the initial interim order). The required contents are as follows:[130]

- the identification details for the proceedings;
- a statement that the application is that of the nominee for an extension of the period under section 256(4) for which the interim order is to have effect;
- an order that the period for which the interim order has effect is extended to a specified date; the particulars of the effect of the interim order (as set out in section 252(2));
- an order that the report of the nominee be delivered to the court no later than two business days before the date fixed for the court's consideration of the report;
- the particulars of any previous orders made under section 255(3) or (4);[131]
- where the debtor is an undischarged bankrupt, an order requiring the applicant to deliver a copy of the order to the OR as soon as reasonably practicable;[132]
- the (new) venue for the court's consideration of the report;
- the date of the order itself.

6.46 After the report has been considered by the court and an extension granted under section 256(5) of IA 1986 to allow the creditors the opportunity to approve the proposal, if the time granted by the court in that order proves insufficient for any reason, the nominee may apply back to the court for a further extension.[133] Where the court grants such a further extension, the same requirements as applied to the original extension will apply.[134]

---

128 IA 1986, s 256(4).
129 Under IR 2016, r 8.7: see above [5.14]–[5.18].
130 IR 2016, r 8.14(a)–(i).
131 IR 2016, r 8.14(f) is silent regarding previous orders under s 256(3A).
132 The precise significance of the words 'and the applicant is not the official receiver' in IR 2016, r 8.14(g) is unclear: the OR could not be the applicant under s 256(4), but if the words are taken to mean 'and the OR was not the original applicant under s 253', it is difficult to see why the OR should not be notified. It is submitted that the better view must be that the OR should be notified whether or not the OR was the original applicant, and that the order should require this.
133 Such an application is treated as being made under s 256(5) of IA 1986.
134 See above [6.37].

In theory and in practice the above variations and extensions are not mutually **6.47** exclusive and the court may be and often is asked to grant more than one such order in succession. Moreover, in theory there is no limit to the number of times the debtor or the nominee (or both in succession) can keep returning to the court to ask for further time, both before and after the filing of the report. There is, however, a limit in practice and the court will not allow the process to be dragged out indefinitely. This is especially true where it appears to the court that the interim order procedure is being used simply (or predominantly) to stave off bankruptcy.[135]

(b) Discharge and cessation of the interim order

The nominee may apply at any time during the above process for the interim **6.48** order to be discharged. If, on such an application, the court is satisfied either that the debtor has failed to comply with the obligations under section 256(2) of IA 1986 to deliver the proposal and the statement of affairs to the nominee or that for some other reason it would be inappropriate for the debtor's creditors to consider the proposal the court may discharge the interim order.[136]

Following the creditors' decision, the nominee must file a report at court **6.49** stating whether or not the creditors approved the proposal (with or without modifications).[137] If the report indicates that the creditors rejected the proposal, the court may, and usually will, discharge the interim order.[138] If the report indicates that the proposal was approved, any interim order that is in force 28 days after the date the report was filed will automatically lapse and cease to have effect after the end of that 28-day period, unless the court directs otherwise for the purposes of dealing with any application pursuant to section 262 of IA 1986.[139]

The standard practice, however, is for the court to make a final order upon **6.50** receipt of the nominee's report, whatever the outcome of the decision. Such an order will record the effect of the report as to whether the creditors approved or rejected the proposal and at the same time provide for the discharge of the interim order: where the result was rejection, the discharge would take effect immediately; in the case of approval, the discharge would be ordered to take

---

135 *Re A Debtor (No. 83 of 1988)* [1990] 1 WLR 708 (reported sub nom. *Re Cove (A Debtor)* [1990] 1 All ER 949).
136 IA 1986, s 256(6).
137 IA 1986, s 259(1), in particular s 259(1)(b). See below [8.48]–[8.49].
138 IA 1986, s 259(2).
139 IA 1986, s 260(4). On such challenges, see Chapter 9 below.

effect at a future specified date.[140] Where there is no bankruptcy order or bankruptcy petition outstanding and as long as the nominee's final report is compliant with the rules, such a final order may be, and usually will be, made on paper without the need for attendance.[141]

---

140   This standard final order is reflected in the wording of IPD, para 14.1(4).
141   IPD, para 14.1(4).

7

THE ALTERNATIVE PROCEDURE

A. PROCEEDING WITHOUT AN INTERIM ORDER

1. The reform and its rationale

From their first introduction in 1986 down to the end of 2002, it was a require- **7.01** ment for any debtor proposing to enter into an individual voluntary arrangement (IVA) under Part 8 of the Insolvency Act 1986 (IA 1986) to first obtain an interim order. An IVA proposed without first securing an interim order was a nullity.[1] Since 1 January 2003, however, it has been possible to enter an IVA by an alternative procedure that does not involve having to obtain an interim order, thanks to reforms introduced by the Insolvency Act 2000 (IA 2000). IA 2000 did so by inserting a new section 256A into IA 1986, which outlines the procedure, and making various consequential amendments to other sections and to the rules, which are now located in Part 8 of the Insolvency (England and Wales) Rules 2016 (IR 2016),[2] so as to bring them into line with the existence of the alternative procedure. These alterations were not perhaps entirely well thought-through and some anomalies still arise due in part to the structure of Part 8 of IA 1986, which is set out in a way that still appears to accord

---

1   *Fletcher v Vooght* [2000] BPIR 435.
2   SI 2016/1024.

primacy to the original interim order procedure, with the alternative procedure somewhat awkwardly bolted on.[3]

7.02 The intention of the reform was to provide a simpler and more cost-efficient mechanism for approving an IVA that placed the procedure firmly in the hands of the Insolvency Practitioner (IP) and removed the court from the routine procedure altogether. It was generally thought that the interim order procedure was cumbersome and potentially off-putting. Under this alternative procedure, the courts will now only become involved where an interested party specifically makes an application to the court in relation to some aspect of the process.[4]

2. Initiating the alternative procedure

(a) The debtor's obligations

7.03 Where a debtor (being an individual) wishes to make a proposal under Part 8 of IA 1986 without first applying for and obtaining an interim order, the debtor may use the alternative out-of-court procedure set out in section 256A of IA 1986. The jurisdiction mirrors that of the interim order procedure, in that the debtor must be either an undischarged bankrupt or able to present an application for their own bankruptcy.[5] The two procedures cannot be used in parallel: if an application for an interim order is pending, the debtor is precluded from making use of the alternative procedure.[6]

7.04 Provided the debtor satisfies one or other of the jurisdictional requirements, the first step for them to take is to choose a person who is a qualified IP or otherwise authorised to act as a nominee with regard to an IVA.[7] The procedure is then formally initiated by the debtor furnishing the nominee with the proposal and statement of affairs.[8] The debtor must take this formal step irrespective of whether the IP whom they have chosen to be the nominee assisted with putting together the proposal or not. However, where the debtor is an undischarged bankrupt, even before taking this formal step they must first have given notice to the Official Receiver (OR) and (if different) their trustee in bankruptcy.[9]

---

3   There are other unintended consequences of this development: see above [3.13]–[3.18].
4   See below [7.15].
5   See, indirectly, IA 1986, s 256A(3); cf. s 255(1)(b) and above [6.14].
6   IA 1986, s 256A(1)(a).
7   The qualification requirements are carried over from the definition in s 253(2) of IA 1986.
8   IA 1986, s 256A(2).
9   IA 1986, s 256A(1)(b), the wording of which has not been updated to reflect what is now IA 1986, s 291A.

Where the debtor is not an undischarged bankrupt, there is no formal require- **7.05**
ment for them to give notice to anyone prior to providing the nominee with the
proposal and statement of affairs. Even if, at the time of initiating this alternative procedure, there is a bankruptcy petition pending against the debtor,
there is no requirement for the debtor to give formal notice of their intention
to propose an IVA to the petitioning creditor. As we shall see below, there is
a requirement for the nominee to notify any such petitioner at a slightly later
stage, so that the procedure will ultimately be brought to the attention of the
petitioner.[10] It is then left to the petitioner to inform the court before which
the petition is pending. It must be noted, however, that (since the matter of the
proposed IVA is not before the court) there is no equivalent under this alternative procedure to the stay that would be imposed on such a petition under the
interim order procedure.[11] In most cases, therefore, the debtor would be well
advised to bring the proposed arrangement to the attention of the petitioning
creditor at the earliest possible opportunity and seek their cooperation in not
actively pursuing the petition.[12]

(b) The initial obligations of the nominee

As in the interim order procedure, the nominee must deliver to the debtor **7.06**
a notice of their consent to act as nominee in respect of the debtor's proposal;
this must be done as soon as reasonably practicable after the nominee has
received the proposal and must state the date on which they received it.[13]
Before taking any further action, the nominee must be able to form the view
that the debtor is eligible to put forward an IVA, being either an undischarged
bankrupt or eligible to apply for their own bankruptcy.[14] If so satisfied, the
nominee must then carefully consider the information the debtor has delivered
for the purposes of compiling a report to send to the creditors.

Where the nominee is of the opinion that further information is required from **7.07**
the debtor in order to be able properly to compile such a report, the nominee
may require the debtor to supply further information and/or documentation in
accordance with the procedures discussed above.[15] In most cases the proposal
will have been put together with the assistance and advice of the IP who will
become the nominee, so that such measures are rarely used.

---

10   See below [7.13].
11   On the relevant provisions under the interim order procedure, see above [6.05].
12   There is no obligation on the petitioner to comply with such a request: see below [7.22].
13   IR 2016, r 8.4(1)–(2).
14   IA 1986, s 256A(3).
15   IR 2016, r 8.7, on which see above [5.14]–[5.18].

3. The report to creditors

(a) Contents

7.08 Having considered the proposal and the statement of affairs, together with any supporting documents supplied by the debtor, the nominee must put together a report to be sent to the creditors explaining, in the view of the nominee, whether or not the arrangement that the debtor is proposing has a reasonable prospect of being approved and implemented and whether the creditors should consider it.[16] There is no prescribed form or template that the nominee is obliged to use when compiling this report. In relation to these general principles, the requirements as to the contents of the report do not differ from those in connection with interim orders.[17] There are, however, some features of the nominee's obligations in relation to the report that are not the same under the alternative procedure.

7.09 Until 6 April 2017, as in the interim order procedure, the report (if it recommended that the proposal be put to the creditors) had to specify the precise date, time and place for the meeting at which it was proposed the creditor's decision should be made.[18] However, as noted above, when the Small Business, Enterprise and Employment Act 2015 (SBEEA 2015) overhauled the procedure for creditor decision-making, this requirement was abolished.[19] Since there is no interim order, the implied imperative for the nominee to provide details of the chosen decision procedure to the court (noted above in connection with such orders) does not arise.[20]

7.10 This being an out-of-court procedure, the creditors' approval, if given, will effectively open the proceedings and, for this reason, under the alternative procedure the nominee must examine the nature of those proceedings within the report. In relation to any proposal considered between 26 June 2017, when the EU Regulation on Insolvency Proceedings 2015 (the EU Regulation) came into force, and the end of 2020, when the UK formally left the EU, the nominee's report had to specify, with reasons, whether the proceedings would be main, secondary, territorial (within the meaning of the EU Regulation) or

---

16   IA 1986, s 256A(3); IR 2016, r 8.19(1).

17   For the contents of the report generally (whichever procedure is followed), see below [8.04]–[8.09].

18   IA 1986, s 256A(3)(c), as originally inserted by the IA 2000 with effect from 1 January 2003; cf. also the wording of s 257(1), as amended by IA 2000.

19   IA 1986, s 256A(3)(c) was omitted and s 257(1), (2), (2A) and (2B) substituted for the old s 257(1)–(2), by SBEEA 2015, Schedule 9 with effect from 6 April 2017. See above [6.33] (in the context of interim orders) and, on the reforms, see below [8.10]–[8.12].

20   Cf. above [6.33]; but see below [8.26].

non-EU proceedings.[21] As noted above, with regard to proceedings opened after 11pm on 31 December 2020, amendments made to IA 1986 and IR 2016 effectively redefined the categorisation of the types of proceedings.[22] As a result of these amendments, the rules now require the report to state whether the proceedings would be 'COMI proceedings, establishment proceedings or proceedings to which the EU Regulation as it has effect in the law of the United Kingdom does not apply'.[23]

In addition, precisely because of the lack of prior court involvement, in contrast **7.11** to the interim order procedure, the report must contain sufficient information to enable a person to identify the appropriate court or hearing centre in which to file any application relating to the proposal, the procedure or the IVA itself.[24]

(b) Delivery

The report must be submitted to the creditors within 14 days of the date on **7.12** which the proposal and statement of affairs were provided to the nominee, unless, upon an application to the court by the nominee, the court allows an extension of time in which to submit the report.[25] Such a necessity may arise, for example, in the context of the nominee having to request further information from the debtor.[26] The nominee must also deliver the report to the debtor within the same 14-day period (unless that period is extended by the court upon the nominee's application).[27] As soon as it becomes clear to the nominee that there is a significant risk that the primary statutory deadline cannot be met, they should make such an application without delay.

Where the report is favourable, the nominee must, when delivering a copy of **7.13** the report to the creditors within the prescribed 14-day period (or such longer period as the court may have allowed), also provide to each creditor the following additional documents: a copy of the proposal (as amended, if applicable); a copy (or a summary) of the statement of affairs; and a copy of the notice of the nominee's consent to act.[28] In addition, the report must be accompanied by

---

21   IR 2016, r 8(19)(1A), as inserted by the Insolvency Amendment (EU 2015/848) Regulations 2017 (SI 2017/702). See above [1.23].
22   See above [1.24].
23   IR 2016, r 8.19(1A), as amended by the Insolvency (Amendment) (EU Exit) Regulations 2019 (SI 2019/146), Sch 1, Part 4, para 85.
24   IR 2016, r 8.19(2). On the appropriate court, see below [7.17].
25   IA 1986, s 256A(3) and (5).
26   See above [7.07].
27   IR 2016, r 8.19(3).
28   IR 2016, r 8.19(4)(b)–(d), respectively.

a statement that no application for an interim order under section 253 of IA 1986 is being made.[29] The nominee must also supply a copy of the report and the same accompanying documents, within the same deadline, to any person who has presented a bankruptcy petition against the debtor.[30] In addition, where the debtor is an undischarged bankrupt, the nominee must deliver a copy of the report, together with a copy of each of the same documents, to the OR and (if other) the debtor's trustee in bankruptcy, within the same time frame.[31]

7.14 Where the report is unfavourable, the nominee must still deliver a copy of the report to each creditor, within the time frame referred to above. At the same time the nominee must deliver a copy of the report to the debtor and provide the debtor with the reasons for the negative opinion contained in the report.[32]

4. Applications to the court

(a) Making an application

7.15 Making a proposal without applying for an interim order is an out-of-court procedure, so the matter is not before the court, until and unless a specific application is made to the court in relation to some aspect of the procedure. Although the procedure is designed to remove the court from the process as a matter of routine, occasions may arise where it is necessary or desirable for an application to be made to the court for directions or some other form of relief. Such an application can be made at any stage of the procedure and in relation to any aspect: the occasion might arise in connection with the proposal, the nominee's report, the creditors' decision procedure or, if the proposal is ultimately approved, some aspect of the IVA itself. The applicant may be the debtor, one or more of the creditors or some other interested party having the right to apply to the court (including the OR and the trustee in bankruptcy, where the debtor is an undischarged bankrupt); it may also be the nominee or (following approval) the supervisor.

7.16 When making any such application, the applicant should use the ordinary insolvency application procedure and the application must be supported by evidence; although there is no longer a prescribed form for such an application,

---

29 IR 2016, r 8.19(4)(a).
30 IR 2016, r 8.15(5)(b). The rule does not specify more precisely, but it is reasonable to assume that this is only a requirement where the petition in question is still pending at the date of the report.
31 IR 2016, r 8.15(5)(a).
32 IR 2016, r 8.15(3) and (6), respectively.

the applicant must follow the prescriptive rules in IR 2016.[33] When filing the application with the court, the applicant must also file any documents required under Part 8 of IR 2016, together with any other documents that the applicant considers may assist the court in determining the particular application being made.[34]

(b)   The appropriate court

Any such application must be made to the appropriate court (or hearing **7.17** centre, if applicable), which is governed by the same principles as apply where an application is made for an interim order.[35] Where the debtor is an undischarged bankrupt, this will be the court or hearing centre that has conduct of the bankruptcy;[36] otherwise the application must be made to the court or hearing centre to which the debtor would have to apply to appeal the adjudicator's refusal to make a bankruptcy order.[37] The application must contain sufficient information to establish that it has been made to the correct court or hearing centre.[38] Where an application is made to the wrong court, this will not be fatal (unless the court so orders); the court has a discretion to hear the application anyway or to transfer it to the appropriate court.[39]

(c)   Examples specific to the alternative procedure

In addition to the generality of matters to which such an application might **7.18** be addressed, there are a number of issues that are specific to the alternative procedure. It has already been noted that the nominee may need to make an application for an extension of time in which to deliver the report to creditors beyond the normal 14 days from the date of delivery to the nominee by the debtor of the proposal and statement of affairs. Where such an application is required, the application must be made in accordance with this procedure.[40]

In addition, the court has specific powers to give directions to replace the **7.19** nominee by another suitably qualified person, either upon the application of the debtor where the nominee has failed to deliver the report as required or has died, or upon the application of the debtor or of the nominee where it is impracticable or inappropriate for the nominee to continue to act as such

---

33   IR 2016, rr 1.6–1.9, 1.35 and the procedural rules in Part 12 of IR 2016.
34   IR 2016, r 8.20(4).
35   Cf. IR 2016, r 8.9(1).
36   IR 2016, r 8.20(2)(a).
37   IR 2016, r 8.20(2)(b), ascertained by reference to r 10.48 of and Sch 6 to IR 2016.
38   IR 2016, r 8.20(3).
39   IR 2016, r 12.31.
40   IA 1986, s 256A(5) and IR 2016, r 8.20.

in relation to the IVA.[41] Where the debtor intends to apply under either of these provisions for the nominee to be replaced, they must give the nominee written notice of such intention at least five business days prior to filing the application with the court.[42] Similarly, where the nominee intends to apply to the court to be replaced under section 256A(4)(b) of IA 1986, they must give the debtor written notice of such intention at least five business days prior to filing the application with the court.[43] The court cannot appoint a replacement upon such an application unless and until the proposed replacement has filed a statement with the court confirming their qualification and their consent to act.[44] These procedural requirements mirror the equivalent provisions relating to replacement of nominees under the interim order regime and, as noted above in that connection, the court may give directions in an appropriate case in relation to varying or dispensing with the notice requirements.[45]

B. THE CHOICE OF PROCEDURE

7.20 Since 1 January 2003, debtors have had a choice as to whether to proceed by way of the traditional procedure of first applying for an interim order or whether to use the alternative procedure, as set out above. Whether it is advisable for the debtor to proceed without first seeking the added protection of an interim order will depend on a number of factors. These are sometimes finely balanced, and in all but the most straightforward cases the debtor would do well to seek urgent professional advice on the matter at the outset. Such advice should be obtained from a qualified IP. For practical reasons, this will usually be the IP whom the debtor proposes to choose as the nominee for the arrangement, although this is not necessarily the case in every instance. In any event, the advice should be sought at the earliest opportunity, so that if an interim order is advisable, the application can be made promptly; otherwise the protection it affords might be reduced or lost entirely.

7.21 The most obvious advantage of first obtaining an interim order is that it provides the debtor with a breathing space by means of a statutory moratorium that prevents legal or other action being taken against the debtor or the property of the debtor that might otherwise upset the efficacy of the IVA.[46]

---

41   IA 1986, s 256A(4).
42   IR 2016, r 8.21(1).
43   IR 2016, r 8.21(2).
44   IR 2016, r 8.21(3).
45   See above at [6.42]–[6.43].
46   See above [6.01].

Put simply, it prevents a hostile creditor from either stealing a march on the other creditors or defeating the purpose of the IVA by making the debtor bankrupt before the creditors as a whole have had a chance to consider the proposal. In some cases, these will be sufficiently strong advantages to justify taking the traditional route of seeking an interim order. But they are not the only considerations.

Where there is a bankruptcy petition pending against the debtor, the protec- **7.22** tion of an interim order, though not required, will undoubtedly be desirable to ensure that no bankruptcy order is made pending the creditors' decision on the proposal. Where the alternative procedure is adopted, such a petition may be dealt with by way of adjournments in the bankruptcy court and it is often possible to obtain the petitioner's cooperation in ensuring that this happens. There is, however, nothing that strictly obliges the petitioning creditor to cooperate in this way, and the debtor may need to make a formal application for an adjournment within the petition. This may be risky and may have cost or other resource implications. In addition, the ultimate fate of such a petition is provided for under the interim order procedure, whereas the position is much less straightforward where the alternative approach is adopted.[47]

Where the debtor is an undischarged bankrupt, it will be desirable for the **7.23** bankruptcy proceedings to be suspended pending the outcome of the creditors' decision; otherwise unnecessary expense could be incurred within the bankruptcy that might diminish the value of the IVA if not undermine it completely. In such circumstances it is also usually prudent to proceed by way of interim order, as the court making the interim order has powers to deal with the conduct of the bankruptcy at the same time.[48] To proceed by way of the alternative route in such circumstances would require the debtor to make an application in the bankruptcy for the bankruptcy proceedings to be stayed. This merely adds an unnecessary extra layer of expense.

More significantly, where an undischarged bankrupt is proposing **7.24** a post-bankruptcy IVA in relation to the bankruptcy debts, they must complete the process prior to obtaining their discharge from bankruptcy.[49] Since April 2004, automatic discharge has taken effect one year after the date of the bankruptcy order (unless suspended), which provides a tight timetable.[50] The

---

47   See below [10.22]–[10.23]; cf. [10.24].
48   IA 1986, s 255(3)–(5): see above [6.29].
49   See above [1.21].
50   IA 1986, s 279(1) as amended by the Enterprise Act 2002.

bankruptcy court has no jurisdiction, in such a case, to suspend discharge at the behest of the debtor merely for the purpose of allowing further time in which to convene the decision-making process for the creditors to consider the proposal. The correct procedure, where there is a risk of discharge coming into effect prior to the creditors' decision date, is for the debtor to make an application for an interim order on which, in an appropriate case, the court could order that discharge be suspended.[51] If there is a realistic prospect that the debtor might be automatically discharged from bankruptcy before the creditors have had an opportunity to reach a decision on the proposal, the debtor would be taking a significant risk by proceeding without seeking an interim order.

7.25 Although under both procedures the nominee has to be of the opinion that the IVA is viable and stands a reasonable prospect of being approved, in choosing the alternative procedure the debtor, in effect, just has to convince the nominee that this is the case. Under the interim order procedure, the court has to be satisfied, upon consideration of the nominee's report and the proposal, that these criteria are met, and in practice that adds a further layer of objective scrutiny to the test.[52] In *Greystoke v Hamilton-Smith*,[53] Lindsey J emphasised that the court's approval under section 256(5) IA 1986 was not a rubber-stamping exercise.[54] By contrast, under the alternative procedure, the nominee must form an opinion, but does not have to be 'satisfied'.[55] In choosing to proceed without an interim order, therefore, the debtor not only runs the risk of allowing a 'selfish' creditor to upset the applecart, but also loses the benefit of the initial court scrutiny that could save the time and expense involved in having the proposal rejected by the creditors anyway.

7.26 On the other hand, the alternative procedure has become more common than the interim order regime and for good reasons. One reason for its attraction is that an application for an interim order will usually take extra time and, possibly more crucially, add an additional layer of cost. As long as the debtor has been well advised at the outset and the out-of-court procedure is run efficiently and with due vigour on the part of the nominee, the added risks in most cases will be slim and the advantages may well outweigh them. In addition, where the debtor has made an application for an interim order in the preceding 12

---

51 Under IA 1986, s 255(3)–(4): see *Bramston v Haut* [2012] EWCA Civ 1637, [2013] BPIR 25; cf. also *Tucker v Atkins* [2013] EWHC 4469 (Ch), [2014] BPIR 1359.
52 See above [6.25].
53 [1997] BPIR 24, at pp 29–31.
54 In *Bramston v Haut* (above) the Court of Appeal came to the view that the proposal was flawed, although it had been approved by the nominee.
55 IA 1986, s 256A(3).

months, that avenue is closed to the debtor, and in such circumstances the only option would be to use the alternative procedure.[56]

In summary, the interim order procedure is usually preferable where the debtor **7.27** is an undischarged bankrupt or there is a bankruptcy petition pending against them. In other circumstances the choice is more finely balanced. Proceeding without first obtaining the protection of an interim order should usually be undertaken only where the debtor is relatively sure that there is no 'rogue' creditor seeking to undermine the process by taking steps that could have been prevented by an interim order. Whenever possible, the likely attitude of the creditors should be sounded as the proposal is being put together. Where it is clear that a sufficient majority of the creditors are likely to be on board, the alternative approach may well be the better option.

---

56   IA 1986, s 255(1)(c); see above [6.15].

PART IV

DECISION AND CHALLENGE

8

THE NOMINEE AND THE DECISION

A. THE NOMINEE'S ROLE

1. Preliminary matters

A debtor contemplating an individual voluntary arrangement (IVA) must des- **8.01** ignate a qualified person to act as nominee in accordance with the Insolvency Act 1986 (IA 1986).[1] The nominee must certify that they are willing to act as such and the date on which they received the debtor's proposal, as required by the Insolvency (England and Wales) Rules 2016 (IR 2016).[2] Although, theoretically, where the debtor is an undischarged bankrupt, the Official Receiver (OR) could be the nominee,[3] in practice the nominee will almost always be an insolvency practitioner (IP). Two or more IPs can act together as joint nominees. In every case the nominee must be bonded (although the premiums for such a bond are reduced to nil if the proposal is subsequently rejected).[4]

---

1   IA 1986, s 253(2) and (impliedly) s 256A(2)-(3), together with s 388(2).
2   IR 2016, r 8.4(1)–(2); see above [6.17] and [7.06].
3   IA 1986, s 389B: see below [11.02].
4   Insolvency Practitioners Regulations 2005 (SI 2005/524), Sch 2 Part 2.

8.02 The nominee's first formal task is to consider the proposal, together with the statement of affairs and any other documentation submitted to them by the debtor for the purposes of preparing a report.[5] They must consider the adequacy of the information provided by the debtor and, if need be, require the debtor to provide further details and supporting documents.[6]

8.03 Where they assisted the debtor in putting together the proposal, as will often be the case, the IP should have ensured that the proposal complies with the rules in accordance with the guidance provided in the relevant Statements of Insolvency Practice (SIPs).[7] In particular, this would mean ensuring that the proposal contains sufficient information to enable the creditors to understand the debtor's financial position and (where appropriate) trading history, including the debtor's background and financial history, what brought on the insolvency, any other attempts the debtor has made to address their financial difficulties and (where relevant and subject to commercial sensitivity) the identification of and documents to support any profit or cash projections; the proposal should also explain any financial or other relationship between the IP/proposed nominee and the debtor. Where the nominee has had no prior involvement, they will have to satisfy themselves that the proposal does adequately deal with these issues.

2. Report on the proposal

8.04 There is no specific form for the report, still less one prescribed by statute. What the report needs to cover will vary from one proposal to another, but a useful checklist is provided in SIP 3.[8] Although, in many cases, following these guidelines will suffice, the report may well need to go further where the circumstances indicate that further investigation is required.[9] It should identify any respects in which the proposal does not comply fully with the statutory requirements. The report must determine whether the proposal is both serious and viable.[10] It must reach clear conclusions and provide sufficient information for the creditors to understand the conclusions reached.

---

5   IA 1986, ss 256(2) and 256A(2); for the procedural formalities, see Chapters 6 and 7 above.

6   See above [5.14]–[5.18].

7   In particular, SIP 3.1 para 14. See above [1.48] and [4.01] and, on SIPs generally, [1.18].

8   In particular SIP 3, para 6.4. See also SIP 3.1.

9   *CFL Finance Ltd v Bass* [2019] EWHC 1839 (Ch), [2019] BPIR 1327, at [100]; although the decision was overturned on appeal (*Gertner v CFL Finance Ltd* [2020] EWHC 1241 (Ch), [2020] BPIR 752), this point was not criticised.

10   *Cooper v Fearnley* [1997] BPIR 20.

The purpose of the report is to inform the creditors (and, in the context of an **8.05** interim order, the court), not to provide the proposal with a seal of approval. In preparing the report, even in cases where they helped the debtor to prepare the proposal, the nominee is expected to cast a 'critical eye' over the debtor's statement of assets and liabilities and to apply an objective judgment, bringing to bear a 'considered opinion of the sort which one would expect of a professional accountant and a licensed insolvency practitioner' upon the proposal.[11]

In compiling the report, the nominee is not expected to undertake a full-scale **8.06** inquiry: it is recognised that they are constrained by limited resources and a tight statutory timetable. Nevertheless, within these limitations, the nominee is expected to carry out a careful review of the material supplied by the debtor; where there are doubts or questions in relation to the information provided by the debtor, the nominee must try to assess the strength and materiality of such concerns and carry out such investigations as may be reasonable so as to be able to address them in the report and reject the proposal if necessary.[12] Such concerns need only be addressed explicitly where the nominee considers that reasonable doubts still remain as to the accuracy of the material that has been presented;[13] but it is good practice for the report to explain the nominee's view on the veracity of the information provided by the debtor and the extent to which it has been verified.[14]

In essence, the report must explain whether there is a reasonable chance of the **8.07** proposal being fully implemented and whether the creditors should consider it.[15] These are two distinct conclusions. Regarding the former, if the proposal is doomed to result in bankruptcy anyway, it would be a waste of time and costs to place it before the creditors. The report should identify the extent to which the debtor is likely to cooperate and any difficulties that are likely to arise in getting in assets such as book debts or work in progress. It must also identify whether there is anything in the proposal that suggests an already manifest and yet unavoidable prospective unfairness.[16] If the proposal is governed by the IVA Protocol, the report must include a statement that the nominee has verified the debtor's income and expenditure in accordance with the Protocol and,

---

11 *Re A Debtor (No 222 of 1990)* [1992] BCLC 137; see also [1993] BCLC 233.
12 *Greystoke v Hamilton-Smith* [1997] BPIR 24; see also *Tradition (UK) Ltd v Ahmed* [2008] EWHC 2946 (Ch) and [2008] EWHC 3448 (Ch), reported together at [2009] BPIR 626.
13 *Shah v Cooper* [2003] BPIR 1018.
14 SIP 3.1, para 15(b).
15 IA 1986, s 256(1) and IR 2016, r 8.15(3); or (where there is no interim order) IA 1986, s 256A(3) and r 8.19(1); see also SIP 3.1, para 15(b) and SIP 3, para 6.2(b).
16 *Greystoke v Hamilton-Smith* [1997] BPIR 24; see also SIP 3, para 6.2(c) and SIP 3.1, para 15(b).

where the debtor is self-employed, it should provide details of the means used to carry out that verification.[17] Such information would be equally desirable in the context of any kind of proposal where the IVA depended to any significant extent on the debtor's income going forward.

8.08 Separately, the report must set out whether there is a reasonable chance that a sufficient majority of the creditors will approve the proposal.[18] It is usually helpful for the nominee to address the views of any significant unsecured creditor, to the extent that these are known.[19] They should not be too quick to take creditor opposition at face value, however: experience shows that even creditors who have initially expressed hostility to the debtor's proposal may change their minds when it comes to the vote itself. Therefore, unless it is clearly futile, the creditors should generally be given the opportunity to decide. In most cases the proposal will contain a comparison of estimated outcomes between the IVA and any other option (usually bankruptcy). The report need not be overly concerned with this comparison,[20] but it must address the question of why creditor support can be expected; the proposal must offer some kind of return for unsecured creditors and, as long as this is not derisory, even a little return might suffice to be worthy of the creditors' consideration.[21] If the debtor has put forward a proposal within the previous 12 months that was rejected, the nominee should say so and include an explanation as to why the current proposal is more worthy of consideration.[22]

8.09 The nominee must take into account information that has come to light since the proposal was finalised, even (perhaps especially) if they helped create it. Such information might include undisclosed assets or liabilities, or, possibly, where the debtor is an undischarged bankrupt, representations made by the OR (or the trustee in bankruptcy). Where there is no interim order in place, the report must additionally contain certain other matters.[23] If favourable, the report no longer has to specify the date, time and place for the creditors' meeting (a requirement abolished by the Small Business, Enterprise and Employment Act 2015 (SBEEA 2015)), but, in an interim order case, the

---

17   IVA Protocol, paragraph 7.9.
18   On the requisite majority, see below [8.46].
19   Cf. SIP 3.1, para 13(c).
20   *Greystoke v Hamilton-Smith* [1997] BPIR 24, at 28; cf. SIP 3.1 paragraph 14(b).
21   *Knowles v Coutts & Co* [1998] BPIR 96; *Gertner v CFL Finance Ltd* [2020] EWHC 1241 (Ch), [2020] BPIR 752.
22   SIP 3, para 6.6.
23   IR 2016, r 8.19(1A) and (2): see above [7.10]–[7.11].

report should still provide the court with the details of the decision procedure the nominee intends to use.[24]

3. The choice of decision procedure

If the report recommends that the proposal be put to the creditors, the nominee **8.10** must choose the appropriate decision-making procedure. Prior to the 2017 reforms, this would have been conducted at a meeting of creditors convened in accordance with the Insolvency Rules 1986 (IR 1986).[25] With effect from 6 April 2017, SBEEA 2015 inserted new provisions into IA 1986 that permitted, for the first time, a range of procedures for creditor decision-making besides physical meetings.[26] How they operate is governed by the rules.[27]

The available decision-making procedures are correspondence, electronic **8.11** voting, virtual meeting, physical meeting or 'any other decision-making procedure which enables all creditors who are entitled to participate in the making of the decision to participate equally'.[28] Subject to restrictions on the use of physical meetings and to any direction given by the court, it is entirely up to the nominee which decision-making procedure to use.[29] In practice, the most commonly used type of procedure is the virtual meeting. Where the nominee opts for an electronic voting procedure, the voting system must not allow any creditor access to any information concerning the vote of any other creditor, and, except where the procedure is used at a physical meeting, the system must enable a creditor to vote at any time between the date of the delivery of the notice and the decision date.[30]

Physical meetings are now the exception: the nominee may not choose this **8.12** option unless a court so directs or a sufficient proportion of creditors require this in accordance with the statutory provisions. A creditor wanting the decision to be made at a physical meeting must send their request in writing to the nominee; it can be made either before or after the nominee sends out notices of the decision-making procedure, but must be made no later than five business days after the date on which the nominee's notice was delivered.[31] If, within that time limit, the creditors who request a physical meeting amount to at least

---

24   See above [6.33]; on the practical consequences, see below [8.25].
25   IR 1986, rr 5.17–5.24.
26   IA 1986, ss 379ZA to 379ZC and Sch 9, para 11A (in relation to the relevant rules).
27   IR 2016, Part 15, supplemented (in the case of IVAs) by further rules in Part 8.
28   IR 2016, r 15.3.
29   IA 1986, s 379ZA(2) and (5). On physical meetings, see below [8.12].
30   IR 2016, r 15.4(b)–(c).
31   IA 1986, s 379ZA(3); IR 2016, r 15.6(1).

10 per cent by value, or 10 per cent by number, or at least 10 creditors request it, the nominee must call a physical meeting.[32] This need not be a coordinated request: any creditor can send a written request to the nominee, but it is only once the aggregate of such requests reaches one of the requisite thresholds that the nominee must accede to the request. It is the responsibility of the nominee to monitor whether such requests have been received by the deadline and if so whether any of the three thresholds have been reached, so as to trigger the necessity for a physical meeting.[33] The calculation of the value of the creditors' debts for this purpose is governed by the general rules applicable to calculating voting rights.[34]

4. Notice of decision procedure

(a) Contents of the notice

8.13 Where the report is favourable, the nominee must seek a decision from the creditors on the proposal unless there is an interim order in force and the court directs otherwise.[35] The nominee thereby becomes the convener.[36] The convener must deliver a notice to every creditor;[37] although there is no mandatory form for such a notice, what it must contain is prescribed.[38] In particular, it must state the following:

- identification details of the proceedings;[39]
- where there is an interim order in force, details of the court or hearing centre in which the nominee filed the report pursuant to s 256 of IA 1986 or, otherwise, of the court or hearing centre in which any application in connection with the proposal or the IVA should be made in accordance with IR 2016, rule 8.20;[40]
- how a person who is entitled to vote may propose modifications and how those will be dealt with by the nominee;[41]
- details of the decision to be made, of the decision-making procedure that will be used and of the arrangements, including venue, for the decision;[42]

---

32 IA 1986, s 379ZA(3), (4), (5)(b) and (7).
33 IR 2016, r 15.6(2).
34 That is IR 2016, r 15.31(1)(e): see r 15.6(8) and below [8.28]–[8.30].
35 IA 1986, s 257(1), (2) and (2A).
36 IR 2016, r 1.2.
37 IR 2016, r 8.22(2) and r 15.8(2): see below [8.17].
38 IR 2016, r 8.22(2)–(3) and (so far as is relevant) r 15.8(3); it must also comply with IR 2016, rr 1.6 and 1.8.
39 IR 2016, r 8.22(3)(a) and r 15.8(3)(a).
40 IR 2016, r 8.22(3)(c) and (b), respectively.
41 IR 2016, r 8.22(3)(d).
42 IR 2016, r 15.8(3)(b)–(c).

- the decision date;[43]
- the date by which the creditor must have delivered proof in respect of their claim, failing which their vote would be disregarded;[44]
- that a creditor whose debt is treated as a small debt within IR 2016, rule 14.31(1) must still deliver a proof of debt by that same date if they wish to vote;[45]
- that a creditor who has opted out from receiving notices may still vote if they deliver a proof of debt by that same date;[46]
- details setting out the effects of the relevant provisions of IR 2016, rules 15.28, 15.31 and 15 34, about creditors' voting rights, the calculations of those rights and the requisite majorities for making decisions, respectively;[47]
- that a creditor may appeal a decision in accordance with IR 2016, rule 15.35, and that such an appeal must be made within 28 days of the relevant date under section 259(1) of IA 1986.[48]

Further information is required as to the details of the decision-making **8.14** procedure and the arrangements that will be used, depending on the type of procedure adopted. Where the choice is other than a physical meeting, the notice must contain a statement that creditors who meet any of the thresholds in section 379ZA(7) of IA 1986 may, within five business days from the date of delivery of the notice, require a physical meeting.[49] Where the nominee opts for electronic voting, the notice must provide the creditors with any necessary information as to how to access the voting system (including any password required).[50] Where the option is for a virtual meeting, the notice must include any necessary information, including telephone number, access code or password required, and must also include a statement that the meeting might be suspended or adjourned by the chair and must be adjourned if the creditors so resolve.[51] In the case of a physical meeting, along with the same details about suspension and adjournment, the notice must identify the venue for the meeting (which must be selected having regard for the convenience of those invited to participate)[52] and state that the nominee has a discretion to

---

43   IR 2016, r 15.8(3)(d). On the date, see below [8.22]–[8.24].
44   IR 2016, r 15.8(3)(e).
45   IR 2016, r 15.8(3)(f), referring back to 15.8(3)(e).
46   IR 2016, r 15.8(3)(g), referring back to 15.8(3)(e).
47   IR 2016, r 15.8(3)(j). See below [8.28]–[8.30] (voting rights) and [8.46] (majorities).
48   IR 2016, r 15.8(3)(n), read with r 15.35(5)(b); see below [9.27]–[9.32].
49   IR 2016, r 15.8(3)(k). See above [8.12].
50   IR 2016, r 15.4(a).
51   IR 2016, r 15.5. On adjournment and suspension, see below [8.34]–[8.36].
52   See IR 2016, r 15.10.

allow remote attendance[53] and that any proxy must be delivered to the nominee before it may be used at the meeting.[54] In addition (if applicable), it must say that a complaint may be made in accordance with IR 2016, r 15.38 and the time in which such a complaint may be made.[55] Where the notice was triggered by the requisite level of creditor requests for a physical meeting, the notice must also state that the original decision procedure has been superseded.[56]

8.15 The notice must be accompanied by a copy of the report, together with copies of the debtor's proposal and statement of affairs (or a summary of the latter, listing the creditors and the amounts of debt owed to each), unless (where there is no interim order) the nominee has already supplied copies of these documents to the creditors.[57]

8.16 Where the nominee intends to publish the results of the creditors' decision exclusively on a website, the notice must explain that the results will be made available on the website, where they may be viewed and downloaded,[58] provide the address of the website and any password necessary to view and download the document and inform the creditors that they may request a hard copy of the document, supplying a telephone number, email address and postal address via which the request may be made.[59] Where this method of publication is chosen, the results must be in a format that enables them to be downloaded within a reasonable time of an electronic request being made for them to be downloaded and they must remain available on the website for a period of two months beyond the end of the IVA or of the release of the last office holder in relation to the IVA.[60] The document containing the results is deemed to have been delivered to the creditors when it is first made available on the website.[61] If the nominee subsequently receives a request for a hard copy of the results document (in accordance with the procedure outlined in the notice), the hard copy must be delivered to the creditor making the request free of charge and within five business days of receiving the request.[62]

---

53   IR 2016, r 15.6(3) and (6)(b).
54   IR 2016, r 15.8(3)(l).
55   IR 2016, r 15.8(3)(m). See below [8.43]–[8.44].
56   IR 2016, r 15.6(4).
57   IR 2016, r 8.22(6); see IR 2016, r 8.19(1) and (4) and see above [7.13].
58   IR 2016, r 8.22(4). See also IA 1986, s 379B.
59   IR 2016, r 8.22(5), read together with r 1.49(2).
60   IR 2016, r 8.22(5), read together with rr 1.49(4)(a) and (b) and 1.51(2).
61   IR 2016, r 8.22(5), read together with r 1.49(5)(a).
62   IR 2016, r 8.22(5), read together with r 1.49(3).

(b) Notice to whom?

The nominee must give notice to every creditor of whose claim the nominee **8.17** is aware in accordance with the rules.[63] This includes not just the creditors mentioned in the statement of affairs but also any other creditors of whose claims the nominee has become aware; the nominee has no discretion and cannot decide whether a particular creditor or would-be creditor should not be given notice.[64] As noted above, the definition of 'creditors' in relation to IVAs is very wide.[65] Notice should be given even to those creditors whose debts are not provable in the IVA,[66] but the omission of creditors who have no right to vote on or participate in the IVA would not be serious.[67] The duty to give notice falls personally on the nominee and cannot be delegated, for example, to the debtor: any failure to give notice is therefore down to the nominee alone.

The requirement is to give notice to each and every creditor individually: it is **8.18** insufficient to give notice to one creditor in the belief that, due to circumstances (known to the nominee) concerning the relationship between that creditor and another, notice would be bound to come to the attention of that other.[68] As a general rule, actual or constructive notice of the decision procedure will not suffice, but where a creditor became aware of the procedure in sufficient time and with sufficient information to be able to participate, this would not necessarily jeopardise the entire process.[69] The nominee cannot rely on the rules of service under the Civil Procedure Rules 1998 (CPR),[70] so that giving notice to a solicitor acting for a particular creditor does not amount to giving notice to that creditor.[71] On the other hand, where a creditor has expressly informed the nominee that they would prefer to receive notice via their solicitor and the solicitors in question have indicated that they are authorised by that creditor to accept notice on their client's behalf, it would suffice to comply with this request.[72]

---

63   IA 1986, s 257(2B); IR 2016, r 8.22(1)–(2).
64   *Re Debtors (Nos 400 IO and 401 IO of 1996)* [1997] BPIR 431.
65   See Chapter 2 above.
66   *Golstein v Bishop* [2013] EWHC 1706 (Ch), [2013] BPIR 708.
67   See *Child Maintenance and Enforcement Commission v Beesley & Whyman* [2010] EWCA Civ 1344, [2011] BPIR 608 (see above [2.28]).
68   *Namulas Pension Trustees Ltd v Mouzakis* [2011] BPIR 1724 (Chesterfield County Court).
69   *Beverley Group plc v McClue* [1996] BPIR 25 – a CVA case where the facts were exceptional.
70   CPR, Part 6.
71   *Namulas Pension Trustees Ltd v Mouzakis* (above); see also *Mytre Investments Ltd v Reynolds (No.2)* [1996] BPIR 464.
72   IR 2016, r 1.40; see also the (*obiter*) comments in *Mytre Investments* (above), at p 471; neither this case nor the *Mouzakis* case (above) involved such express authorisation.

8.19 Where notice was not properly given to creditors who found themselves bound by the IVA, this does not automatically invalidate the IVA; but where the votes of such creditors would (on aggregate) have been sufficient to change the result of the vote, this could amount to a material irregularity that might result in the decision being revoked.[73] If a creditor, to whom the nominee had not sent notice, became aware of the decision procedure and was subsequently permitted by the convener or chair to vote in the procedure, this too would not invalidate the procedure. In *Re Debtors (Nos 400 IO and 401 IO of 1996)*,[74] the debtor unsuccessfully challenged the rejection of the proposal on the basis that the nominee had been right not to send notice to a particular creditor, but wrong subsequently to have admitted that creditor's vote.

8.20 Given the central importance of notice and the rigour with which the courts have tended to scrutinise this, it is essential for the nominee to seek to obtain the correct address for each creditor. With institutional creditors, like banks, it is often sensible to send notice to the local branch or office, marked for the attention of the individual officer or employee who has been dealing with the debtor, as well as the head or regional office. As a matter of good practice, the nominee should keep a record and evidence of notice (for example, proof of postage) so as to be in a position to prove notice was given in case this is subsequently challenged. Providing the nominee can show the notice was properly sent, the onus of proving non-receipt rests on the creditor.[75]

8.21 In cases where the nominee has reason to believe that delivery of notice to a particular creditor might entail difficulties, they should consider using recorded delivery, possibly in addition to ordinary first-class post; it may also be advisable, where there is concern that a creditor might later cause trouble, to check by telephone that such a creditor has actually received the notice. In an extreme case, it may be prudent to use a personal service through a process server, who can then supply an affidavit of service. In exceptional circumstances the court may order that notice be provided by advertisement instead, but otherwise notice of the decision procedure should not be advertised or gazetted.[76]

(c) Timing

8.22 As soon as the nominee, or (in an interim order case) the court, has determined that the decision of the creditors should be sought, the nominee must seek

---

73 See IR 2016, r 15.15. On revocation, see Chapter 9 below.
74 [1997] BPIR 431.
75 IR 2016, r 1.42(3) (formerly IR 1986, r 12.10, or, more recently, r 12A(3)); see *Lombard NatWest Factors Ltd v Arbis* [2000] BPIR 79.
76 IR 2016, r 15.12; note that r 15.13 does not apply to IVAs.

such a decision by delivering notice to the creditors. The notice must stipulate a date for the decision procedure and this date must be not less than 14 days from the date of the delivery of the notice and not more than 28 days from the relevant date: where there is an interim order, the relevant date is the date of the court's consideration of the report; otherwise, it is the date the nominee received the proposal and supporting documents from the debtor.[77]

The above requirements are mandatory and strictly applied; the minimum **8.23** requirement means 14 'clear days' and non-compliance could not be cured by simply adjourning a decision procedure wrongly convened for a date within the 14-day period to a date after it had expired.[78] Where the nominee delivers the notice by post, the day on which the notice is posted and the date of the decision procedure itself are to be discounted and allowance must also be made for the days deemed to be required by the postal service: two days for first class postage and four for second class.[79]

Formerly, under IR 1986, the relevant rule required that the notices 'shall be **8.24** sent by the nominee, at least 14 days before the day fixed for' the meeting.[80] The current requirement is that '[t]he decision date must be not less than 14 days from the date of delivery of the notice', which provides somewhat greater clarity.[81] The old wording led to additional complications in calculating the required minimum period for giving notice, as it was held that 'sent to' (in this context) included delivery, and where the creditor could show that delivery had not been achieved within the requisite window, the IVA could be invalidated.[82] Failure to provide notice to a particular creditor at least 14 clear days before the decision procedure would now be much less likely to endanger the IVA; in effect the aggrieved creditor would have to challenge the IVA on the basis that the failure to provide proper notice to them amounted to a material irregularity.[83] Nevertheless, a wholesale disregard of this requirement could still be fatal. Given the strictness of the notice requirements, to avoid difficulties it is best practice for the nominee to err on the side of giving slightly more than 14 days' notice.

---

77   IR 2016, r 8.22(7); see also r 15.11(1).
78   *Mytre Investments Ltd v Reynolds (No.2)* [1996] BPIR 464.
79   IR 2016, 1.42 and see Ch.9 of Part 1 of IR 2016 generally.
80   IR 1986, r 5.13(2) as originally drafted and r 5.17(2) from 1 January 2003.
81   IR 2016, r 8.22(7).
82   *Skipton Building Society v Collins* [1998] BPIR 267.
83   See IA 1986, s 260(2)(b) and IR 2016, 15.15; note also IA 1986, s 262(8). See Chapter 9 below.

8.25 Where the interim order procedure is being followed, if the creditors' decision is sought before the court has had a chance to consider the report, the creditors' approval would be incurably invalid and the resulting IVA a nullity.[84] Under current law, the order directing the nominee to convene a decision procedure will give details of that procedure;[85] in *Re N (A Debtor)*,[86] decided under the law as it was prior to 6 April 2017, it was held that if the meeting of creditors was held otherwise than in accordance with the court order, it would not be valid. Although that would no longer be the case, having regard to the current statutory provisions and the modern approach of the courts to invalidity,[87] where the nominee finds that it is simply not possible to comply with the details of the arrangements in the court order, it might be necessary to apply back to court for that order to be reviewed or varied (and, if necessary, for permission to rely on revised notices and for extensions of time and an extension of the interim order), supported by evidence explaining why compliance had become impossible.[88]

8.26 Where the alternative procedure is being followed, the position prior to 6 April 2017 was similar to that in interim order cases and, if it became impracticable for the meeting to be held strictly in accordance with the details in the report, the nominee would have had to make application for permission to deliver an amended report that contained a new timetable for the decision procedure. Since 6 April 2017, the decision procedure must conform to the details set out in the nominee's notice to the creditors, delivered along with the report.[89] Where that has become impracticable, the nominee should send out new notices, revoking the earlier notices, and (if necessary) apply to the court for any relevant extensions.

8.27 Where the threshold for triggering a physical meeting is met, there are additional requirements that pertain in relation to the timing: the nominee must send the notice summoning the meeting not later than 3 business days after any of the three thresholds referred to above has been reached.[90] Such meetings are now rare, and it is not yet clear what the consequences would be if this provision were not strictly complied with.

---

84 *Vlieland-Boddy v Dexter Ltd* [2003] EWHC 2592 (Ch), [2004] BPIR 235.
85 IR 2016, r 8.16(e). On the former position under IR 1986, see above [6.33] and cf. [8.09].
86 [2002] BPIR 1024. The *ratio* of the decision is firmly rooted in the wording of s 257(1) as it was then in force (prior to 6 April 2017): see above [6.33].
87 See below [9.10]–[9.12].
88 Pursuant to IA 1986, s 375(1). This would not be necessary where the reason was that a physical meeting was now required (see above [8.12] and below [8.27]).
89 See above [8.15].
90 IR 2016, r 15.6(5). See above [8.12].

B. THE DECISION

1. Conduct of the decision procedure

(a) Determining voting rights

The nominee's role does not cease upon delivering notice of the decision pro- **8.28** cedure but extends to the conduct of the procedure itself. Where the procedure is to be conducted at a meeting, the nominee (as convener) will automatically become the chair of that meeting.[91] In presiding over the procedure, the nominee has to determine the extent to which each creditor should be admitted for voting purposes.[92] The starting position is that every creditor who has notice of the decision procedure is entitled to vote in respect of that creditor's debt.[93] The relevant date for calculating whether a person is a creditor and if so the amount of their claim depends on whether the debtor is an undischarged bankrupt: if so, it is the date of the bankruptcy order;[94] otherwise, it is the date of the interim order or, where the alternative procedure has been followed, the date of the decision itself.[95] The value accorded to such claims for voting purposes is a matter for the nominee, who may (subject to certain constraints set out below) admit or reject a claim in whole or in part.[96] For the purposes of arriving at this decision, the nominee is entitled to call for documentation or other evidence in support of the claim.[97]

Where the debt is wholly secured, its value for voting purposes must be nil **8.29** (unless the security is surrendered); where it is partly secured (or partially surrendered), its value for these purposes will be the value of the unsecured part.[98] If the debt is unliquidated or its amount is unascertained, the nominee should value it at £1 for voting purposes unless they decide to put a higher value on it, in which case they should admit it for that higher value.[99] When considering whether to put a higher value on the debt for voting purposes, the nominee is not under a duty to conduct an investigation and should not speculate; however, where the creditor has supplied evidence to support a value for the claim higher than £1, the nominee is under an obligation to consider it and,

---

91   IR 2016, r 15.21(1).
92   IR 2016, r 15.33(1).
93   IR 2016, r 15.28(5).
94   IR 2016, r 15.31(1)(e)(ii).
95   IR 2016, r 15.31(1)(e)(i)(aa)–(bb).
96   IR 2016, r 15.33(2).
97   IR 2016, r 15.28(4).
98   IR 2016, r 15.31(4)–(5).
99   IR 2016, r 15.31(3).

if that evidence is sufficiently clear to enable them safely to ascribe a higher minimum value, they should do so.[100]

8.30 If the debt is disputed or the nominee is in any doubt as to whether a claim should be admitted, they should mark it as objected to and allow the creditor to vote in respect of it (subject to such vote subsequently being declared invalid in the event that the objection is sustained).[101] The nominee must, however, be very careful not to confuse or elide this decision with the one relating to unliquidated or unascertained debts: a liquidated claim cannot be accorded a value of £1 by reason of being disputed; it must be accorded its full value and marked as disputed, even where this would mean the IVA is defeated.[102] Conversely, an unliquidated claim may be accorded a value higher than £1 where there is evidence to support this, even if it is also disputed and marked as such.[103]

8.31 The nominee must be neutral and should be scrupulously careful not to take sides, or be seen to take sides, between creditor and debtor or between one creditor and another, when making decisions as to whether or to what extent to admit or exclude a debt for voting purposes.[104] The extent of the nominee's duties as chair was considered in *Tradition (UK) Ltd v Ahmed*.[105] Although this was a rather extreme case, involving allegations against the nominee of vote-rigging and partisanship, it is illustrative of the norms that the court will expect of IPs in their role as nominee and in particular as chair. When deciding whether to admit claims for voting purposes, particular care must be taken where there is evidence to suggest that the creditor has different competing claims potentially conflicting with the debt being relied on for the purposes of the vote or that the claim on which the voting right would depend may no longer exist at the time of the decision.[106]

---

100 *Re Newlands (Seaford) Educational Trust* (aka *Chittenden v Pepper*) [2006] EWHC 1511 (Ch), [2006] BPIR 1230, a CVA case; and *National Westminster Bank v Yadgaroff* [2011] EWHC 3711 (Ch), [2012] BPIR 371. See also *Leighton Contracting (Qatar) WLL v Simms* [2011] EWHC 1735 (Ch), [2011] BPIR 1395 (CVA) and *Sofaer v Anglo Irish Asset Finance Plc* [2011] EWHC 1480 (Ch), [2011] BPIR 1736.

101 IR 2016, r 15.33(3).

102 *AB Agri Ltd v Curtis* [2016] BPIR 1297.

103 See *Sofaer v Anglo Irish Asset Finance Plc* [2011] EWHC 1480 (Ch), [2011] BPIR 1736.

104 *Smurthwaite v Simpson-Smith & Mond* [2006] EWCA Civ 1183, [2006] BPIR 1504, at [33], *per* Jacob LJ.

105 [2008] EWHC 2946 (Ch) and [2008] EWHC 3448 (Ch), reported together at [2009] BPIR 626.

106 See *Smurthwaite v Simpson-Smith & Mond (No.2)* [2006] BPIR 1483; *CFL Finance Ltd v Rubin* [2017] EWHC 111 (Ch) [2017] BPIR 326. See further below at [9.14].

(b)   Conduct and control of the decision procedure

In almost every case the nominee has overall control of the decision procedure, **8.32**
as convener or chair. In relation to the conduct of a virtual or physical meeting,
the chair has a fairly wide discretion, including allowing persons other than
creditors to have a voice and deciding whether and, if so, what questions may
be put to the debtor.[107] Where the nominee has had to convene a physical
meeting, they may permit a creditor to participate in the meeting without
being physically present, provided the nominee has received a request for such
remote attendance in advance of the meeting.[108]

Creditors are entitled to make use of proxies, provided that the proxy complies   **8.33**
with certain minimum standards and contains the necessary information and
the creditor has delivered it to the nominee before the meeting begins.[109]
A creditor is entitled to vary the terms of their proxy.[110] The nominee (as
convener/chair) must take care only to apply proxy votes strictly in accordance
with the terms of the proxy.[111] Formerly, under IR 1986, the chair could not,
as proxy-holder, vote to increase or reduce the fees or expenses of the nominee
or supervisor unless expressly mandated to do so by the proxy.[112] That rule has
been recast so as to spell this prohibition out in more elaborate detail under IR
2016, but to similar effect.[113] The rights in regard to the inspection of proxies
are also strictly governed by the rules.[114] There are, in addition, specific rules
about the representation of corporate bodies at such meetings.[115]

(c)   Adjournment and suspension

Subject to any direction given by the court, the nominee (as chair), may – and,   **8.34**
if the creditors so resolve, must – adjourn a meeting (virtual or physical).[116] The
adjournment can only be for a maximum of 14 days and, although a procedure
can be adjourned more than once, any successive adjournment must not be to
a date more than 14 days after the date of the original meeting, unless the court
so orders.[117] Although the discretion accorded to the chair regarding adjourn-

---

107   IR 2016, r 15.22.
108   IR 2016, r 15.6(6)(a) and (7).
109   See IR 2016, Part 16, in particular rr 16.2 and 16.4.
110   *Re Cardona, IRC v Cardona* [1997] BPIR 604.
111   See *Smith-Evans v Smailes* [2013] EWHC 3199 (Ch), [2014]1 WLR 1548 and *Narandas-Girdhar v
       Bradstock* [2016] EWCA Civ 88, [2016] 1WLR 2366, [2016] BPIR 428.
112   IR 1986, r 5.20.
113   IR 2016, r 16.7.
114   IR 2016, r 16.6.
115   IR 2016, rr 16.8–16.9.
116   IR 2016, r 15.23(1).
117   IR 2016, r 15.23(1)–(2).

ments is wide (subject to the provisos mentioned above), it is not unlimited. In *Tradition (UK) Ltd v Ahmed*,[118] the court held that the nominee was not entitled to adjourn merely for the purposes of carrying out further investigations into creditor claims. It should be borne in mind, however, that this decision was made under the somewhat more restrictive provisions of IR 1986.[119] The court in that case went on to consider whether the nominee had any residual power under the common law to adjourn such a meeting and found that they did, but only in very limited circumstances, for example for the purposes of restoring order or to deal with logistical problems.[120] It is likely that such contingencies would now largely be governed by the rules in relation to suspension (not then available).[121] The provisions of IR 1986 dealing with adjournments in the context of IVAs also included a stipulation that any proposal that had not been approved following a final adjournment would be deemed rejected.[122] There is no equivalent provision under IR 2016.

8.35 Where the decision procedure is adjourned, the nominee must be sure to provide notice, with full details of the adjournment, to all creditors (not just to the creditors who attended first time). Under IR 1986, the nominee was also required to notify the court:[123] there is no equivalent under IR 2016, but where there is an interim order in place, it may be necessary to obtain an extension of that order from the court in circumstances where the adjournment might take the decision beyond or perilously close to the expiry of the interim order. IR 2016 contains no provisions for where the nominee does not appear to chair a meeting that has been convened (or adjourned) for the purposes of allowing the creditors to consider a proposal.[124] The situation is, thankfully, too rare to have attracted judicial comment. There may also be circumstances, lying outside the strict confines of acting as nominee or chair, where the IP will owe the debtor a duty of care to advise about the possibility of obtaining an adjournment.[125]

---

118 [2009] BPIR 626, at [234]–[238].

119 IR 1986, r 5.24.

120 *Tradition (UK) Ltd v Ahmed* [2009] BPIR 626, at [239]–[243].

121 See below [8.36].

122 IR 1986, r 5.24(5), applied in *Bonney v Mirpuri* [2013] BPIR 412; it is submitted that the alternative reasoning in that case, based upon the court's discretion, would still be relevant under IR 2016.

123 IR 1986, r 5.24(4).

124 IR 2016, r 15.25 does not apply to voluntary arrangements.

125 *Prosser v Castle Sanderson (a firm)* [2002] EWCA Civ 1140; [2002] BPIR 1163 established that the IP, when not acting as chair, might owe the debtor such a duty, but it was unnecessary to determine in that case whether they had breached such a duty as there was clearly no recoverable loss involved.

Until 2010, other than by way of adjournment, there was no express power for **8.36**
the chair to suspend a meeting. A new provision was inserted into what was
then IR 1986 to permit suspension for very limited period (not exceeding one
hour).[126] There was no flexibility.[127] Under the equivalent provision in IR 2016,
a somewhat less rigid power is granted to the chair to suspend the meeting:
the suspension may exceed one hour only in exceptional circumstances, but
can never extend beyond the same day.[128] In addition, the chair may suspend
a meeting in circumstances where someone has become 'excluded'.[129]

2. Modifications

When considering the debtor's proposal, any creditor is entitled to propose **8.37**
modifications to the terms.[130] The range of potential modifications is very
wide, subject to certain restrictions (discussed below) and to the overriding
proviso that no modification is permitted that would have the effect of rendering the proposal no longer within the ambit of Part 8 of IA 1986 altogether.[131]
Notwithstanding the statutory wording, it is likely that an IVA with such
modifications would not be void *ab initio*, but would rather be liable to be set
aside (pursuant to section 262 of IA 1986); however this remains somewhat
controversial.[132]

There are further specific restrictions as to what modifications may be per- **8.38**
missible. No modification can affect the rights of secured creditors or interfere with the relative priority of preferential creditors, save with the express
consent of the creditor concerned.[133] Moreover, every modification must have
the support of the debtor.[134] If the debtor does not accept the modification,
the approval of an IVA containing such a modification would be, at the very
least, open to challenge. There are authorities that go further and suggest that
a proposal modified without the debtor's consent is incapable of being validly

---

126 IR 1986, r 5.24(4A), inserted by the Insolvency (Amendment) Rules 2010.
127 See *Re Forstater* [2015] BPIR 21, but the result depended on what was then IR 1986, r 5.24(5), on which see
     above [8.34].
128 IR 2016, r 15.27.
129 See below [8.41].
130 IA 1986, s 258(2), subject to subsections (3)–(7).
131 IA 1986, s 258(3).
132 See below [9.10]–[9.12].
133 IA 1986, s 258(4), (5) and (7). On secured creditors, see *Webb v MacDonald* [2010] BPIR 503. Such an IVA,
     though clearly open to challenge by the creditor concerned, would not be void: see below [9.11].
134 IA 1986, s 258(2).

approved and any purported approval would be a nullity.[135] It now appears this goes too far.[136]

8.39 Modifications may include changes to the fees and expenses recoverable by the nominee and/or supervisor. Where a creditor proposes such a modification on the basis that the fees suggested in the proposal are excessive, the nominee (as convener/chair) has no authority to disregard such a proposed modification; the fact that the nominee and the debtor consider the fees in the proposal to be appropriate is irrelevant.[137] Modifications may also include a change to the proposed supervisor from the debtor's nominee, though this is rare. If such a modification is put forward, the proposed alternative must provide confirmation that they are qualified to act in relation to the debtor and consent to act as such a supervisor: where the decision is being taken at a meeting, this must be provided at or before the meeting; otherwise, it must be delivered to the nominee by the creditor proposing the change prior to the decision.[138]

8.40 Certain creditors who find themselves frequently being asked to approve IVAs, in particular HMRC, have some standard modifications they will often try to introduce. Where any such creditor has a substantial stake in the decision, consideration should be given at the outset to including such common requirements within the proposal, and in any event the likely impact of such modifications should be taken into account.

3. Excluded persons

(a) Procedure for dealing with exclusion

8.41 Where someone, who has been invited to attend a virtual meeting or to attend a physical meeting remotely, has taken all the steps necessary to attend in accordance with the arrangements put in place by the nominee but nevertheless finds themselves unable to attend all or part of the meeting, such a person is referred to as an 'excluded person'.[139] Once the chair is aware of the fact that there is one or more excluded persons, they have a range of options: they can continue the meeting, declare it to be void and reconvene the meeting or declare the meeting valid up to the point where the person became excluded

---

135 See *Reid v Hamblin* [2001] BPIR 929; *Re Plummer* [2004] 767.
136 See *Narandas-Girdhar v Bradstock* [2016] EWCA Civ 88, [2016] 1 WLR 2366, at [33]–[53], *per* Briggs LJ, discussed below at [9.10]–[9.12].
137 *Royal Bank of Scotland plc v Munikwa* [2020] EWHC 786 (Ch).
138 IA 1986, s 258(3) in combination with IR 2016, r 8.23(1)–(2).
139 IR 2016, r 15.36(1).

and adjourn the meeting.[140] Alternatively, the chair may suspend the meeting for up to one hour, to allow the fault to be rectified.[141] Where, in such circumstances, the chair decides to continue the meeting, the meeting will be valid unless (upon a complaint by the excluded person) the chair subsequently decides to declare the meeting void and hold the meeting over again, or the court directs otherwise.[142]

A creditor who claims to be an excluded person may request an indication of **8.42** what occurred during the period of their exclusion. Such a request must be made as soon as reasonably practicable and, in any event, not later than 4pm on the business day following the exclusion; if made during the meeting, it must be made to the chair, and if after, to the convener.[143] In practice, in both cases, this will be the nominee who, if satisfied that the request is from a genuine excluded person, must supply the information requested as soon as reasonably practicable and, in any event, by no later than 4pm on the business day following receipt of the request.[144]

(b) Making a complaint

Any excluded person may complain that they have been adversely affected by **8.43** the exclusion to the nominee (chair or convener, as the case may be), provided they do so by no later than 4pm on the business day following the exclusion or, if the complainant requested an indication (as discussed above), on the business day following receipt of that indication.[145] The nominee must consider the complaint as soon as reasonably practicable. If satisfied both that the complainant is an excluded person and that the excluded person has suffered prejudice as a result of the exclusion, the nominee must take appropriate action to remedy the prejudice.[146]

The appropriate action will depend on the circumstances. If a vote was taken **8.44** during the period of exclusion and the complainant asserts how they intended to vote, as long as the nominee is satisfied that the excluded person's vote, had it been cast as intended, would have affected the outcome of the vote, the nominee must count the excluded person's vote in the way indicated and

---

140   IR 2016, r 15.36(2).
141   IR 2016, r 15.36(4).
142   IR 2016, r 15.36(3). On the complaints procedure, see below [8.43]–[8.45].
143   IR 2016, r 15.37(1)–(3).
144   IR 2016, r 15.37(4).
145   IR 2016, r 15.38(1)–(3).
146   IR 2016, r 15.38(4).

amend the record of the result accordingly.[147] If, by the time this adjustment is made, the nominee has already reported the result of the decision, they must deliver a corrected report, giving the reasons for the correction; otherwise the report must include details of the change and the reasons for it.[148] Where there was more than one excluded person, the nominee must take into account the combined effect of their respective votes.[149] Where no vote was taken during the period of the exclusion, the above does not apply. Equally, if the nominee, upon considering the complaint, is not satisfied that the vote of the excluded person (had it been made in accordance with the intentions expressed in the complaint) would have made any difference to the outcome, no correction is required.

8.45 In every case, the nominee must deliver notice of their decision to the complainant as soon as reasonably practicable after reaching that decision.[150] If the complainant is dissatisfied with the nominee's decision, they may apply to the court for directions, provided the application is made not more than two business days from the date of receipt by the complainant of notice of the nominee's decision.[151] Such application must be made to the court in which the interim order was made, if there is one; otherwise, it must be made to the appropriate court in accordance with the rules.[152]

C. OUTCOME AND APPROVAL

1. Approval and requisite majorities

8.46 To become binding, the proposal (and any modification to it) must be approved by the creditors in a decision procedure by a requisite majority, meaning that at least 75 per cent (in value) of the creditors who participated in the procedure voted in favour; such a decision does not count as a requisite majority, however, if more than half the total value of creditors who are not associates of the debtor voted against it.[153] For these purposes, the total value of creditors who are not associates is the total value of such claims that have been admitted by the nominee for voting purposes.[154] A creditor is only to be classed

---

147   IR 2016, r 15.38(5) and (6)(a)–(b).
148   IR 2016, r 15.38(6)(c)–(d). On this report, see below [8.48]–[8.49].
149   IR 2016, r 15.38(7).
150   IR 2016, r 15.38(8).
151   IR 2016, r 15.38(9).
152   If there is no interim order, the appropriate court is governed by IR 2016, r 8.20.
153   IR 2016, r 15.34(6)(a)–(b), respectively.
154   IR 2016, r 15.34(7)(c).

as an associate, for these purposes, if the nominee so decides, either in reliance upon the information provided by the debtor in their statement of affairs or otherwise in accordance with the rules.[155]

If the vote attains the requisite majority, the IVA is approved and comes into **8.47** effect forthwith upon the close of the decision procedure. The immediate effect of such approval is that it takes effect as if made by the debtor and binds every creditor who, in accordance with the rules, was entitled to vote in the decision procedure or would have been so entitled if they had had notice of the procedure, as if they were a party to the arrangement.[156] The result is susceptible to challenge in certain circumstances but, absent such challenge, the IVA will not be invalidated by any irregularity in relation to the decision procedure.[157] Another immediate consequence of approval is that the nominee (or their replacement) automatically becomes the supervisor of the IVA.[158] At this point the nominee will become entitled to payment of their expenses and fees.[159]

2. Reporting the outcome

Once the creditors have reached a final decision on the proposal, the nominee **8.48** (as convener or chair) must compile a report on the outcome of the decision procedure, stating whether the proposal was approved or rejected and, if approved, whether this was with any, and if so what, modifications.[160] The report must also list every creditor that voted in the decision procedure, recording the value accorded to each creditor and how they voted (in favour, against or abstained) on each resolution, together with such further information as the nominee thinks appropriate.[161] If the proposal was approved, the rules also require the report to state whether the resulting proceedings are main, territorial or non-EU.[162]

Where there is an interim order, the nominee must file a copy of the report **8.49** with the court within four business days of the decision date, whereupon the

---

155 IR 2016, r 15.34(7)(a)–(b); see also r 1.2(2) and IA 1986, s 435.
156 IA 1986, s 260(2). On this statutory 'hypothetical contract', see above, [2.14].
157 IA 1986, s 262(8). For the challenge procedure see Chapter 9 below.
158 IA 1986, s 263(2); on the role of supervisor, see Chapter 11 below.
159 On the nominee's fees and expenses, see below [11.13].
160 IR 2016, r 8.24(1) and (2)(a); see also IA 1986, s 259(1).
161 IR 2016, r 8.24(2)(b) and (d).
162 IR 2016, r 8.24(2)(c). Curiously, unlike IR 2016, rr 8.3(q) and 8.19(1A), this provision was not amended as a result of Brexit (see above [1.24]), presumably by oversight.

court will endorse the report with the date of filing.[163] The rules do not mention the function of the report where the debtor has chosen to use the alternative procedure. In practice, in such cases, the nominee provides each creditor with a copy of the report by way of complying with the notice requirement.[164]

8.50   In every case, the nominee is required to give notice of the outcome of the vote to everyone who was invited to consider the proposal and to whom notice of the decision procedure was given, as well as any other creditor.[165] Where there is an interim order, they must do so as soon as reasonably practicable after filing the report with the court; otherwise, they must do so within four business days of the decision date.[166] If the debtor is an undischarged bankrupt, the nominee must also notify the outcome of the decision, by the same deadline, to the OR and any trustee.[167] The nominee's final task, where the outcome is favourable, is to report this to the Secretary of State for the purposes of registration.[168]

---

163   IA 1986, s 259(1)(b); IR 2016, r 8.24(3)–(4).
164   See below [8.50].
165   IA 1986, s 259(1)(a); IR 2016, r 8.24(5)(a)–(b).
166   IR 2016, r 8.24(6).
167   IR 2016, r 8.24(5)(c) and (6).
168   IR 2016, r 8.26. By this point, in most cases, the nominee will have become the supervisor: see below [11.04].

9

CHALLENGE

A. INTRODUCTION

Where a debtor has put forward a proposal for an individual voluntary arrange- **9.01** ment (IVA) that is referred to the creditors for approval, there are a number of ways in which the procedure can be challenged or subjected to scrutiny. The most common of these is a challenge brought by way of an application under section 262 of the Insolvency Act 1986 (IA 1986), upon which there is a significant body of case law that is considered in detail below. There are a number of other ways in which the procedure and the debtor's conduct can be subjected to scrutiny, including under the provisions of Part 15 of the Insolvency (England and Wales) Rules 2016 (IR 2016),[1] and these will be considered more briefly at the end of this chapter.

---

1   SI 2016/1024.

B. CHALLENGING THE CREDITOR DECISION

1. Who may challenge?

9.02 Following the conclusion of the decision procedure convened to consider the debtor's proposal under section 257 of IA 1986, the result of that decision procedure may be challenged by way of an application to the court.[2] Such an application may be brought by the debtor, any creditor entitled to vote in the decision procedure (or who would have been so entitled if they had had notice of it), or the nominee (or any replacement nominee).[3] Where the debtor is an undischarged bankrupt, it may also be brought by the trustee in bankruptcy or the Official Receiver (OR).[4] In addition, in an appropriate case concerning the IVA of a person regulated by the Financial Conduct Authority or the Prudential Regulation Authority, the appropriate regulator is also entitled to apply under this provision or to be represented at the hearing of an application by any other person.[5]

9.03 For these purposes, an applicant who was entitled to vote does not have to prove to the court that they are indeed a creditor: it is sufficient that they received notice of the decision procedure and were allowed to vote.[6] Nevertheless, the court will need to be satisfied that the applicant has sufficient interest in the relief being sought before granting any such relief.[7] The interest does not have to be financial, but it does have to be real.[8] It should, however, be borne in mind that where the applicant does have the necessary standing to bring the application (for example, by reason of being a creditor), the fact that they may have no legitimate interest in the outcome of the challenge or the relief that might be granted does not go to jurisdiction, but rather to the court's discretion as to whether to grant the relief: in the words of Lord Millett in *Deloitte & Touche AG v Johnson*,[9] '[t]his is not a matter of jurisdiction. It is a matter of judicial restraint.' Although said in a slightly different context, this has been applied in the corporate equivalent of section 262 of IA 1986.[10] Equally, where the challenger's interests (even if legitimate) are contrary to the those of the

---

2 IA 1986, s 262(1).

3 IA 1986, s 262(2)(a)–(c).

4 IA 1986, s 262(2)(d).

5 Financial Services and Markets Act 2000, s 357(5), (6).

6 *Sea Voyager Maritime Inc v Bielecki* [1999] 1 BCLC 133.

7 *Nero Holdings Ltd v Young* [2021] EWHC 1453 (Ch), at [73], a CVA case under IA 1986, s 6.

8 *Brake v Lowes; Brake v Swift* [2020] EWCA Civ 1491, [2021] BPIR 1, at [79]; see also *Bentinck v Fenn* (1887) LR 12 App Cas 652, at 669. Both were applied in *Nero Holdings Ltd v Young* (above).

9 [1999] 1 WLR 1605 (PC), at 1611.

10 *Nero Holdings Ltd v Young* [2021] EWHC 1453 (Ch), at [53]–[54] and in particular at [73].

creditors as a whole, this may warrant rejecting the application and where the challenger's motives for bringing the application are collateral to the statutory purpose of section 262, the application may amount to an abuse of process.[11] Conversely, where a would-be challenger is not in fact a creditor, for the purposes of an IVA, and was not entitled to vote, they will not be permitted to challenge the IVA, even if the terms of the IVA were apparently detrimental to them.[12]

2. Grounds

(a) The two grounds

Section 262 of IA 1986 provides two distinct grounds on which a challenge **9.04** may be brought: (a) the IVA unfairly prejudices the interests of a creditor;[13] (b) there was some material irregularity in the creditors' decision procedure by which the creditors decided whether or not to approve the debtor's proposal.[14] The application may invoke either ground or both grounds simultaneously.[15] Unfair prejudice cannot be relied upon unless the decision procedure resulted in approval;[16] where the proposal was rejected, therefore, the only available ground is material irregularity. It is mostly in the context of applications under this provision (and its corporate equivalent) that the courts' approach to the core principles, discussed above, has been developed.[17]

(b) Unfair prejudice

The first ground covers any situation where the terms of the IVA, as approved **9.05** (whether in the proposal or some modification to it), operate to the detriment of a particular party or parties, such that their interests have been unfairly prejudiced. In essence, this includes any party whose rights against the debtor might have been prejudiced in a way that singles them out unfairly. Such prejudice can arise in many different contexts, but among the parties more likely to find themselves prejudiced in this way are secured creditors whose interests have been unfairly prejudiced without proper consent and the debtor's spouse (especially, but not exclusively, in the context of divorce).[18] Other creditors

---

11   *Nero Holdings Ltd v Young* (above), at [73] and [98]–[104]; see also *Discovery (Northampton) Ltd v Debenhams Retail Ltd* [2019] EWHC 2441 (Ch), [2020] BCC 9, at [132]–[139].
12   *Child Maintenance and Enforcement Commission v Beesley and Whyman* [2010] EWCA Civ 1344, [2011] BPIR 608, overturning the decision at first instance, which had allowed the challenge.
13   IA 1986, s 262(1)(a).
14   IA 1986, s 262(1)(b).
15   IA 1986, s 262(1).
16   IA 1986, s 262(1)(a).
17   See above [2.01]–[2.11].
18   See above at [2.32]–[2.36].

who often perceive themselves as being treated unfairly are landlords whose interests have been adversely affected in a way they consider to be disproportionate. Such landlord challenges are not common in the context of IVAs, but they do occur.[19] In *Doorbar v Alltime Securities Ltd*,[20] it was pointed out that the prejudice must be to the rights of the landlord as creditor and not merely to their rights as landlord. For obvious reasons, however, challenges by landlords are encountered far more frequently in the context of CVAs; given that the same principles apply in both contexts, these CVA-landlord challenges are none the less instructive.[21]

9.06 As to what amounts to unfair prejudice, two fundamental points must be understood. First, the prejudice must stem from the terms of the proposal itself (with or without modifications), and not from misleading information deployed at the meeting, for example as to the status of certain creditors.[22] Secondly, the prejudice has to be tangible and not theoretical or speculative.[23] In *Re Timothy*,[24] it was accepted that it was at least arguable that failing to include a provision within the debtor's IVA for the debt he owed to the Child Support Agency in respect of maintenance for his daughter to survive the IVA (for the daughter's benefit) could amount to unfair prejudice; however, the court rejected the challenge on the basis that it had been brought too late.

9.07 For the purposes of determining such challenges, the courts have regularly applied two tests, usually referred to as 'vertical' and 'horizontal' comparators.[25] The former compares the actual position of the creditors under the voluntary arrangement with what their position would most likely have been if the approval had not happened. Although in most cases this hypothetical comparator would be their position if the debtor were to have been made (or to have remained) bankrupt, in some circumstances it might instead be their position under an alternative IVA on different terms. In all cases, however, the

---

19   For example, *Re Naeem (A Bankrupt) (No. 18 of 1988)* [1990] 1 WLR 48 (where the challenge was upheld at first instance, but overturned on appeal).

20   [1996] 1 WLR 456.

21   For landlord challenges under s 6 of IA 1986, see in particular: *Discovery (Northampton) Ltd v Debenhams Retail Ltd* [2019] EWHC 2441 (Ch), [2020] BCC 9; *Lazari Properties 2 Ltd v New Look Retail Ltd* [2021] EWHC 1209 (Ch), [2021] BPIR 920; *Carraway Guildford (Nominee A) Ltd v Regis UK Ltd* [2021] EWHC 1294 (Ch), [2021] BPIR 1006; *Nero Holdings Ltd v Young* [2021] EWHC 1453 (Ch); cf. also *March Estates plc v Gunmark Ltd* [1996] BPIR 439 (not strictly a s 6 case, but also relevant).

22   *Re A Debtor (No. 259 of 1990)* [1992] 1 WLR 226.

23   *National Westminster Bank plc v Scher* [1998] BPIR 224.

24   [2005] EWHC 1885 (Ch), [2006] BPIR 329; on the question of time limits, see below [9.15]–[9.16].

25   For a detailed and helpful explanation of how the comparators work in the context of CVAs (for these purposes, identical to IVAs) and the relevant case law, see *Lazari Properties 2 Ltd v New Look Retail Ltd* [2021] EWHC 1209 (Ch), [2021] BPIR 920, at [106]–[199], especially [107]–[115].

comparator used must be a realistic option. Satisfying the vertical comparator test is not, however, sufficient to preclude a finding of unfair prejudice: the court must go on to consider the horizontal comparator – that is, the position of the creditors as between themselves. In *Re A Debtor (No. 101 of 1999)*,[26] an arrangement was approved by a majority consisting largely of friends who had agreed to postpone their debts until after the IVA, leaving the Crown departments to prove for approximately 19 pence in the pound; this was found to be unfairly prejudicial, even though this figure was better than they would achieve on bankruptcy, as the comparison with the friendly creditors under the IVA outweighed the comparison between the two potential outcomes.

Differential treatment of creditors within the IVA is the touchstone by which **9.08** the unfairness of any prejudice is assessed, but it is not enough in itself to indicate that there has been unfair prejudice: rather, the presence of such differentiation will give rise to an inquiry as to the reasons why it has arisen and the effect that the different treatment will have.[27] There are circumstances where differential treatment of creditors can be justified on the facts.[28] Indeed, there are even cases where differential treatment is necessary in order to avoid unfair prejudice.[29] It is therefore necessary for the court to probe beneath the mere existence of differential treatment and conduct a deeper investigation into whether and to what extent such differences might be unfair. It is only after weighing up all the relevant facts that a court can come to a proper conclusion as to whether there was unfair prejudice.

(c) Material irregularity

The second ground, material irregularity in connection with the decision pro- **9.09** cedure, covers a multitude of sins, from the provision of notice of the decision procedure, through the control of the procedure itself, including voting rights and the use or misuse of proxies, to the report to the court (and notice to creditors) at its conclusion. It is, however, confined solely to the decision procedure convened by the nominee under section 257 of IA 1986 for the purposes of enabling the creditors to consider the proposal: any complaint about some subsequent decision procedure, convened by the supervisor (for example, in

---

26 [2000] BPIR 998.

27 *Re A Debtor (No. 101 of 1999)* (above), at 1006; see above [2.09].

28 See, for example, *IRC v Wimbledon Football Club Ltd* [2004] EWHC 1020; *Discovery (Northampton) Ltd v Debenhams Retail Ltd* [2019] EWHC 2441 (Ch), [2020] BCC 9; *Lazari Properties 2 Ltd v New Look Retail Ltd* [2021] EWHC 1209 (Ch), [2021] BPIR 920; but cf. *Carraway Guildford (Nominee A) Ltd v Regis UK Ltd* [2021] EWHC 1294 (Ch), [2021] BPIR 1006 (where the differentiation was not justified).

29 See *Sea Voyager Maritime Inc v Bielecki* [1999] 1 BCLC 133, on which see above [2.11].

relation to a proposed variation to the IVA), lies outside the ambit of section 262 altogether.[30]

9.10 The ambit of this second ground is less clear-cut. In particular, there have been conflicting views expressed in the authorities as to whether there are 'irregularities' that are so fundamental as to vitiate the approval of an IVA entirely without the necessity to invoke the procedure under section 262, with its strict time limits. Some clarification has been afforded by the comments of Briggs LJ in *Narandas-Girdhar v Bradstock*.[31] Although these comments are persuasive and were supported by the other two members of the court (in the sense that they agreed with the judgment of Briggs LJ) and although it was clearly intended to provide, and did provide, some much-needed general guidance on these issues, strictly speaking these comments were *obiter*.[32]

9.11 According to this analysis, the starting point is to recognise that there are in reality two separate considerations in play here. The first concerns instances where there was no proposal (properly speaking) put to the creditors for their consideration. Into this category fall those cases where the court's sanction (in the form of an interim order and/or an order for the meeting of creditors to be convened) was not obtained, in the days when such sanction was *de rigueur*;[33] likewise, those where the purported proposal was not in fact a proposal within the meaning of Part 8 of IA 1986 at all.[34] In such cases the fundamental defect arises prior to the commencement of the decision procedure under section 257 and renders the entire process a nullity and the resulting IVA void. This is therefore considered to be wholly outside the ambit of section 262 altogether. By contrast, where the irregularity arises, not from the outset, but during and in relation to the decision procedure itself, then such an irregularity, however 'material' or fundamental, will not of itself invalidate the entire process and the IVA will be valid unless and until successfully challenged under section 262 of IA 1986. This analysis places considerable weight on section 262(8) of IA 1986, which provides that, except pursuant to the challenge mechanism under section 262, no irregularity in relation to a creditors' decision procedure con-

---

30   *Linfoot v Adamson* [2012] BPIR 1033, at [53].
31   [2016] EWCA Civ 88, [2016] 1 WLR 2366, [2016] BPIR 428, at [33]–[53]. On the relevant time limits, see below [9.15].
32   For this reason, the headnote of the report in [2016] 1 WLR 2366, describing *Re Plummer* [2004] BPIR 767 as being 'disapproved of', is technically more accurate than that in [2016] BPIR 428, stating that *Re Plummer* was 'overruled': see below [9.11].
33   Thus, *Fletcher v Vooght* [2000] BPIR 435; *Vlieland-Boddy v Dexter Ltd* [2003] EWHC 2592 (Ch).
34   See *IRC v Bland* [2003] EWHC 1068 (Ch), [2003] BPIR 1274.

ducted under section 257 of IA 1986 will invalidate the approval of an IVA.[35] In *Somji v Cadbury Schweppes plc*,[36] the Court of Appeal held that a declaration granted at first instance that the IVA was void (at common law), by reason of the materially misleading picture the debtor had presented to the creditors during the meeting, had been granted in error (although the appeal was dismissed for other reasons). This decision, which predates *Narandas-Girdhar v Bradstock*,[37] is thus aligned with the analysis of Briggs LJ in the latter case.

This way of approaching section 262 of IA 1986 has some startling repercussions and is not without its critics. It apparently applies to any defects, however grave, in the nominee's report of the result of the decision procedure, even if the nominee's report stated that the IVA had been approved on the basis that the required majority of 75 per cent of creditors had voted in favour of approving the proposal, when in fact it subsequently transpires this was wrong.[38] More controversially, it equally applies where the debtor had not been given the opportunity during the decision procedure to object to modifications. In *Re Plummer*,[39] the court had held that such lack of approval by the debtor was fatal to the IVA, which was therefore void, placing reliance on section 258(2) of IA 1986, which prohibits the creditors from approving any modification that had not been consented to by the debtor. The Court of Appeal in *Narandas-Girdhar v Bradstock*,[40] on the facts of that case, found that the debtor had approved the modifications; however, Briggs LJ went on to say that *Re Plummer* had been wrongly decided.[41] This obviously presents something of a problem.[42] The analysis does not dovetail entirely satisfactorily with those cases that have held that material irregularity can arise out of the proposal itself or even the statement of affairs, which are not part of the decision procedure.[43] Nor is it clear how it is to be reconciled with cases where a decision procedure

9.12

---

35   It must be noted, however, that this does not take into account similar challenges under either IR 2016, r 15.35 (below at [9.27]) or default petitions (below at [12.29]), neither of which mechanisms contain an equivalent provision.

36   [2001] 1 WLR 615, [2001] BPIR 172 (CA), at [33]–[34].

37   Above.

38   See *Smith-Evans v Smailes* [2013] EWHC 3199 (Ch), [2014] 1 WLR 1548, approved by the Court of Appeal in *Narandas-Girdhar v Bradstock* (above).

39   [2004] BPIR 767; see also *Reid v Hamblin* [2001] BPIR 929, decided (somewhat oddly) in the context of an application pursuant to s 263(3), which appears to have overlooked by Briggs LJ in *Narandas-Girdhar v Bradstock* (above).

40   [2016] EWCA Civ 88, [2016] 1 WLR 2366, [2016] BPIR 428.

41   [2016] EWCA Civ 88, [2016] 1 WLR 2366, at [53].

42   See s 258(2) of IA 1986 (above [8.38]) and the extra-judicial commentary by S Barber in 'Involuntary Arrangements' [2014] 27 Insolv. Int. 133.

43   For example, *Re A Debtor (No. 87 of 1993) (No. 2)* [1996] BPIR 64; *IRC v Duce* [1999] BPIR 189; *Fender v IRC* [2003] BPIR 1304.

was no longer in existence at the time of the supposed approval.[44] On a strict application of the reasoning, it means that where the proposal is structured so as to take it outside Part 8 of IA 1986 altogether, any approval would be void; whereas, where elements having this effect (or other prohibited terms) are introduced by way of modifications, it remains valid unless challenged.[45] Notwithstanding these difficulties, the consensus appears to be that this exegesis has put this issue to bed, as the Court of Appeal clearly intended that it should. It is therefore reasonable to suppose that this guidance will be followed in the future (until or unless revisited by the Court of Appeal or the Supreme Court).

9.13 What constitutes 'material' for these purposes, in relation to the irregularity, has been explored in a number of cases. In essence, where the challenge is in relation to the conduct of the decision procedure itself, in particular to the admission (or otherwise) of debts for voting purposes, the irregularity will be 'material' if, had the correct procedure been followed, this would have, or at least would likely have, made a difference to the outcome.[46] In the context of a challenge based on misleading information (or the withholding of significant information), 'material' signifies that the irregularity would be likely to have made a significant difference to the way the creditors would have considered or assessed the terms of the proposal.[47] That is not the same as asking whether a new vote would end up with the same result.[48] The term is to be construed widely and was capable of including breaches of the good faith principle that is a vital element of the IVA procedure.[49] Material irregularity can also cover behind the scenes deals between the debtor and one or more creditors, the provision of misleading or false information or a material non-disclosure by the debtor.[50]

---

44 *Re Forstater* [2015] BPIR 21 (although this decision rested in part on a provision that has since been repealed: see above [8.34]).

45 See above [8.37]–[8.38], in relation to IA 1986, s 258(3)–(4).

46 *Doorbar v Alltime Securities Ltd* [1996] 1 WLR 456.

47 *Somji v Cadbury Schweppes plc* [2001] 1 WLR 615, [2001] BPIR 172, at [25]; although this test was set out in the context of IA 1986, s 276(1)(b) (see below [12.19]), it has since been applied in this context: see *Fender v IRC* [2003] BPIR 1304, at [11]; *Monecor (London) Ltd v Ahmed* [2008] BPIR 458, at [17]; *National Westminster Bank plc v Kapoor* [2011] EWHC 255 (Ch), [2011] BPIR 836 (on this issue, upheld on appeal).

48 *Monecor (London) Ltd v Ahmed* [2008] BPIR 458, at [17].

49 *Somji v Cadbury Schweppes plc* (above), at [24]; *Fender v IRC* (above). On good faith, see above at [2.02]–[2.07].

50 *Somji v Cadbury Schweppes plc* (above); *Kapoor v National Westminster Bank plc* [2011] EWCA Civ 1083, [2011] BPIR 1680; *Golstein v Bishop* [2016] EWHC 2187 (Ch) & [2016] EWHC 2804 (Ch), reported together at [2017] BPIR 51; *Gertner v CFL Finance Ltd* [2018] EWCA Civ 1781, [2018], BPIR 1605.

Many such cases involve scrutiny of the decisions taken by the nominee in the **9.14**
course of the decision procedure. This can include the failure of the nominee
to give proper notice of the procedure to a creditor,[51] as well as the conduct of
the procedure itself, for example in determining the voting rights of creditors,[52]
or in relation to the use of proxies,[53] or to the proper conduct of procedure
for tabling modifications.[54] Breaches of good faith on the part of the debtor
have also been held to be capable of amounting to material irregularities.[55]
In some cases, the alleged irregularity can be extreme, including allegations
of vote-rigging and collusion.[56] In *Smurthwaite v Simpson-Smith & Mond
(No.2)*,[57] the court found that, in circumstances where the debtor's partner
asserted a claim to have a beneficial interest in a property that the debtor
included in the IVA, it would clearly amount to a material irregularity for
the chair to allow the partner to vote on the basis of a debt based on the same
factual matrix unless the nominee had already formed the view that the claim
to that beneficial interest was unsustainable. Where the decision procedure has
been so wrongly conducted as to make it clear that the IVA could not properly
remain in force, the correct course is for the office-holder to apply to court for
the approval to be revoked; in the right circumstances, even though no such
application has been made, the court can intervene to order revocation, upon
the office-holder's undertaking to issue the necessary application.[58] However,
the irregularity does not have to be so extreme, so long as it is material in the
operative sense.[59] Thus, where a problem with a proxy could easily have been
sorted by suspending a meeting for up to an hour, not to have done so could
amount to a material irregularity.[60]

---

51 For example, *Namulas Pension Trustees Ltd v Mouzakis* [2011] BPIR 1724.
52 For example, *Re A Debtor (No. 222 of 1990), ex p. Bank of Ireland* [1992] BCLC 137; *Fender v IRC* [2003] BPIR 1304; *Roberts v Pinnacle Entertainment Ltd* [2003] EWHC 2394 (Ch), [2004] BPIR 208; *Coutts & Co v Passey* [2007] BPIR 323 (on which, see above [2.27]); *Commissioners of HMRC v Early* [2011] EWHC 1783 (Ch), [2011] BPIR 1590; *National Westminster Bank v Yadgaroff* [2011] EWHC 3711 (Ch), [2012] BPIR 371.
53 For example, *Rowbury v OR* [2015] EWHC 2276 (Ch), [2016] BPIR 477.
54 *RBS plc v Munikwa* [2020] EWHC 786 (Ch).
55 Thus, in *Kapoor v National Westminster Bank plc* [2011] EWCA Civ 1083, [2011] BPIR 1680 and *Gertner v CFL Finance Ltd* [2018] EWCA Civ 1781, [2018], BPIR 1605 (on both of which see above [2.06]–[2.07]).
56 See, for example, *Tradition (UK) Ltd v Ahmed* [2008] EWHC 2946 (Ch) and [2008] EWHC 3448 (Ch), reported together at [2009] BPIR 626.
57 [2006] BPIR 1483; cf. (on appeal) [2006] EWCA Civ 1183, [2006] BPIR 1504.
58 *Re N (A Debtor)* [2002] BPIR 1024, admittedly an extreme case.
59 For example: *Re Cardona* [1997] BPIR 604; *Roberts v Pinnacle Entertainment Ltd* [2004] BPIR 208; *Commissioners of HMRC v Early* [2011] EWHC 1783 (Ch), [2011] BPIR 1590; *National Westminster Bank v Yadgaroff* [2011] EWHC 3711 (Ch), [2012] BPIR 371.
60 *Rowbury v OR* [2015] EWHC 2276 (Ch), [2016] BPIR 477.

3. Procedure and relief

(a) Timing

9.15 In order to provide finality and certainty to the procedure, for the benefit of both the debtor and the creditors, a challenge pursuant to section 262 of IA 1986 must be brought within certain time limits. The primary limitation is 28 days from the date of the creditors' decision or, where there was an interim order, from the date on which the nominee's report of the decision was filed at court.[61] In the interests of justice this is extended, in the case of a creditor who was not given notice of the decision procedure, to 28 days from the date on which the creditor in question became aware of the decision. Subject to that proviso, such a creditor may even bring a challenge after the IVA has come to an end, as long as (a) the IVA has run its full course and did not end prematurely and (b) the challenge is on the grounds of unfair prejudice and not merely procedural irregularity.[62]

9.16 The time periods under section 262(3) of IA 1986 are strict, but in an appropriate case may be extended pursuant to section 376 of IA 1986. Nevertheless, finality and certainty remain paramount considerations and the reasons for the delay must be cogent and the delay as minimal as possible.[63] The conduct of the parties may also be a factor to be taken into account in deciding whether to extend time,[64] as may the merits of the challenge itself.[65] It is not clear whether the court would now apply an even stricter test, by analogy with *Denton v TH White Ltd*,[66] as has been done in the context of IR 2016, rule 15.35(4).[67]

(b) Procedure

9.17 The application must be made using a standard Insolvency Act application, supported by evidence.[68] Where there is an interim order in place, the application must be made to the court seized of the interim order; otherwise to the appropriate court in accordance with the rules.[69]

---

61 IA 1986, s 262(3)(a).
62 IA 1986, s 262(3)(b).
63 *Tager v Westpac Banking Corp* [1998] BCC 73; but cf. *Tanner v Everitt* [2004] EWHC 1130 (Ch), [2004] BPIR 1026; *Re Timothy* [2005] EWHC 1885 (Ch), [2006] BPIR 329 (both refusing the extension).
64 *Warley Continental Services Ltd v Johal* [2004] BPIR 353.
65 *Re Timothy* (above).
66 [2014] EWCA Civ 906, [2014] 1 WLR 3926.
67 See below [9.29].
68 IR 2016, r 1.35.
69 IR 2016, r 8.20.

The court must determine the issues on the evidence before it. Where the **9.18** court is concerned with material irregularity in relation to the value accorded by the nominee to debts for voting purposes, the court is not merely concerned to review the nominee's decision but should also assess the proper value to be accorded in light of all the evidence.[70] Where the dispute concerns a creditor who was allowed to vote, but the debt was marked 'objected to', the court must decide whether the objection should be sustained.[71] The general rules of civil evidence apply, as modified by IR 2016, including as to the admissibility of hearsay evidence.[72] Such applications are not, however, full-blown actions and the general rules governing disclosure are of limited application.[73] A creditor may seek to obtain further information from the nominee/supervisor in relation to bringing a challenge pursuant to section 262 of IA 1986, but there is a limit to how far they can press this. In one case, after the court had dismissed an application for specific disclosure against the nominee, brought by a disgruntled creditor, the latter sought unsuccessfully to have the court review that decision pursuant to section 375(1) of IA 1986.[74] Where a challenge to the approval of an IVA is erroneously mounted other than pursuant to section 262, it may be possible for it to be amended so as to bring it within the section.[75]

In principle, an application under section 262 is susceptible, in an appropriate **9.19** case, to being struck out or summarily determined.[76] Where the strike-out application goes to jurisdiction (typically where it is alleged that the applicant is not within the ambit of section 262(2) of IA 1986), the court would determine this at the interlocutory stage. Where it is alleged that the substantive application is an abuse of process, on the basis that the challenger is motivated by a collateral purpose, this could properly ground a strike-out application;[77] but, save in the most clear-cut of examples, the court will be reluctant to deter-

---

70 *Golstein v Bishop* [2016] EWHC 2187 (Ch) & [2016] EWHC 2804 (Ch), reported together at [2017] BPIR 51 (applying *Re Mercury Tax Group Ltd (In Administration)* [2010] EWCA Civ 1379, [2011] BPIR 480).

71 *National Westminster Bank Plc v Sher* [1998] BPIR 224.

72 The Civil Evidence Act 1995 and the Civil Procedure Rules 1998 (CPR) supersede the decision in *Re A Debtor (No. 87 of 1993) (No. 1)* [1996] BPIR 56, which held hearsay evidence inadmissible on such applications.

73 Under the CPR.

74 *Smurthwaite v Simpson-Smith & Mond* [2005] EWHC 447 (Ch), [2006] BPIR 1469; see also on appeal, [2006] EWCA Civ 1183, [2006] BPIR 1504.

75 *Zelouf v Khanna and Herron* [2016] EWHC 205, [2016] BPIR 1288, a very curious case where a dispute arose as to the terms of the order.

76 See, for example, *Monecor (London) Ltd v Ahmed* [2008] BPIR 458 (although in this case the summary relief was refused).

77 See *Nero Holdings Ltd v Young* [2021] EWHC 1453 (Ch), at [100]–[101], citing *Aabar Block SARL v Maud* [2016] EWHC 2175, at [83]–[90].

mine such issues at the interlocutory stage.[78] Where the issue is whether the applicant lacks a legitimate interest in the relief sought, this is quintessentially a matter of discretion for the trial judge, and the court would be most unlikely to determine it on the basis of strike out or summary judgment.[79]

9.20 There is another way in which an application under section 262 might come to a premature end. Once the 28-day deadline for making such an application has elapsed, the debtor will be aware of whether any such applications have been made and, if so, by whom. At that stage, there is nothing to prevent the debtor, or some other party that has an interest in retaining the IVA, from buying off any challenger (if necessary, by paying their debt in full) in return for an agreement to drop the application.[80]

(c) Relief

9.21 Where the court is satisfied that the challenger has succeeded on either of the grounds referred to above, it may apply a range of remedies: it can revoke or suspend any approval attained as a result of the decision procedure;[81] or it can direct any person (usually the nominee) to seek a new decision from the creditors by means of a decision procedure for the approval of any revised proposal the debtor may care to make or (where the ground was material irregularity) of the debtor's original proposal.[82] The court has a wide discretion, ranging from taking no action to making a combination of the possible orders.[83] This flexibility allows the court, in an appropriate case, to recognise that material irregularities have occurred without necessarily having to revoke the IVA. Such an application can still be pursued and the arrangement can potentially still be revoked even after the termination of the IVA.[84]

9.22 In *Monecor (London) Ltd v Ahmed*,[85] the Court of Appeal provided some clarification on the relationship between revocation and suspension and the effect of directing a renewal of the decision procedure. Where the court directs the renewal of the decision procedure, such procedure takes effect as if under section 257 of IA 1986, for all purposes, including the effect of section

---

78 *Nero Holdings Ltd v Young* (above), at [103]–[105].

79 Ibid., at [73], [96]–[97], [110]. On 'legitimate interest', see above [9.03].

80 See *Nero Holdings Ltd v Young* [2021] EWHC 1453 (Ch), at [32]; this is precisely what had happened in this case, although one of the challengers had refused to take up the offer.

81 IA 1986, s 262(4)(a).

82 IA 1986, s 262(4)(b)(i)–(ii).

83 [2008] BPIR 458; noted in *Narandas-Girdhar v Bradstock* [2016] EWCA Civ 88, [2016] 1 WLR 2366. See also *IRC v Duce* [1999] BPIR 189.

84 *Carraway Guildford (Nominee A) Ltd v Regis UK Ltd* [2021] EWHC 1294 (Ch), [2021] BPIR 1006.

85 [2008] BPIR 458.

260(2).[86] Any creditor entitled to vote in the original procedure can do so in the renewed procedure; this remains the case whether the approval is revoked or suspended; a suspension does not mean that the only creditors who could be bound by the later decision are those that were bound by the original decision.

Where the court directs a renewed decision procedure to take place, it may also **9.23** extend, or (if necessary) renew, any interim order there may have been for such period as it thinks appropriate, so as to allow time for the renewed decision procedure and the 28-day grace period that would follow the new report.[87] If, after directing that a new decision procedure be convened to consider a revised proposal or reconsider the debtor's original proposal, the court becomes satisfied that the debtor does not intend to submit (or resubmit) such a proposal, the court will then revoke or suspend any approval previously given.[88]

In addition, when granting any relief under section 262(4) or (5) of IA 1986, **9.24** the court has a wide discretion to provide any such other directions as it may consider necessary or helpful, including in particular with respect to anything done under the IVA since the time of the decision to approve and also anything done in relation to the debtor that could not have been done if an interim order had been in place at that time.[89] This can include (in the case of revocation) an order that the nominee return all their fees (qua nominee and qua supervisor).[90] The breadth of this discretion is intended to enable the court to ensure that any order made under section 262 does not prejudice any party more than is strictly necessary to do justice for all concerned.

If the court makes an order revoking or suspending the approval of an IVA, **9.25** the applicant must deliver a sealed copy of that order to the supervisor of the IVA and, unless the applicant is the debtor, also to the debtor.[91] If the debtor is an undischarged bankrupt, the applicant must also deliver a sealed copy of the order to the OR and any trustee (unless that person is the applicant).[92] Within five business days of the date of the order, the applicant must also deliver notice of the order to the Secretary of State; if the order includes suspension, the applicant must also deliver notice of the expiry of the suspension to the Secretary of State within five business days of the expiry of the suspen-

---

86   *Davis v Price* [2014] EWCA Civ 26, [2014] 1 WLR 2129.
87   IA 1986, s 262(6).
88   IA 1986, s 262(5).
89   IA 1986, s 262(7). See *IRC v Duce* [1999] BPIR 189, at 204.
90   *Carraway Guildford (Nominee A) Ltd v Regis UK Ltd* [2021] EWHC 1294 (Ch), [2021] BPIR 1006.
91   IR 2016, r 8.27(1) and (2)(a)–(b).
92   IR 2016, r 8.27(2)(c).

sion.[93] As soon as reasonably practicable, the debtor (or, where the debtor is an undischarged bankrupt, the trustee) must deliver notice that the order has been made to any person to whom notice had been delivered to consider the proposal by a decision procedure, or who appears to be affected by the order.[94] Where the court directs the matter to be considered further by a decision procedure, the applicant must deliver notice that such an order has been made to the person directed in the order to seek such a decision;[95] in addition, the debtor (or, where the debtor is an undischarged bankrupt, the trustee) must, within five business days of delivery of a copy of the order (or such longer time as the court may allow), deliver a notice to the court advising that it is intended to make a revised proposal to the creditors or to invite re-consideration of the original proposal (if applicable).[96]

(d) Costs

9.26 The court has a wide discretion in relation to the costs of challenges brought under section 262 of IA 1986. Where the challenge fails, the applicant will inevitably have to pick up the costs. In certain circumstances the costs of a successful challenge may be ordered against the debtor or to be paid out of the funds in the IVA. As a general rule, however, the court will not order the costs of a successful challenge to be paid by the office-holder personally.[97] This remains the case even where it is the nominee's conduct (as convener or chair) that gave rise to the challenge. The court will only depart from this position in the most exceptional cases, where the conduct complained of has fallen sufficiently far short of what could reasonably be expected of a professional in such circumstances.[98] Where the court takes the view that the nominee ought to have applied to court for the approval to be revoked, the court may direct that the nominee should be personally responsible for the costs of that application, once issued.[99] The court's discretion to order the office-holder to pay the costs of the application is flexible and is not necessarily an all or nothing decision: in an appropriate case, the court may order the nominee to be responsible for some of the costs (either by proportion or by reference to a particular issue).[100]

---

93   IR 2016, r 8.27(5) and (6).

94   IR 2016, r 8.27(4)(a).

95   IR 2016, r 8.27(3).

96   IR 2016, r 8.27(4)(b).

97   See *Re Naeem (A Bankrupt) (No. 18 of 1988)* [1990] 1 WLR 48, at 51. Cf. below at [9.32].

98   *Re A Debtor (No. 222 of 1990) ex p. Bank of Ireland (No 2)* [1993] BCLC 233; *Harmony Carpets v Chaffin-Laird* [2000] BPIR 61; *Smurthwaite v Simpson-Smith & Mond (No.2)* [2006] EWCA Civ 1183, [2006] BPIR 1504 (and see at first instance at [2006] BPIR 1483). Cf. *Tradition (UK) Ltd v Ahmed* [2009] BPIR 626, where the conduct, though below standard, was held not to be so lamentable as to warrant such an order.

99   *Re N (A Debtor)* [2002] BPIR 1024.

100   For example: *Fender v IRC* [2003] BPIR 1304 (65%); *AB Agri Ltd v Curtis* [2016] BPIR 1297 (50%).

C. OTHER AVENUES OF REDRESS

1. Appeals concerning decision procedures

(a) The jurisdiction

Any decision made under Chapter 8 of Part 15 of IR 2016 by the convenor **9.27** or chair of a decision procedure is subject to an appeal to the court by the debtor or any creditor.[101] Chapter 8 of Part 15 is concerned with creditors' voting rights and the decisions taken by the convener or chair in relation to the admission and calculation of claims for voting purposes and the requisite majorities for any particular kind of vote. This jurisdiction does not therefore cover every kind of decision potentially made by a convener or chair: it does not cover decisions in relation to the choice of decision procedure or their various requirements, nor in relation to notices convening the decision procedure or the conduct of meetings (virtual or physical), including appearances, adjournments or suspension;[102] nor does it cover decisions by the chair in relation to the use of proxies.[103] On the other hand, (in the context of IVAs) it is not confined to decisions made in the context of the decision procedure under section 257 of IA 1986 in relation to a proposed IVA, but extends equally to any relevant decision by the supervisor (under IR 2016, Part 15, Chapter 8) as convener or chair of any subsequent decision procedure (for example, one convened for the purposes of allowing the creditors to consider a proposed variation or to give directions to the supervisor).[104]

The jurisdiction is therefore both narrower and wider than section 262 of IA **9.28** 1986 (discussed above) or than the equivalent provisions of the Insolvency Rules 1986 (IR 1986) in relation to IVAs that it replaced.[105] The former is concerned with any material irregularities (not solely decisions of the convener or chair under Chapter 8 of Part 15 of IR 2016) arising in the context of a decision procedure convened under section 257; it has no application to any decision made in the context of any other form of decision procedure.[106] In addition, to be eligible to challenge under section 262 of IA 1986, a creditor must have been entitled to vote in the decision procedure (or at least would

---

101 IR 2016, r 15.35(1).
102 As such decisions fall within Chapters 2, 3, 6 and 7 of Part 15 of IR 2016.
103 As, with the exception of IR 2016, r 15.28(2), such decisions fall within Part 16 of IR 2016.
104 See below [11.12]. IR 2016, r 15.35 is not confined to IVAs but extends to any kind of insolvency procedure under Parts 1 to 11 of IA 1986. On the separate regime for complaints by someone claiming to be an excluded person, see above [8.45].
105 IR 1986, r 5.22(3), (5)–(7); r 5.23(7).
106 See above [9.09].

have been so entitled had they had notice of it); but for the purposes of this appeal procedure, a 'creditor' is not so confined.[107] The former equivalent provisions under Part 5 of IR 1986 were both narrower (being confined to IVAs) and wider (in that they also dealt with the chair's use of proxies).[108] In the context of decisions by the nominee in the decision procedure convened under section 257, there is likely to be considerable overlap between such an appeal and a challenge under section 262; indeed, in that context, it has been doubted that such appeals (at least as they existed under IR 1986) form an entirely separate avenue of challenge.[109] Given the differences noted above, however, the scope of this observation is perhaps rather limited.

(b) Procedure

9.29 The application must be made by way of an Insolvency Act application.[110] Where there is an interim order, the appeal lies to the court that made that order; otherwise, it must be made in accordance with the rules.[111] Appeals in relation to decision procedures convened after the IVA has been approved must be brought within 21 days of the date of the decision to which the appeal relates.[112] If the decision under appeal was made in the context of a decision procedure relating to a proposed IVA, such an appeal must be made within 28 days of the relevant date: where there is no interim order, the relevant date is the date on which the nominee delivered notice of the result of the decision to the creditors; otherwise, it is the date on which the nominee filed the report on the result with the court.[113] There is power for the courts to extend these time limits, but this has been applied sparingly. In *Edwards v Tailby*,[114] it was held that such extensions should be considered strictly in accordance with the guidance for relief from sanctions provided in *Denton v TH White Ltd*.[115] However, the power to grant an extension in that case was technically under the CPR, under which *Denton* was also decided;[116] it is not entirely clear that the same

---

107 See *Re Cranley Mansions Ltd; Saigol v Goldstein* [1994] 1 WLR 1610 (a CVA case decided under equivalent provisions in IR 1986).

108 They concerned any decisions under IR 1986, rr 5.21(3), 5.22 or 5.23.

109 See *Narandas-Girdhar v Bradstock* [2016] EWCA Civ 88, [2016] 1 WLR 2366, [2016] BPIR 428, at [54]–[56] *per* Briggs LJ, referring to IR 1986, r 5.22: note in particular r 5.22(5).

110 IR 2016, r 1.35.

111 See above [7.17].

112 IR 2016, r 15.53(4).

113 IR 2016, r 15.35(5)(b).

114 [2021] 7 WLUK 558 (ChD, 30/07/21) a case concerning an appeal in the context of decision procedure in an administration, governed by IR 2016, r 15.35(4).

115 [2014] EWCA Civ 906, [2014] 1 WLR 3926.

116 IR 2016, Sch 5 para 3; because the case concerned an administration, s 376 of IA 1986 would not apply.

considerations would necessarily apply in the context of an IVA where the extension is sought pursuant to section 376 of IA 1986.

The nature of such an application is not a true appeal and the court is required **9.30** to form its own view, rather than simply review the decision taken at the time; for the same reason, the evidence that can be put before the court is not limited to the information available to the convener or chair at the time of the decision complained about.[117]

Subject to one proviso, the court has a discretion as to what relief, if any, to **9.31** grant on such an application. Where it accepts that the appeal is well-grounded, it may reverse or vary the nominee's decision or declare any votes invalid, and, where it does so, it may order another decision procedure to be convened or may make such other order as it sees fit.[118] However, it may only make such an order (in the context of an IVA) where it considers that the circumstances that led to the appeal gave rise to unfair prejudice or material irregularity.[119] This proviso, together with the time limits referred to above, helps to underline the parallel between such an application and one under section 262 of IA 1986.[120] It appears, however, that the proviso applies even where the decision to which the appeal relates was made in the context of a later decision procedure convened by the supervisor.

The applicant appeals at their own costs risk, and the office holder will not **9.32** be personally liable for the costs unless the court so orders, which will be the exception rather than the rule even where the appeal succeeds.[121] In the equivalent provision under IR 1986, however, the court had no discretion to order costs against the chair, irrespective of the circumstances.[122]

2. Alternative options

(a) Bankruptcy petition

In addition to the routes outlined above for challenging an IVA, where the **9.33** debtor has provided misleading or false information to the creditors, or has withheld material information from them, any creditors bound by the IVA

---

117 It is therefore analogous to the appeals against office holders' decisions on proof (IR 2016, r 14.8). See *Revenue and Customs Commissioners v Maxwell* [2010] EWCA Civ 1379, [2012] BCC 30, a case concerning an administration under a similar provision in IR 1986.
118 IR 2016, r 15.35(3).
119 Ibid. Derived from IR 1986, r 5.22(5).
120 There is, however, no equivalent provision to IA 1986, s 262(8) here, nor does s 262(8) refer to this provision.
121 IR 2016, r 15.35(6), again echoing IR 2016, r 14.9.
122 IR 1986, r 5.22(7).

aggrieved by such conduct have another string to their bow. Such conduct on the part of the debtor also provides possible grounds on which to present a bankruptcy petition.[123] There is nothing to prevent a creditor bound by the IVA from presenting a petition on this basis even after the time limits under section 262 of IA 1986 and rule 15.35 of IR 2016 have passed.

(b) Criminal sanctions

9.34 In addition, a debtor who makes any false representation or fraudulently does or omits to do anything for the purposes of inducing the creditors to approve their proposal for an IVA commits an offence punishable by imprisonment and/or a fine.[124] This remains the case even if the proposal is rejected by the creditors. If, at any stage of the procedure, the nominee or the supervisor becomes aware of any such potentially criminal behaviour, they are obliged to report this to the Secretary of State.[125]

9.35 Prosecutions relating to these provisions are exceedingly rare. In principle, however, there would be nothing to prevent a creditor or an office-holder from bringing, or at least threatening to bring, a private prosecution with a view to seeking a compensatory contribution to the IVA from the debtor, or, following conviction, a compensation order (usually subsumed within a confiscation order under the Proceeds of Crime Act 2002).

(c) Antecedent transactions

9.36 One of the more significant differences between IVAs and bankruptcy is that there are no statutory powers granted to the supervisor of an IVA comparable to those accorded to the trustee in bankruptcy in regard to applying to the court for relief in connection with inappropriate antecedent transactions entered into by the debtor.[126] Nor does the supervisor have the investigatory powers of a trustee nor anything comparable to the powers of compulsion that are available to trustees.[127] The absence of these powers is a factor that the court bears in mind when considering challenges under section 262 of IA 1986.[128]

---

123   IA 1986, s 276(1). See *Somji v Cadbury Schweppes plc* [2001] 1 WLR 615, [2001] BPIR 172 (CA) and below at [12.28]–[12.29].
124   IA 1986, s 262A, inserted by the Insolvency Act 2000 (IA 2000), with effect from 1 January 2003.
125   IA 1986, s 262B, also inserted by IA 2000.
126   Primarily, IA 1986, ss 339 and 340. This is why the debtor is required to deal with any such transactions in the proposal: see above [4.24].
127   Primarily, IA 1986, ss 363 and 366. Note also the range of bankruptcy offences.
128   See above [2.06]–[2.07]. On s 262, see above [9.02]–[9.26].

Nevertheless, where it appears that the debtor, prior to entering into the IVA, **9.37**
has given away assets or otherwise entered into a transaction at an undervalue
with the purpose (or with a substantial purpose)[129] of putting assets beyond
the reach of, or prejudicing the interests of, their creditors, an application may
be made to the court for an order restoring the position to what it would have
been had the transaction not been entered into and protecting the interests
of persons prejudiced by the transaction (referred to as 'victims').[130] Such
an application can be brought by any person who is (or is capable of being)
a victim, whether or not that person is bound by the IVA, or, where a victim
is bound by the IVA, by the supervisor.[131] This is a class action: in every case
such an application would be treated as made on behalf of every victim of the
transaction.[132] The definition of 'victim' is deliberately wide, and the debtor
does not need to have had the applicant, or indeed the class of 'victims' for
whose benefit the application is brought, specifically in mind at the date of
the transaction.[133] The application must be made to the High Court or to the
appropriate court.[134] Upon such an application, the court has wide powers in
relation to the possible relief it can grant for the benefit of the creditors, subject
to certain limitations.[135]

Notwithstanding the terminology used, such an 'application' must in fact be **9.38**
brought by way of a claim under CPR Part 7, even where it is brought by the
office-holder, and procedurally it is subject to the CPR rather than IR 2016
(including as to issue fees, disclosure and evidence).[136] For these reasons and
by reason of the difficulties presented by the need to establish the prohibited
purpose, this avenue of redress is rarely deployed in the context of IVAs, but
where the asset base of the IVA has been thoroughly depleted by the transac-
tion(s) in question, it might have its place. It is mentioned here for complete-
ness, but such applications have a long history and voluminous jurisprudence,
which are beyond the scope of this work.[137]

---

129 'Substantial' rather than 'dominant': *IRC v Hashmi* [2002] EWCA Civ 981, [2002] BPIR 974; *4Eng Ltd v Harper* [2009] EWHC 2633 (Ch), [2010] BPIR 1.
130 IA 1986, s 423.
131 IA 1986, s 424(1)(b).
132 IA 1986, s 424(2).
133 *Sands v Clitheroe* [2006] BPIR 1000; *Gordian Holdings Ltd v Sofroniou* [2021] EWHC 235 (Comm), [2021] BPIR 808.
134 The appropriate court in this context means the court that made the interim order, where there was one, or otherwise that indicated by IR 2016, r 8.20.
135 IA 1986, s 425. The relief is essentially restitutionary, not compensatory (see *Johnson v Arden* [2018] EWHC 1624, [2019] BPIR 901); nor is it punitive (*Deansgate 123 LLP v Workman* [2019] EWHC 2 (Ch), [2019] BPIR 341, at [57], although the comment is *obiter*).
136 See *Manolete Partners Plc v Hayward and Barrett Holdings Ltd* [2021] EWHC 1481 (Ch).
137 For a helpful summary, see *4Eng Ltd v Harper* [2009] EWHC 2633 (Ch), [2010] BPIR 1.

PART V

IMPLEMENTATION

10

EXTANT BANKRUPTCY PROCEEDINGS

A. SUBSISTING BANKRUPTCY

1. Transition from bankruptcy to IVA

Where a debtor, whose proposal for an individual voluntary arrangement **10.01** (IVA) has been approved, was an undischarged bankrupt at the date of the approval, the transition from bankruptcy to IVA is governed by the Insolvency Act 1986 (IA 1986) and the Insolvency (England and Wales) Rules 2016 (IR 2016).[1] Together, these cover a number of issues, from the transfer of the assets from the bankruptcy estate, the settling of fees due to the Official Receiver (OR) and the trustee in bankruptcy in connection with the administration of the bankruptcy, to the annulment of the bankruptcy and the various consequences that follow from that.

As soon as reasonably practicable after the IVA has been approved by the **10.02** creditors of an undischarged bankrupt, the trustee in bankruptcy (who may be the OR) must do all that is required to put the supervisor of the IVA in

---

1   IR 2016 (SI 2016/1024), Part 8.

possession of the assets included in the IVA.[2] Before taking possession of such assets, the supervisor must deliver an undertaking to the trustee to discharge the balance due to the OR and/or trustee out of the first realisation of the assets or to discharge such balance directly upon taking possession of those assets.[3] The balance so referred to is the balance due to the trustee (or to the OR) by way of fees or expenses properly incurred and payable (in accordance with IA 1986 and/or IR 2016) and on account of any advances made in respect of the bankrupt's estate, together with interest thereon at judgment rate.[4] The supervisor is entitled to deduct from the realisation of any such assets the proper costs and expenses of such realisation. Subject to these deductions, the OR and any trustee have a charge on the assets included in the IVA in respect of such balance.[5] Any sums due to the OR in this way take priority over sums due to any trustee.[6]

10.03 In addition, from time to time during the course of the implementation of the IVA, as and when the supervisor is able to realise any assets, the supervisor must discharge any and all guarantees given by any trustee (or the OR) for the benefit of the bankrupt's estate out of such realisations and also pay any expenses of the OR and/or trustee.[7] Any such guarantees and any assets in relation to which such realisations are anticipated ought to have been identified in the proposal and the requisite arrangements made explicit.

10.04 As discussed in the previous chapter, the approval of the IVA of a debtor who is an undischarged bankrupt may be challenged under section 262 of IA 1986. If, upon such a challenge, the court makes an order revoking or suspending the approval (whether or not it also directs a further decision procedure),[8] the debtor or their trustee in bankruptcy must deliver notice of the order and (where applicable) notice of the debtor's intentions regarding any revised proposal or resubmission of the original proposal in accordance with the rules.[9]

---

2   IR 2016, r 8.25(1). The wording of r 8.25 reflects the fact that, prior to 6 April 2017, the OR would have assumed control of the bankrupt's estate when a bankruptcy order was made without becoming the trustee; since that date, however, the OR will automatically become the trustee upon the making of a bankruptcy order, unless the court appoints a different trustee: IA 1986, s 291A(1).

3   IR 2016, r 8.25(2).

4   IR 2016, r 8.25(3); 'judgment rate' here means the rate specified in accordance with s 17 of the Judgments Act 1838 as at the date of the bankruptcy order.

5   IR 2016, r 8.25(4).

6   IR 2016, r 8.25(5).

7   IR 2016, r 8.25(6).

8   Pursuant to IA 1986, s 262(4) or (7): see above [9.21]–[9.24].

9   IR 2016, r 8.27(4)(a) and (b): see above [9.25].

2. Annulment following the approval of an IVA

(a) The jurisdiction

Once the creditors have approved an IVA in respect of a debtor who is an **10.05** undischarged bankrupt, the debtor can seek to have their existing bankruptcy annulled and the court has specific powers to annul the bankruptcy and give further directions concerning the conduct of the bankruptcy in order to facilitate the implementation of the IVA.[10] For many years the provisions governing these powers were somewhat clumsy: in particular the rules that governed the procedure at the time, namely the Insolvency Rules 1986 (IR 1986), simply imported wholesale and without modification the rules then in force dealing with what amounts to a quite different form of annulment under section 282 of IA 1986.[11] This was highly unsatisfactory. As a result, with effect from 1 April 2004, section 261 was completely revised and a new set of rules, specifically governing annulment pursuant to section 261, was inserted into IR 1986.[12] With some minor modifications since that time, these rules remain the governing provisions, now slightly recast within IR 2016.[13] This procedure and the issues surrounding it are set out below.

(b) Procedure

(i) The debtor's application

To obtain an annulment of their bankruptcy, the debtor must file an applica- **10.06** tion at court.[14] Although the statutory provisions are silent as to the appropriate court and the appropriate respondent, the application should be made to the court seized of the bankruptcy and the usual practice is for the respondents to be the trustee in bankruptcy and the creditor upon whose petition the bankruptcy order was made. At first sight, the wording of section 261 of IA 1986 might suggest that, to be eligible to invoke this jurisdiction, the debtor must still be an undischarged bankrupt as at the date of the application (or even, more strictly, as at the date of the annulment order). This interpretation is, however, too narrow: on a purposive construction of the provisions of s 261 and having regard to the wording of section 282(3) of IA 1986 (which on its face is not specifically confined to applications under section 282), it is clear

---

10   IA 1986, s 261 (as amended).

11   IR 1986, r 6.212A (repealed in 2004).

12   IR 1986, 5.21 ff, inserted by the Insolvency (Amendment) Rules 2003 (SI 2003/1730); the recast s 261 was substituted by EA 2002.

13   For the modern rules, see IR 2016, rr 8.32–8.37. With the abolition of required forms, these rules now include a prescriptive formula for the order itself: IR 2016, r 8.34 (see below).

14   IA 1986, s 261(2)(a).

that as long as the debtor was still an undischarged bankrupt as at the date of the decision to approve the IVA (a prerequisite), it does not matter if they have since been discharged from their bankruptcy prior to making the application.[15]

10.07 The annulment application cannot be made until after the end of the period specified in section 262(3)(a) of IA 1986, being the primary period in which the creditors' decision can be challenged under section 262 of IA 1986; nor can it be made while any such challenge application is pending or any appeal in respect of such an application is pending or may be brought.[16] There is no reference to an application to appeal against a decision made by the convener or chair in the course of the decision procedure at which the IVA was approved.[17] Nevertheless, the time limits that govern such an application are equivalent to those under section 262(3)(a), and if an annulment application were to be made when such an application was pending (or an appeal of any decision made upon it were outstanding), the court would simply stay the annulment application pending the final determination of that challenge application or appeal application.[18] In practical terms, this means waiting at least 28 days from the date of the decision or, in the case of an IVA approved following an interim order, 28 days from the date on which the report on the decision was made to the court by the nominee, before issuing an annulment application. If, during that period, an application under section 262 (or under IR 2016, rule 15.35) is made, the debtor would have to wait, additionally, until at least 21 days after the date of the determination of that application;[19] if, during those 21 days, an appeal against that decision were launched, the debtor would have to await the determination of that appeal before applying to annul.

10.08 The annulment application must be supported by a witness statement. The statement must, at a minimum, set out the following three pieces of information: (a) that the IVA has been approved; (b) the date on which it was approved; and (c) that the 28-day period for making an application stipulated in section 262(3)(a) has elapsed and that no such application or appeal remains to be disposed of (that is, that the temporal conditions for making the application are satisfied).[20]

---

15 *Re Johnson* [2006] BPIR 987, distinguishing *Re Ravichandran* [2004] BPIR 814 and *Demarco v Perkins and Bulley Davey* [2006] EWCA Civ 188, [2006] BPIR 645, on which see above at [1.21] and also below [10.21].
16 IA 1986, s 261(3). On the time limits under s 262(3), see above [9.15].
17 Under IR 2016, r 15, 35: see above [9.27]–[9.32].
18 On timings, see IR 2016, r 15.35(5)(b) and above [9.29].
19 On the time limit for appeal, see IR 2016, r 12.61(2).
20 IR 2016, r 8.32(1).

Once the debtor has filed the application and witness statement with the **10.09**
court, the court will deliver a notice of the venue for the hearing to the debtor,
who must then, not less than five business days before the date fixed for the
hearing, deliver a copy of the notice to each of the OR, the trustee (if other
than the OR) and the supervisor of the IVA.[21] Any of these may attend or be
represented at the hearing and bring to the court's attention any matters that
seem to any of them to be relevant.[22] At any point in this procedure the court
has a wide discretion to give such directions as it thinks appropriate in relation
to the conduct of the bankruptcy pending the determination of the annulment
application.[23]

(ii) The OR's application

If the debtor does not make an application in accordance with section 261(2)(a) **10.10**
of IA 1986, the OR may make an application for annulment of the bankruptcy
order in the debtor's place in accordance with the rules and subject to certain
conditions.[24] The OR must not make such an application until at least 42 days
have passed since the date on which the nominee filed their report in relation
to the creditor's approval with the court, in a case where an interim order was
in place, or delivered their report in relation to the creditor's approval to the
creditors, where the alternative procedure was used.[25] Moreover, as with a debt-
or's annulment application, the OR may not make such an application if any
application challenging the IVA under section 262 of IA 1986, or any appeal
relating to such a challenge application, is still pending.[26] The OR's annulment
application must be supported by a report from the OR, filed together with the
application, stating the grounds on which the application is made and that, as
far as the OR is aware, no such challenge application or appeal remains to be
disposed of.[27] The report must also confirm that the requirements as to timing
referred to above, in reference to the nominee's report, are satisfied.[28]

On receipt of the OR's application, the court will deliver a notice of the venue **10.11**
to the OR, who must, not less than five business days before the date fixed for
the hearing of the application, send a copy of the notice together with a copy

---

21   IR 2016, r 8.32(2)–(3).
22   IR 2016, r 8.32(4).
23   IA 1986, s 261(4); cf. the equivalent discretion under s 255(3), although here there is no fetter to the discre-
      tion (in contrast to s 255(4)–(5), on which see above [6.29]).
24   IA 1986, s 261(2)(b) and IR 2016, r 8.33.
25   IR 2016, r 8.33(2).
26   IA 1986, s 261(3). In relation to pending applications under IR 2016, r 15.35, see above [10.07].
27   IR 2016, r 8.33(1)(a) and (c).
28   IR 2016, r 8.33(1)(b), referring to the requirements of r 8.33(2).

of the application and the report to the debtor.[29] As with a debtor's application, the court is empowered to give directions in relation to the bankruptcy proceedings while the annulment application is pending.[30]

(c)   The annulment order

10.12   If the court is satisfied that the conditions are met, then it must grant the annulment.[31] The consequences of the annulment are somewhat complex and, given the abolition of prescribed forms under IR 1986, it is not surprising therefore that the contents of the annulment order is rigidly prescribed by the rules.[32] Unless the court determines that the order should be presented in some other fashion, the contents of the annulment order should be set out in the order provided in the relevant rules.[33]

10.13   The order must identify the proceedings in which it is made and state that it is made under section 261 of IA 1986.[34] It must give the name and address of the applicant, cite the fact and date of the approval of the IVA and record that there has been no application for the suspension or revocation of the IVA under section 262 of IA 1986 and that the time for any such application has expired.[35] Where the applicant is the OR (under section 261(2)(b) of IA 1986), the order must also contain a statement that the relevant time period has expired.[36] It must then order that the bankruptcy order made against the debtor, identified by date and the name of the debtor, be annulled and, if appropriate, order that the bankruptcy petition or application on which the debtor was made bankrupt (identified by the date of presentation or issue, respectively) be dismissed.[37]

10.14   The annulment order must also contain a number of further matters, consequential upon the annulment. It must include the following orders: that the trustee in bankruptcy should be released;[38] that the registration of the bankruptcy petition or application as a pending action at HM Land Registry (HMLR), identified by the date of registration and the reference number, be

---

29   IR 2016, r 8.33(3) and (4).
30   IA 1986, s 261(4).
31   IA 1986, s 261(2) is couched in mandatory terms.
32   IR 2016, r 8.34(1), which is new to IR 2016.
33   IR 2016, r 1.8(2).
34   IR 2016, r 8.34(1)(a)–(b).
35   IR 2016, r 8.34(1)(c)–(e), respectively.
36   IR 2016, r 8.34(1)(f); for the relevant period, see r 8.33(2) and above [10.10].
37   IR 2016, r 8.34(1)(g)–(h), respectively.
38   IR 2016, r 8.34(1)(i); the time for such release to take effect is determined in accordance with IR 2016, r 8.37 (on which see below [10.18]). The introductory words in r 8.34(1)(i), 'where there is a trustee', relate to bankruptcies commenced prior to 6 April 2017 (see above [10.02]).

vacated;[39] that the registration of the bankruptcy order at HMLR (identified by the date of registration and the reference number) be vacated.[40] In addition, the annulment order must also contain the following: the date on which the annulment order is being made;[41] a notice to the debtor to the effect that if they wish the annulment order to be gazetted and advertised in the same manner as the bankruptcy order, they must deliver a notice to that effect to the OR within 28 days;[42] a notice to the debtor reminding them that it is both their responsibility and in their interest to ensure that any registration of the bankruptcy petition or application as a pending action and any registration of the bankruptcy order and any enquiries relating to any of the above at HMLR are cancelled (providing the debtor with the relevant contact details at HMLR and referring to relevant HMLR guidance).[43]

3. Consequential matters following annulment

Once the annulment order is made, the court must send a sealed copy of **10.15** the order to the debtor, the OR, the trustee (if other than the OR) and the supervisor of the IVA.[44] If notice of the bankruptcy order had been given to the creditors by the OR, then upon receiving the sealed copy of the annulment order, the OR must deliver notice of the annulment to the creditors as soon as reasonably practicable, for the expenses of which the OR is entitled to a charge over the debtor's property.[45]

In addition, the debtor has the right to require the OR to cause a notice of **10.16** the annulment order to be gazetted and advertised in the same manner as the original bankruptcy order; this request must be made in writing not more than 28 days after the date of annulment order.[46] The OR must comply with such a request as soon as reasonably practicable and the notice must state the name of the debtor, the date of the bankruptcy order, the fact that it has been annulled and the date of that order and the grounds on which it was annulled.[47] If, prior to being able to get the annulment order gazetted, the debtor has died or become mentally incapacitated, their personal representative or a suitable

---

39   IR 2016, r 8.34(1)(j).
40   IR 2016, r 8.34(1)(k).
41   IR 2016, r 8.34(1)(l).
42   IR 2016, r 8.34(1)(m), in accordance with IR 2016, r 8.36: see below [10.16].
43   IR 2016, r 8.34(1)(n).
44   IR 2016, r 8.34(2).
45   IR 2016, r 8.35(1)–(3).
46   IR 2016, r 8.36(1).
47   IR 2016, r 8.36(2)–(3).

person appointed by the court (respectively) may stand in the debtor's stead to make the request.[48]

10.17 The debtor should be aware that the annulment order does not, of itself, automatically serve to cancel any registration of the bankruptcy petition or application as a pending action or any registration of the bankruptcy order and any enquiries relating to any of the above at HMLR. The debtor must write directly to the registrar at HMLR to ensure this is done, providing a copy of the annulment order and following the HMLR guidance as reference in the annulment order.[49]

10.18 The annulment order will mean that the trustee in bankruptcy must vacate office,[50] but this does not release the trustee nor does it relieve them of their statutory obligations, in particular the duty to file a final report.[51] The court will determine the date of the trustee's release, having regard to the trustee's compliance with that duty.[52] For this reason, the annulment order itself will normally provide for the trustee's release to take effect once the final report has been duly filed.

4. Duty of office-holders relating to annulment

(a) The trustee's duties

10.19 The trustee in bankruptcy of an undischarged bankrupt seeking to enter an IVA will be aware, at all stages, of the progress of the bankrupt's attempts to exit their bankruptcy by way of an IVA: where the interim order procedure is followed, the trustee (if the trustee is not the applicant) will be provided with notice of the application;[53] in every case they will be furnished with a copy of the proposal and the nominee's report on the proposal,[54] as well as notice of the result of the creditors' decision.[55] The trustee will also be on notice of the bankrupt's application to annul.[56] Part of the rationale for providing that the trustee be kept in the loop in this way is to enable the trustee to minimise any additional burden on the bankruptcy estate, pending the anticipated annulment, including in particular keeping to a minimum the fees that the trustee

---

48   IR 2016, r 8.36(4); see above [3.13] and [3.22], respectively.
49   Cf. above [10.14] and IR 2016, r 8.34(1)(n).
50   IA 1986, s 298(9).
51   See below [10.20].
52   IR 2016, r 8.37(4).
53   IR 2016, 8.8(4)(b).
54   IR 2016, r 8.15(5), or r 8.19(5)(a), depending on which procedure is being followed.
55   IR 2016, r 8.24(5)(c).
56   IR 2016, r 8.32(3)(b).

might otherwise run up. Where a trustee ignores this and, in full awareness of the debtor's attempts to exit the bankruptcy by way of an IVA, pursues a course of action that needlessly incurs additional expense, such action (at its worst) could amount to misfeasance and, in any event, it would be open to the debtor to challenge the trustee's fees and expenses.[57]

In addition, as noted above, the trustee is under a duty to cooperate fully with **10.20** the supervisor and, as soon as reasonably practicable after the date of approval of the IVA, to do all that is required to put the supervisor in possession of the assets included within the IVA.[58] Following the annulment order, the trustee must bring the bankruptcy to an orderly conclusion, accounting for all their transactions in connection with the bankruptcy estate and as soon as reasonably practicable thereafter delivering a copy of their final account, including a summary of the trustee's receipts and payments, to the Secretary of State and file a copy with the court.[59] The trustee would be expected to carry out these duties with the minimum of additional expense.

(b) Duty of nominee where the ability to annul has been lost

Where the nominee is aware that the reason (or a principal reason) why the **10.21** debtor is proposing an IVA is to enable them to annul their bankruptcy in the manner described above, the nominee owes the debtor a common law duty to progress the IVA in sufficient time to achieve this aim. The nominee's failure to do so could result in the debtor becoming discharged from their bankruptcy before the proposal could be approved by the creditors. This would mean that the creditors would be precluded from approving the IVA in respect of the bankruptcy debts and the debtor's ability to proceed with the IVA as contemplated and then pursue a subsequent annulment (pursuant to section 261) would be lost forever. Such circumstances could give rise to a claim in negligence by the debtor against the nominee.[60] If the debtor still wished to proceed to annul their bankruptcy, they would have to find the sums necessary to pay off the bankruptcy debts and expenses in full and then apply in the normal way pursuant to section 282(1)((b) of IA 1986. It is important to note, however, that if the debtor brings a claim in negligence against the nominee on this basis and that claim succeeds, the debtor would only be entitled to general

---

57   See IA 1986, s 303(1), s 363(1) and, potentially, s 304(1)(b).

58   See above [10.02].

59   IR 2016, r 8.37(1)–(3). On the trustee's release being conditional upon compliance with these duties, see above [10.18].

60   See *Demarco v Perkins and Bulley Davey* [2006] EWCA Civ 188, [2006] BPIR 645. Such circumstances are, however, rare: more often it is simply that the debtor is unable to prepare the groundwork for making a viable proposal in time (e.g., *Leopard v Robinson* [2020] EWHC 2928 (Ch), at [110]).

damages, assessed on the difference between there having been an annulment under section 261 and there being no annulment at all; they would not be entitled to special damages in the sum needed to achieve an annulment under section 282(1)(b).[61]

B. OUTSTANDING BANKRUPTCY PETITION

1. Where the interim order procedure has been followed

10.22 Where a bankruptcy petition presented against a debtor who is making a proposal to enter into an IVA remains outstanding as at the date of the approval of the IVA, the debtor will need to ensure that the petition is dealt with. This is considerably more straightforward where the debtor has chosen to proceed with the IVA by way of an interim order. As noted above, where the interim order procedure has been followed, the debtor is required to notify the petitioning creditor and the court has express powers to deal with such a petition while the application for an interim order is pending; once the interim order is made it will provide for the petition to be stayed.[62] To ensure maximum efficiency and to minimise costs, it is standard practice for the petition and the interim order proceedings to be listed together in parallel, so that any orders or directions given in one set of proceedings are properly reflected in the other.

10.23 Where an interim order that stayed the bankruptcy petition automatically lapses under s 260(4) of IA 1986, that petition will be deemed to have been dismissed on the same date unless the court orders otherwise.[63] This deeming provision does not, however, expressly include any reference to the vacation of the registration of the bankruptcy petition as a pending action at HMLR. In practice, the court will usually have listed the petition alongside the interim order and, when ordering the discharge of the interim order at a suitable date in the future (usually on paper, without a hearing), will include an order expressly dismissing the petition on the same date and directing that the registration of the bankruptcy petition as a pending action at HMLR (identified by the date of registration and the reference number) be vacated.[64]

---

61 *Demarco v Perkins and Bulley Davey* (above).
62 See Chapter 6 above.
63 IA 1986, s 260(5). On s 260(4), see above at [6.49].
64 Such a direction is standard upon the dismissal of a petition; but cf. IR 2016, r 8.34(1)(n), on which see above [10.14].

2.   Where the alternative procedure has been followed

The position is different where the debtor decided against obtaining an interim **10.24** order and chose instead to follow the alternative procedure under section 256A of IA 1986. Under this out-of-court procedure, there are no equivalent provisions dealing with a pending bankruptcy petition; nor is there any provision equivalent to section 260(5) automatically dismissing such a petition in the event of the creditors' approval of the IVA. Instead, the debtor would have had to ensure that the court before which the petition was pending had stayed the petition (with liberty to apply back in the event that the IVA was approved). Following the approval, the debtor would need to attend the next hearing of the petition to have it dismissed in the event that the matter could not be dealt with on paper. Precisely because these arrangements are more complicated and potentially more costly, it will usually be a good idea for a debtor who is an undischarged bankrupt to avail themselves of the more efficient procedures built into the interim order procedure.

11

IMPLEMENTATION AND SUPERVISION

A. COMMENCEMENT OF THE IVA

1. Initial Implementation

11.01 Once the creditors have approved the proposal in accordance with the provisions of the Insolvency Act 1986 (IA 1986) and the Insolvency (England and Wales) Rules 2016 (IR 2016),[1] with or without modifications, the individual voluntary arrangement (IVA) comes into force immediately and binds every creditor who was entitled to vote in the creditors' decision procedure or would have been so entitled if they had had notice of it.[2] The nominee will automatically become the supervisor upon the approval taking effect, unless (unusually) there was a modification to provide otherwise.[3] This means that in the vast majority of cases the supervisor will already be fully familiar with the terms of the IVA, having been the nominee and presided over the decision procedure and, very likely, also having previously advised the debtor on the terms of the proposal in the first place. Such continuity obviously lends itself to greater efficiency.

---

1   SI 2016/1024.
2   IA 1986, s 260(2). On the binding effect and the statutory hypothesis behind it, see Chapter 2 above.
3   IA 1986, s 263(1)–(2).

Where the debtor is an undischarged bankrupt, section 389B(1) of IA 1986 **11.02** permits the Official Receiver (OR) to assume the role of both nominee and then supervisor. This provision was introduced to help facilitate the introduction of 'fast track' IVAs, which never really got off the ground.[4] When the latter were finally abolished,[5] section 398B was preserved, but in practice it is seldom, if ever, used. In general, the supervisor must be a qualified insolvency practitioner (IP), who must be licensed and regulated by one of a number of recognised professional bodies.[6] In implementing the terms of the IVA, the supervisor will be expected to follow the guidance set out in the relevant 'Statement of Insolvency Practice' (SIP), in particular SIP 3.1, as well as the Code of Ethics.[7] Among the very first tasks that the supervisor should undertake is to ensure that all the creditors are made aware of the final form of the IVA as approved, including any and all modifications.[8] This should be done at the outset, by providing a copy of the proposal together with all the accepted modifications to every creditor bound by the IVA of whom the supervisor is aware.

Immediately following the approval, there ensues a 28-day grace period during **11.03** which an application may be brought to challenge the approval.[9] The potential consequences of such a challenge, if successful, have already been dealt with above.[10] If no such challenge is mounted, or if one or more challenges are mounted but are subsequently disposed of, the IVA will continue on its course under the supervision of the supervisor. The supervisor cannot simply await the passing of the initial grace period, still less the subsequent period of limbo pending the final disposal of any such application as may be brought, in order to start implementing the IVA. As soon as reasonably practicable after the IVA has been approved, the debtor must cooperate fully in putting the supervisor in possession of the assets included in the IVA.[11] Where the debtor is an undischarged bankrupt, special rules apply for dealing with the transfer of assets from the trustee to the supervisor for the purposes of the IVA.[12] Depending on the terms of the IVA, the supervisor will usually need to take action in relation to some such assets even prior to the expiry of the grace

---

4 IA 1986, s 389B was inserted by the Enterprise Act 2002 (EA 2002), along with ss 263A–263G (introducing fast track IVAs), with effect from 6 April 2004: see above [1.29].
5 By the Small Business, Enterprise and Employment Act 2015 (SBEEA 2015).
6 See IA 1986, Part 13 and above [1.18].
7 See above [1.18].
8 See SIP 3.1, para 16(a).
9 IA 1986, s 262; IR 2016, r 15.35.
10 See Chapter 9 above.
11 IR 2016, r 8.25(1).
12 See above [10.02].

period. Where a challenge is mounted, the supervisor should take care only to take such actions as are strictly necessary for the proper implementation of the IVA pending the conclusion of the challenge. In the event that a challenge is subsequently upheld, the court will give suitable directions as to any such actions that may have been taken by the supervisor in the meantime.[13]

2. Registration

11.04 One of the first tasks that the supervisor must carry out (although technically the obligation lies with the nominee) is to report to the Secretary of State, in order to register the IVA with the Insolvency Service.[14] This report must provide the identification details of the debtor, together with the debtor's gender, date of birth and any name by which the debtor has been known other than that under which they entered the IVA, the date on which the IVA was approved and the name and address of the supervisor.[15]

11.05 The report should be provided as soon as reasonably practicable and in any event within 14 days of the date the nominee's report of the outcome was filed at court, in the case of an IVA with an interim order, or the date notice was delivered to the creditors where the alternative procedure was followed.[16] Notwithstanding this requirement, there can sometimes be a time lag involved in the registration process (at both ends), often due to issues related to the infrastructure and information technology. Such technical issues can occasionally lead to quite significant delays, stretching to weeks or even months, between commencement and formal registration.

B. IMPLEMENTATION AND SUPERVISION

1. The role of the supervisor

(a) General principles

11.06 The primary role of the supervisor is to ensure that the IVA is carried out in accordance with its terms.[17] The standard of competence that a supervisor is expected to attain in carrying out these functions is similar to that which per-

---

13   IA 1986, s 262(7): see above [9.24].
14   IR 2016, r 8.26.
15   IR 2016, r 8.26(3).
16   IR 2016, r 8.26(2).
17   See SIP 3.1, para 16(b).

tains to nominees at an earlier stage in the proceedings. In *Pitt v Mond*,[18] an unsuccessful claim against an IP, the primary focus was on the duty owed by the IP to the debtor as nominee in relation to the possibility of falls in property prices, but the case also touched upon the role of the supervisor.

Each IVA is unique and the extent of the supervisor's powers and duties will **11.07** vary from one IVA to another. Although the role can sometimes involve a fairly light touch, at the very least it will require the supervisor to ensure that the IVA is conducted in accordance with its terms and that dividends due to creditors are duly paid. As already noted, there are some useful broad distinctions to be drawn between different relatively common categories of IVAs. One such category is the consumer IVA.[19] Another is the trading IVA, under which the debtor's business is allowed to continue, usually under the supervision of the supervisor. It is important to note, however, that in most cases the business will remain that of the debtor and, in contrast to the analogous position in bankruptcy, the assets and income of the business will not automatically vest in the supervisor (although the supervisor may be required to carry on the business in the debtor's name) and will only be applied for the benefit of the IVA to the extent that the terms of the IVA so provide.[20] IA 1986 contains specific provisions dealing with the supply of utilities in connection with a business being run under the auspices of an IVA.[21] If the debtor's business employed other individuals, the debtor would be expected to have regard for the duties and rights of the employees, in order to ensure the efficient running of the business. Where there is a trading IVA, the supervisor will be required to keep additional accounting records, summaries of which will need to be included in the reports.[22]

A crucial function of the supervisor is to ensure that the debtor complies with **11.08** the terms of the IVA. The progress of the IVA should be carefully monitored and any departures from terms identified and addressed at earliest opportunity.[23] If the supervisor becomes aware of any such departure from the terms or breach on the part of the debtor, they must deal with this in accordance with the terms of the IVA; typically, this will oblige the supervisor to notify the debtor forthwith, requiring the debtor to remedy the breach and, if appropri-

---

18   [2001] BPIR 624; see above [4.03].
19   See above [4.08]–[4.10].
20   Cf. the bankruptcy case of *Leopard v Robinson* [2020] EWHC 2928 (Ch).
21   IA 1986, s 372 and, especially, s 372A (which relates to IVAs only).
22   See below [11.17]–[11.18].
23   See SIP 3.1, para 16(c)–(d).

ate, to provide an explanation.[24] Where the breach is irremediable or is not remedied within the appropriate time frame, the supervisor may be required to take action to terminate the arrangement.[25]

11.09 The supervisor will need to ensure that the assets of the IVA are properly dealt with in accordance with the terms of the IVA. Generally speaking, the supervisor is usually given fairly wide powers in relation to dealing with the assets in the IVA.[26] Depending on the terms of the IVA, the supervisor may hold these assets on trust.[27] In some cases the supervisor may hold power of attorney to deal with assets and, where that is the case, would in general be expected to use that power if the need arose.[28] The terms of the IVA may also empower the supervisor to claim assets acquired by the debtor during the course of the IVA in a similar manner to after-acquired property in the context of bankruptcy.[29]

11.10 Another key function of the supervisor is to deal with the apportionment of the dividends to be paid to creditors under the terms of the IVA. At an early stage (subject to any challenge under section 262 of IA 1986 or IR 2016, rule 15.35), the supervisor should remind the creditors and any other person to whom the debtor may be indebted of the deadlines specified in the IVA for submitting proofs of debt for dividend purposes in such form as the supervisor may require.[30] Since Part 14 of IR 2016, dealing with proofs and dividends in the context of bankruptcy, does not directly apply to IVAs, the procedure for admitting or rejecting proofs and for the payment of dividends will be governed by the terms of the IVA.[31] The IVA often contains a term expressly dealing with appeals to the court in respect of any decision on proofs by the supervisor, but even where this is not the case, anyone affected by such a decision could apply under the general statutory provision (discussed below).[32]

11.11 If the terms of the IVA confer a discretion in any matter upon the supervisor, they must ensure that such discretions are exercised where the need arises and that this is actioned in a timely manner.[33] The supervisor will also need to ensure that any such discretion is exercised in a way that is fair and objec-

---

24   See Standard Conditions, paras 70–71.
25   See below, [12.07]–[12.10].
26   See Standard Conditions, para 13(1); note in particular the breadth of 13(1)(9).
27   See Standard Conditions, para 29; see also above [2.16].
28   See *Masters v Furber* [2013] EWHC 3023 (Ch), [2014] BPIR 263.
29   See above [4.44].
30   This would normally be set out in the proposal: see Standard Conditions, paras 31–32.
31   See Standard Conditions, paras 33–48 and 49–58.
32   IA 1986, s 263(3): see below [11.24]. The provisions of IR 2016, rr 14.7–14.9 do not apply to IVAs.
33   See SIP 3.1, para 16(e).

tively justifiable, favouring neither the debtor nor any particular creditor. The supervisor should deal with any enquiries raised by the debtor or any creditor promptly and to the best of their ability (within such restraints as time and expense may allow).[34]

Where the IVA includes terms for the setting up of a creditors' committee, **11.12** the supervisor will need to implement these and act in accordance with the decisions made by such a committee.[35] Where this is not the case, or where the decisions that are required lie outside the scope of the committee, the supervisor may need to seek a creditor decision by convening some kind of decision procedure: again (ideally), this should be detailed in the terms of the IVA.[36] If no such provisions exist, the supervisor may need to seek directions from the court.[37] The court cannot, however, direct the supervisor to do anything that lies outside the scope of the IVA.[38]

(b) Office-holder's fees and expenses

The supervisor must discharge the fees and expenses properly due to the **11.13** nominee out of the funds held within the IVA.[39] In practice, since the supervisor will usually have previously acted as nominee, this amounts to an entitlement to recoup their own fees and expenses incurred while acting as nominee. The amount due to the nominee will be dictated by the terms of the IVA.[40]

The supervisor's fees and expenses are equally governed by the terms of the **11.14** IVA and, in principle, will need to be agreed in advance when drafting the proposal (although this may become subject to modifications). The terms of the IVA usually provide for the remuneration to be calculated on one of three bases: a fixed sum, a percentage of funds brought into the IVA or on a time-cost basis (by reference to the time spent by the supervisor and the supervisor's staff).[41] Where the chosen basis is time-costs, the IVA may specify the appropriate fee-scales or allow a mechanism for how these may be determined and any disputes resolved.[42] Sometimes, where the fees are not fixed in advance, the terms may impose a cap to the level of fees that can be recovered

---

34 See SIP 3.1, para 16(g).
35 See Standard Conditions, para 59.
36 See Standard Conditions, paras 61–69.
37 See below [11.31].
38 See below [11.32].
39 IR 2016, r 8.30(a)–(b).
40 Where the nominee's remuneration is based on time-costs, see below [11.15].
41 See above [4.30].
42 See Standard Conditions, para 17(1) and (3).

by the supervisor. Where the terms of the IVA impose a fixed fee or provide for a specific cap, the court has no power to vary that provision.[43]

11.15 Where the nominee or the supervisor is entitled, under the terms of the IVA, to remuneration based on the time spent, they must provide specified details of the basis of those time-costs in a statement if requested to do so in accordance with the rules.[44] If, at any time while acting as such nominee or supervisor or within two years of ceasing to act in either capacity, a request is made by the debtor or (following approval of the IVA) any person bound by the IVA, the IP must, within 28 days of such a request, deliver to that person, free of charge, a statement covering the relevant period, setting out the total number of hours spent on the matter by the IP personally or their staff during the relevant period and providing, for each grade of staff engaged on the matter, the average hourly rate at which work carried out by staff at that grade was charged and the number of hours spent by each grade of staff.[45] The relevant period is, in the case of a nominee or supervisor who has ceased to act as such, from the date of their appointment to that office down to the date on which they ceased acting as such;[46] where the IP is still in the relevant office at the date of the request, the relevant period consists of one or more complete periods of six months beginning with the date of appointment to that office and ending most nearly before the date of receiving the request.[47]

11.16 Categories and levels of expenditure or other costs will either be specifically sanctioned by the terms of the IVA or, more usually, the IVA will spell out how these are to be determined. Even where an expense is not specifically sanctioned by the terms of the IVA, however, it is recoverable if it would be payable, or corresponds to those that would be payable, in the debtor's bankruptcy.[48] The supervisor should keep careful records of all expenditure and provide full disclosure of these and any income directly or indirectly derived from the IVA in their reports.[49] The terms of the IVA may require the supervisor to provide forecasts and estimates of expenditure, but even where this

---

43 *Re a Block Transfer by Kaye and Morgan; Re Paul Murphy* [2010] BPIR 602. Conversely, where the Standard Conditions are incorporated and the restriction has been imposed by a creditor decision (rather than by the terms of the IVA itself), the court might have jurisdiction to arbitrate the dispute under para 17(3) of the Standard Conditions. On variation, see below [11.20]–[11.23].

44 IR 2016, r 8.38(1).

45 IR 2016, r 8.38(2), (3) and (5).

46 IR 2016, r 8.38(4)(a).

47 IR 2016, r 8.38(4)(b).

48 IR 2016, r 8.30(c).

49 See SIP 3.1, para 16(h). On records and reports, see below [11.17]–[11.18].

is not the case it is good practice to do so. If costs exceed such estimates, the supervisor should make this clear in their next report.[50]

(c) Record keeping and reporting

The supervisor is generally expected to maintain full accounts and records **11.17** of the IVA and its progress. As noted above, such records should include all items of expenditure and remuneration, full disclosure of which should be provided in the supervisor's reports.[51] It is in any event a formal requirement for all supervisors to keep full accounts and records where the terms of the IVA authorise or require the supervisor to carry on the business of the debtor, to realise the assets of the debtor or to administer or dispose of funds belonging to the debtor (or, for as long as the debtor remains an undischarged bankrupt, any equivalent dealings with a business, assets or funds in the bankruptcy estate).[52] All such accounts and records must include records of all receipts and payments of money and, more generally, of all the supervisor's dealings in or in connection with the IVA.[53] In circumstances where a person has been appointed supervisor in succession to another, the successor supervisor is required to preserve any such accounts and records of any prior supervisor as may be in the successor supervisor's possession.[54]

In addition, the terms of the IVA will usually require the supervisor to provide **11.18** reports periodically (usually every 12 months) to the debtor and to the creditors. The supervisor's reports must provide details of the progress of the IVA and the prospects of its successful implementation, covering each 12-month period of the IVA starting with the period to the first anniversary of the approval of the IVA, and must be delivered to the debtor and every creditor bound by the IVA within two months of the end of the period which it covers.[55] Where the supervisor is authorised or required by the IVA to carry on the debtor's business on behalf of or in the name of the debtor, or to deal with the debtor's assets or funds (as above), the report must include a summary of the receipts and payments, the accounts of which they are required to maintain, or, where there have been no such receipts and payments within the relevant period,

---

50   See SIP 3.1, para 16(i). See below [11.18].
51   See above [11.16]. The court censured the supervisor's failings in this regard in *Varden Nuttall Ltd v Nuttall* [2018] EWHC 3868 (Ch), [2019] BPIR 738.
52   IR 2016, r 8.28(1). In practice, this will cover the vast majority of IVAs.
53   IR 2016, r 8.28(2) and the Insolvency Practitioners Regulations 2005 (SI 2005/524), as amended (IPR 2005), Reg 13. (Note that Reg 13 of IPR 2005 was amended and Sch 3 to IPR 2005 (setting out minimum requirements) repealed with effect from 1 October 2015 by the Insolvency Practitioners (Amendment) Regulations 2015 (SI 2015/391).
54   IR 2016, r 8.28(3). On the appointment of successor supervisors, see below [11.33].
55   IR 2016, r 8.28(4)–(6).

must say so.[56] The supervisor is also required to produce a final report dealing with the receipts and expenditures of the IVA after the IVA has come to an end.[57]

11.19 The supervisor is required to preserve the accounts and records for six years after their release.[58] At any time, either during the course of the IVA or after its full implementation or termination, the Secretary of State may require the supervisor to produce for inspection (at the supervisor's premises or elsewhere) the supervisor's accounts and records in relation to the IVA and copies of any such reports.[59] The Secretary of State may also require such accounts and records to be audited, and in that case the supervisor must provide such further information and assistance as may be required for the purposes of that audit.[60]

(d) Variations

11.20 Neither IA 1986 nor IR 2016 contains any provision that allows the terms of the IVA, once approved, to be subsequently varied. In consequence, the court has no power, whether upon an application under section 263(3) of IA 1986 or upon an application by the supervisor for directions under section 263(4), to vary or amend the terms of an IVA.[61] The debtor and the creditors are none the less at liberty to agree to an express term allowing the IVA to be varied, and it is prudent, and indeed common in modern IVAs, for the proposal to contain such a provision.[62] To be effective so as to bind the parties, any such variations must be approved in the appropriate way by a formal decision procedure and would require both the consent of the debtor and the support of at least 75 per cent of the creditors, by value, in the same way as in the original approval.[63]

11.21 By reason of the statutory requirements for an IVA, special care needs to be applied when seeking approval of variations and putting them into effect.[64] Clearly, no variation can be validly introduced that would render the entire arrangement outside the ambit of Part 8 of IA 1986 or that was incapable

---

56   IR 2016, r 8.28(8).
57   IR 2016, r 8.31: see below [12.32]–[12.33].
58   IPR 2005, Reg 13(5).
59   IR 2016, r 8.29(1). See also IPR 2005, Reg 15 and note that this right thereby also extends to the recognised professional body of which the IP is a member.
60   IR 2016, r 8.29(2).
61   *Re a Block Transfer by Kaye and Morgan; Re Paul Murphy* [2010] BPIR 602, at [8]–[10] in reliance on *Re Alpha Lighting Ltd* [1997] BPIR 341 (CA), and *Re Beloit Walmsley Ltd* [2008] EWHC 1888 (Ch), [2008] BPIR 1445 (both CVA cases). Although *Re FMS Financial Management Services* [1989] BCC 191, apparently reached a different conclusion, it has been confined to its exceptional facts by these later authorities.
62   See Standard Conditions, para 81.
63   As explicitly provided in Standard Conditions, para 81(1)–(2), read together with para 66(2).
64   In this regard, note also SIP 3.1, para 16(f).

of being approved in the original decision procedure,[65] and it is common to include specific terms to that effect in the proposal.[66] Caution must be exercised when seeking to introduce variations. Any variation that unfairly prejudiced one or more creditors or that was obtained by means of a material irregularity in the procedure that brought it into effect would be vulnerable to attack and could jeopardise the entire arrangement.[67] This should therefore be avoided.

There is no reason why the express power to vary could not include variations **11.22** that affected the rights of third parties, but in so far as the IVA, as so varied, purported to bind any third party, the variation would only be effective if expressly consented to by the third party in question.[68] A variation affecting the rights of a third party, consented to by the third party, is capable of being enforced as against that third party by the supervisor. Thus, where an IVA was varied so as to include a property jointly owned by the debtor and his wife and the wife subsequently refused to agree to hand over her share of the proceeds of the sale of the property to the supervisor, the supervisor was entitled to enforce that arrangement as a collateral contract between the supervisor and the wife.[69]

In the absence of any express power to vary its terms, an IVA may not be **11.23** varied by the parties; but, in keeping with the contractual nature of an IVA, the parties can nevertheless agree amongst themselves to act in accordance with a varied set of provisions. Thus, in *Raja v Rubin*,[70] a variation was purportedly approved by all but one creditor, Mr Raja, notwithstanding the absence of any express power to vary in the IVA. Mr Raja issued an application under section 263(3) of IA 1986 for a declaration that the purported variation was void. At first instance, Sir John Vinelott rejected as misconceived the supervisor's contention that the power to vary could be implied into the terms of the IVA,[71] but held that there was no reason the creditors who stood to benefit from the IVA could not agree terms with the debtor, amounting in effect to a contract to abide by such a variation, and dismissed the application on the basis that Mr Raja, having renounced his right to participate in the dividends available

---

65   *Re a Debtor (No 638 IO of 1994)* (1998) The Times, 3 December; see also *Horrocks v Broome* [1999] BPIR 66.
66   See Standard Conditions, para 81(3) and (5).
67   Under IA 1986, s 263(3) (below [11.24]–[11.30]), or IR 2016, r 15.35 (see above [9.27]–[9.32]). Cf. Standard Conditions, para 81(4).
68   Thus, Standard Conditions, para 81(2).
69   *Stericker v Horner* [2012] BPIR 645. The supervisor's chosen route of enforcement (bankruptcy) failed only because the court found that the sums due to him from the wife did not constitute a liquidated sum.
70   [2000] Ch 274 (CA).
71   This point was not contested on appeal; a similar submission was equally rejected by HHJ Pelling QC in *Re a Block Transfer by Kaye and Morgan; Re Paul Murphy* [2010] BPIR 602, at [11]–[14].

in the IVA, had no legitimate interest in blocking it. The Court of Appeal agreed, emphasising that such an agreement could only take effect in contract and not under the statute.[72] Unless such an agreement receives the unanimous approval of all those entitled to participate in the IVA, however, it may be of limited value.

2. The role of the court

(a) Control of the supervisor

11.24 The court has the power to intervene upon the application of the debtor, any creditor of the debtor or any other person who is dissatisfied with any act, omission or decision of the supervisor. In certain circumstances, the appropriate financial regulator may also apply or be heard on such an application.[73] On such an application, the court may review any such decision, act or omission and may give directions to the supervisor.[74] The supervisor's role is in many ways akin to that of a trustee in bankruptcy, albeit that they are not appointed by the court. Like a trustee in bankruptcy, the supervisor is subject to the control of the court. By analogy, therefore, case law under the equivalent provision in relation to the control of trustees applies in much the same way to supervisors.[75] Moreover, the analogy can also be extended to other provisions of IA 1986 designed to enable the court to control office-holders in corporate insolvency,[76] even where the office-holders were not appointed by the court.[77] The role of supervisor is a statutory creation and the arrangement is a statutory contract: therefore, even though the supervisor's powers are largely governed in each case by the terms of the IVA itself, the court will always be willing to intervene where an office-holder has exceeded the powers conferred on them, expressly or impliedly, by statute.[78]

11.25 The control of office-holders by the court reaches beyond the strict application of the statutory controls referred to above and, in the right circumstances, can

---

72 It did, however, overturn the original decision in relation to indemnity costs.
73 Financial Services and Markets Act 2000, s 357(5) and (6): see above [9.02].
74 IA 1986, s 263(3).
75 The bankruptcy equivalent is IA 1986, s 303(1); the parallel between the two provisions was explicitly drawn in *Linfoot v Adamson* [2012] BPIR 1033.
76 See IA 1986, s 168(5), and para 74 of Schedule B1, in relation to liquidators and administrators, respectively.
77 For example, out-of-court appointments are now the norm for administrators.
78 See *Lehman Brothers Australia Ltd v MacNamara* [2020] EWCA Civ 321, [2021] Ch 1, [2020] BPIR 550, at [81]. This case concerned administrators challenged under para 74 of Sch B1 to IA 1986 and *ex parte James* (on which, see below). In *Manolete Partners Plc v Hayward and Barrett Holdings Ltd* [2021] EWHC 1481 (Ch), at [6], CICCJ Briggs appeared to cast doubt on whether a (CVA) supervisor was an 'office-holder'; if this was what the judge meant, it is clearly wrong (see, e.g., IA 1986 s 372, IR 2016, r 12.36).

involve the courts refusing to allow the office-holder to assert their full legal rights where to do so would be unconscionable or unjust. This is often referred to as the rule in *ex parte James*.[79] The authorities make clear that this is a matter of arriving at an outcome that is morally fair, rather than legally right. The rule only comes into play where the estate would otherwise in effect be unjustly enriched, where the person in whose favour the order is sought would not simply be entitled to prove in the insolvency for the loss suffered and where the legal position would lead to an outcome that would seem obviously unjust to any right-thinking person; but the court will only intervene to the extent required to prevent such injustice.[80] Although its application does sometimes require investigation into the proper standards of honesty and fair dealing on the part of the office-holder, it does not depend on any adverse findings of this nature.[81] There is no requirement for the office-holder to have acted unconscionably; it is enough that the result of their conduct would be objectively unfair.[82] Indeed, the rule's application often arises in relation to mistaken understandings.[83] Although some judicial doubt has been cast on whether the supervisor of an IVA is technically an officer of the court, the better view is that they are and that (even to the extent that they may not be) they are susceptible to the rule in *ex parte James* as office-holders.[84]

Although there is no statutory guidance as to who, other than the debtor or **11.26** a creditor, might have standing to bring such an application, the ambit of the phrase 'any other person [who] is dissatisfied' has been considered in various authorities. In *Brake v Lowes; Brake v Swift*,[85] the Court of Appeal rejected the suggestion that trustees of a family trust could themselves, merely by reason of having been unsuccessful bidders in an auction of property by a trustee in bankruptcy, be dissatisfied so as to bring them within the ambit of this phrase.

79　After the decision of the Court of Appeal in *In re Condon, ex parte James* (1874) 9 Ch App 609; [1874–80] All ER Rep 388.

80　See, for example, *In re Wizgell, ex parte Hart* [1921] 2 KB 835; *Re Clark* [1975] 1 WLR 559; *Re Lehman Brothers International (Europe), Lomas v Burlington Loan Management Limited* [2015] EWHC 2270 (Ch); *Lehman Brothers Australia Ltd v MacNamara* [2020] EWCA Civ 321, [2021] Ch 1.

81　See, for example, *Re Robinson, Leonard v Robinson* [2020] EWHC 2928 (Ch), at [140]–[146].

82　*Lehman Brothers Australia Ltd v MacNamara* (above), at [64]–[69].

83　Thus in *ex parte James* itself and in *Re Robinson* (above); see also *Allen v Young* [2017] BPIR 1116 and *HMRC v Sanders* [2021] EWHC 1843 (Ch).

84　*King v Anthony* [1999] BPIR 73, at 78 *per* Brooke LJ; see also *Appleyard Ltd v Ritecrown Ltd* [2009] BPIR 235, at [38] (a CVA case). By contrast, the comment of HHJ Purle QC in *Masters v Furber* [2013] EWHC 3023 (Ch), [2014] BPIR 263, at [11], casting doubt on the issue, was *obiter* (made in the context of an application by the supervisor, on which see below [11.31]). On supervisors as office-holders, see above [11.24] and (on the application of *ex parte James*, by analogy with administrators) see *Lehman Brothers Australia Ltd v MacNamara* [2020] EWCA Civ 321, [2021] Ch 1.

85　[2020] EWCA Civ 1491, [2021] BPIR 1, in the context of IA 1986, s 303(1).

The applicant must have a real connection to the insolvency in question and a substantial interest in the relief being sought.[86] Similarly an applicant who brings such an application for an entirely collateral purpose is unlikely to be granted relief, although the court will be slow to infer such purpose where there is a legitimate interest engaged.[87] It has also been doubted that the court would entertain an application brought by a third party who had entered a contract with the supervisor (in relation to assets to be included in an IVA by way of variation) complaining about the supervisor's conduct in entering into such a contract or arranging such a variation.[88]

11.27 Part 8 of IA 1986 provides a self-contained statutory scheme and therefore a creditor who wishes to complain about the conduct of the supervisor in carrying out the functions imposed by the terms of the IVA or to obtain assistance from the court to enforce those terms has no legal recourse other than by an application under section 263(3); there is no parallel common law duty of care.[89] In addition, the supervisor owes no duty of care to post-IVA creditors in relation to matters not strictly within the IVA.[90] When considering the supervisor's conduct and determining whether to intervene in respect of a decision, act or omission of the supervisor, the correct test to be applied was one of objective fairness and there was no additional hurdle that the conduct had to be discriminatory, still less unconscionable.[91]

11.28 Such complaints in relation to the decisions or conduct of the supervisor have much in common with challenges brought under section 262(1) of IA 1986.[92] They are, however, quite distinct procedures and cannot be elided.[93] The approach the court will take on considering whether to revoke an IVA on grounds of material irregularity in connection with the original decision procedure is not the same as that to be applied to complaints arising during the course of the IVA. The latter cover a wide range of possible matters, many of which will be much less serious.

---

86 See (in a CVA context) *Nero Holdings Ltd v Young* [2021] EWHC 1453 (Ch), in reliance upon *Deloitte & Touche AG v Johnson* [1999] 1 WLR 1605 (PC), in particular at 1611A–G, *per* Lord Millett. See also *Raja v Rubin* [2000] Ch 274 (CA) (above [11.23]) and *Discovery (Northampton) Ltd v Debenhams Retail Ltd* [2019] EWHC 2441 (Ch), [2020] BCC 9, at [132]–[139].

87 *Nero Holdings Ltd v Young* [2021] EWHC 1453 (Ch).

88 *Stericker v Horner* [2012] BPIR 645, at [37]–[38]; although strictly *obiter*, these comments are persuasive.

89 *King v Anthony* [1999] BPIR 73 (CA).

90 *Heritage Joinery v Krasner* [1999] BPIR 683, in which such a claim was dismissed.

91 See *Lehman Brothers Australia Ltd v MacNamara* [2020] EWCA Civ 321, [2021] Ch 1 (see above).

92 On which, see Chapter 9 above.

93 *Linfoot v Adamson* [2012] BPIR 1033.

On the application of the debtor or any creditor, the court could determine the **11.29** issue of whether an apparent default by the debtor did or did not constitute an act (or omission) resulting in the failure of the IVA and make declarations accordingly; at the same time, on a finding of failure, the court can give a direction to the supervisor to issue a certificate of non-compliance.[94] In an appropriate case the court would examine the terms of the IVA closely to see whether there had been non-compliance, even where the supervisor had certified the IVA as having completed successfully. In *Timmins v Conn*,[95] the supervisor had wrongly certified full compliance on the erroneous basis that an asset included in the IVA (the debtor's home), which had not been realised, had been excluded. Nevertheless, the creditor's claim against the supervisor for consequential loss failed on the facts. Moreover, the creditor had chosen to pursue this application without joining the debtor; although the supervisor had successfully applied to join the debtor as a respondent, the creditor (bizarrely) had succeeded in reversing this. The court observed that, given such declaratory relief would impact directly on the debtor, it was wholly inappropriate for a creditor to seek any such relief against the supervisor alone without joining the debtor. For an unusual, but instructive case involving allegations of dishonesty against a supervisor, see *Varden Nuttall Ltd v Nuttall*.[96]

An applicant whose complaint against the supervisor is unsuccessful will inevi- **11.30** tably bear the costs of and occasioned by the application. It does not, however, follow that where such an application succeeds the applicant will be awarded their costs, either against the supervisor personally or against the funds in the IVA. The court retains a wide discretion in relation to costs. In *Bhogal v Knight*,[97] a district judge had upheld the creditors' complaint that their proof of debt had been wrongly excluded for dividend purposes by the supervisor but had made no order as to costs; Falk J dismissed the appeal on the basis that the district judge had not strayed outside the wide ambit of his discretion in relation to costs.[98]

---

94 *Ing Lease (UK) Ltd v Griswold* [1998] BCC 905.
95 [2004] EWCA Civ 1761, [2005] BPIR 647.
96 [2018] EWHC 3868 (Ch), [2019] BPIR 738 (a case brought under Part 7 of the CPR, rather than under IA 1986, s 263(3), but the issues were very similar).
97 [2018] EWHC 2952 (Ch), [2019] BPIR 41.
98 Cf. *Raja v Rubin* [2000] Ch 274 (see above [11.23]), where the decision to award costs against the unsuccessful applicant on the indemnity basis was overturned by the Court of Appeal.

(b)   Directions sought by the supervisor

11.31   At any time, the supervisor may seek directions from the court.[99] The terms of the IVA may themselves provide for occasions where it would be appropriate for the supervisor to seek directions from the court, potentially including provisions that would allow the supervisor to apply to the court for determination of a matter where the supervisor and the creditors were in disagreement.[100]

11.32   A supervisor may wish to seek clarification from the court under this provision in relation to the validity or appropriateness of a proposed course of action before taking action in a way that might prove difficult or costly to undo. Such an application might, for example, relate to the proper construction of the terms of the IVA.[101] The court was prepared to provide guidance to the supervisor in *Re a Debtor (No 638 IO of 1994),*[102] where the supervisor was concerned about the validity of a variation to the terms of the IVA that had been proposed by the debtor and its potentially prejudicial effect to a particular creditor, even though the supervisor considered that the variation would be in the interests of the creditors as a whole. It is important to note, however, that on an application for directions the court has no power to vary the terms of the IVA, even where it might be expedient and/or in the interests of the creditors as a whole for it to do so.[103]

C. RETIREMENT, REPLACEMENT AND REMOVAL

11.33   Circumstances may arise during the course of the IVA where a supervisor can no longer practicably continue in office. Apart from when a supervisor dies in office, these may include the supervisor's cessation of practice as an IP (whether immediate or prospective and whether by reason of retirement or the revocation of their licence for professional misconduct), or on grounds of ill-health or some other change in circumstances rendering it impractical for the supervisor to continue in office. It may also be that the debtor or, more usually, the (or some) creditors wish to remove or replace a supervisor, who might or (more usually) might not accept that this should happen. In

---

99   IA 1986, s 263(4); cf. the equivalent provision in bankruptcy, s 303(2).
100   For example, Standard Conditions, para 17(3): see above [11.14].
101   *Horrocks v Broome* [1999] BPIR 66.
102   (1998) The Times, 3 December.
103   *Re Alpha Lighting Ltd* [1997] BPIR 341 (CA); see also *Re Beloit Walmsley Ltd* [2008] BPIR 1445 (both CVA cases under the equivalent provision in s 7(4)(a) of IA 1986). See also *Re a Block Transfer by Kaye and Morgan; Re Paul Murphy* [2010] BPIR 602 (above [11.20]).

most IVAs, such eventualities are anticipated within the terms of the IVA.[104] Usually, in such circumstances, it will be necessary to appoint a replacement, although this might not be strictly necessary where there are joint supervisors. Unless that is the case, absent express mechanisms in the IVA, or in the event of any difficulty in their implementation rendering it inexpedient, difficult or impracticable for an appointment to take place without the intervention of the court, the court may appoint a suitably qualified person to act as supervisor of the IVA, either in substitution for an existing supervisor or to fill a vacancy.[105]

There is no express provision under IA 1986 (or IR 2016) for a creditor or the **11.34** debtor to apply to the court for the removal of the supervisor.[106] To an extent, this may be a reflection of the fact that, unlike in other insolvency proceedings, the choice of supervisor is the result of agreement between the debtor and the creditors. Any application for the removal and replacement of a supervisor would have to be made under a combination of section 263(3) and (5) of IA 1986 and, unless the incumbent supervisor acquiesces, would have to show cogent grounds. Whenever the order sought is to remove or replace a supervisor, the supervisor in question should be served with the application and where that has not happened, the appropriate course is to adjourn the application.[107]

In general, the courts have shown themselves very reluctant to replace **11.35** office-holders:[108] the conduct of the office-holder is material, but ultimately it is a question of what best serves the interests of the creditors as a whole.[109] Where the office-holder has been generally honest and efficient, the court should be very slow to remove them at the behest of a disgruntled creditor and it is appropriate to take into account the almost inevitable undesirable consequences of additional costs and delay in doing so.[110] The court is entitled to have due regard for the likely impact of removal on the IP's professional reputation;[111] but the office-holder should be 'efficient, and vigorous and unbiased' and the court should have no hesitation in removing them if satisfied that they had failed to live up to those standards, at least unless it can be rea-

---

104   See Standard Conditions, paras 18–21.
105   IA 1986, s 263(5).
106   Cf. IA 1986, s 298 (removal of a trustee in bankruptcy).
107   *Clements v Udal* [2001] BPIR 454.
108   See *Re Birdi; Miles v Price* [2019] EWHC 291 (Ch), [2019] BPIR 498.
109   *Re Edennote Ltd* [1996] 2 BCLC 389 at 398; *Doffman & Isaacs v Wood & Hellard* [2011] EWHC 4008 (Ch), [2012] BPIR 972, at [13]–[14].
110   *AMP Music Box Enterprises Ltd v Hoffman* [2002] EWHC 1899 (Ch), [2003] 1 BCLC 319, at [27]; see also *SISU Capital Fund Ltd v Tucker* [2005] EWHC 2170 (Ch) and [2005] EWHC 2321 (Ch), reported together at [2006] BPIR 154.
111   *Re Edennote Ltd* (above); *Doffman & Isaacs v Wood & Hellard* (above) at [23].

sonably confident that the IP will live up to those requirements in the future.[112] Recently, the courts have shown themselves to be a little less reluctant to hold office-holders to account,[113] but the hurdle remains high.

11.36 Where there are joint supervisors, such an order may replace one or more without having necessarily to replace all the joint supervisors, and the court may also use such an order to increase the total number of supervisors.[114] The appointment of a joint office-holder is often a better option than straight replacement;[115] but in an appropriate case the appointment of an additional supervisor could be used as part of a two-stage process to replace a supervisor.[116] Any person who is appointed to the office of supervisor or who ceases to hold that office (whether under a court order or otherwise) must give notice to the Secretary of State as soon as reasonably practical after the event;[117] at the same time, they should also give notice to the debtor and to the creditors.[118]

11.37 If an IP who is the supervisor of a number of IVAs (and potentially the office-holder in a number of other insolvencies as well) dies in office or retires from practice or otherwise is either unable or unwilling to continue in office, the court may make a block transfer order, transferring the office of supervisor in all or some of the cases being administered by that IP (along with some or all of any other offices held by the outgoing IP) to a replacement office-holder.[119] The procedure is far from automatic and the court will consider the application and the cases to which it relates with care before determining what orders to make and in favour of whom, although weight would be given to the choice of the outgoing office-holder's professional body.[120] In making such a block transfer order the court may make an order in relation to what proportion (if any) of the costs of such an application should be borne by each insolvency proceedings (including each IVA) to which the application relates, having regard (among other things) to the reasons for the application, the number of cases to which it relates, the value of the assets comprised in each such case and the nature and extent of the costs involved.[121] Where the application relates to IVAs in which the fees and expenses of the supervisor are limited (either by

---

112 *AMP Music Box Enterprises Ltd v Hoffman* (above), at [23]. Apparent bias might suffice.
113 See *Lehman Brothers Australia Ltd v MacNamara* [2020] EWCA Civ 321, [2021] Ch 1.
114 IA 1986, s 263(6).
115 See *Doffman & Isaacs v Wood & Hellard* [2011] EWHC 4008 (Ch), [2012] BPIR 972, at [22].
116 *Clements v Udal* [2001] BPIR 454.
117 IR 2016, r 8.26(4), as reflected in Standard Conditions, para 20(4).
118 See Standard Conditions, para 20(4).
119 The procedure is governed by IR 2016, rr 12.35–12.38.
120 See *ICAEW v Webb* [2009] EWHC 3461 (Ch); *ACCA v Koumettou* [2012] EWHC 1265 (Ch).
121 IR 2016, r 12.38(4).

being fixed in advance or, more usually, by reference to a cap) and those limits have already been reached, this may present some problems for the incoming supervisor.[122]

The provisions in the rules governing block transfers were first introduced into **11.38** the predecessor of IR 2016, the Insolvency Rules 1986 (IR 1986), in 2010.[123] Block transfers had been happening for some considerable time prior to this, however. Thus, in *Re Bullard & Taplin Ltd*,[124] an IP who was the supervisor of an IVA and simultaneously the office-holder in a number of other insolvencies, needed to resign his offices (following the take-over of his firm) in favour of partners in the new firm. The court readily accepted that effecting this by one application rather than a series of meetings in each insolvency was expedient, so as to empower the court to make the order sought. The High Court can do this even if the interim order for the IVA in question had been made in the County Court, by ordering the proceedings to be transferred to the High Court.[125] In an appropriate case, the professional body of the supervisor has standing to apply to the court for an order to replace the supervisor with another.[126]

---

122 See *Re a Block Transfer by Kaye and Morgan; Re Paul Murphy* [2010] BPIR 602.
123 IR 1986, rr 7.10A–7.10D, inserted by the Insolvency (Amendment) Rules 2010 (SI 2010/686).
124 [1996] BCC 973.
125 Pursuant to what is now IR 2016, r 12.30(3) and s 41(1) of the County Courts Act 1984: see *Re Bullard & Taplin Ltd* (above), at pp 976–978; *Re Abbot* [1997] BCC 666.
126 *Re Stella Metals Ltd* [1997] BPIR 293 (another case involving transfer from the County Court) and see *ICAEW v Webb* [2009] EWHC 3461 (Ch); *ACCA v Koumettou* [2012] EWHC 1265 (Ch).

12

ENDING THE IVA

A. COMPLETION AND EFFLUXION OF TIME

12.01 An individual voluntary arrangement (IVA) made under Part 8 of the Insolvency Act 1986 (IA 1986) can come to an end in a number of ways. As already noted above, it may be revoked for material irregularity or unfair prejudice,[1] or it may be brought to an end by or as a result of the death of the debtor.[2] As we shall see below, it may also be terminated in the event of material default by the debtor under the terms of the IVA, resulting in a bankruptcy order made upon the petition of the supervisor or one or more creditors bound by IVA;[3] or it may be brought to an end by a bankruptcy order made on the petition of a creditor whose debt lies outside the IVA.[4] In the absence of any of the above, however, the IVA will come to its natural end in accordance with its terms (including as to duration).

---

1   See Chapter 9 above.
2   See above [3.10]–[3.14]; see also below [12.18].
3   IA 1986, s 264(1)(c), on which below [12.13]–[12.29].
4   IA 1986, s 264(1)(a), on which below [12.30].

The hoped-for result is that the IVA will successfully run its full course and **12.02** come to its natural end in accordance with the terms of the IVA. The duration of the IVA is determined by the proposal as approved (with or without modifications). An IVA necessarily comes to an end by effluxion of time at the conclusion of the duration stipulated in the IVA unless there is a power to extend the duration and that power is properly exercised prior to the end of the primary term; if a power to extend the duration is not properly exercised prior to that date, the power lapses and any purported extension exercised thereafter would be of no effect.[5] Nor does the court have any power to extend the IVA once it has expired.[6] Where an IVA does come to end by effluxion of time, it does not follow that it has concluded successfully: if the debtor has not managed to do all that was required of them prior to the conclusion, it may well be that the creditors who were formerly bound by the IVA are entitled to enforce their debts by other means, including seeking a bankruptcy order against the debtor.[7]

An IVA does not constitute an unconditional composition of the debtor's **12.03** debts and the debtor is not automatically released from the debts caught by the IVA upon it coming to an end by effluxion of time: they are only released if and when the supervisor issues a notice or certificate of completion confirming that the debtor has fulfilled all their obligations under the IVA.[8] The effect of a certificate of completion is, usually, that the debtor will be released from his IVA debts, analogous to the discharge from bankruptcy; but, like discharge, this does not necessarily mean that the debts cease to exist.[9] Even then, as long as the IVA is not brought to an end prematurely, if at the date it ceases to have effect there are sums that remain due under the arrangement to any creditor who is bound by the IVA purely by virtue of section 260(2)(b)(ii) of IA 1986 (that is, in circumstances where they did not have notice of the decision procedure but would have been entitled to vote had they received such notice), the debtor becomes personally liable to pay any such creditor the amount payable to them under the arrangement.[10]

Although a certificate of completion generally signifies the conclusion of the **12.04** IVA, any trusts under which funds or property (including choses in action)

---

5   *Strongmaster Ltd v Kaye* [2002] EWHC 444 (Ch), [2002] BPIR 1259. This may be subject to para 8(5) of the Standard Conditions, if incorporated.
6   *Re Alpa Lighting Ltd* [1997] BPIR 341 (CA); *Strongmaster Ltd v Kaye* (above).
7   This was the result in *Strongmaster Ltd v Kaye* (above).
8   *Co-operative Bank plc v Phillips* [2017] 1320 (Ch), [2017] BPIR 1156.
9   See *Green v Wright* [2017] EWCA Civ 111, [2017] BPIR 430.
10   IA 1986, s 260(2A).

were held for the benefit of the IVA creditors may, on a true construction of the terms of the arrangement, survive even the issue of a certificate of completion. Thus, in *Green v Wright*,[11] where the terms of the IVA expressly dealt with the treatment of moneys arising under a PPI claim for the benefit of the IVA creditors, it was held that the post-IVA receipts arising under the PPI claim were to be distributed to the IVA creditors even though the IVA had come to an end and a certificate of completion had been issued. Although an unusual case, this illustrates the point that, notwithstanding that the duration of an IVA must be specified in the proposal, practical completion may in part depend on the fulfilment of certain steps, including a (final) distribution to creditors. Difficulties can arise where contingent debts remain uncrystallised. Where uncrystallised contingent claims remain outstanding after many years, the court may consider it appropriate to direct the supervisor to make a final distribution and bring the arrangement to an end without setting aside a reserve to satisfy potential future contingencies.[12] While such situations are likely to be rare in the context of IVAs, they are at least theoretically possible.

B. DEFAULT AND TERMINATION

1. Default

12.05 Regrettably, many IVAs do not end satisfactorily. As noted in an earlier chapter, government statistics show that failure rates remain high.[13] Where the debtor defaults on the terms of the IVA, this is likely to result in failure. Not all defaults, however, necessarily result in premature termination of the IVA: the terms of the IVA may provide for the supervisor to have a discretion to issue a certificate of substantial compliance in cases where the default is not egregious and, in the event that such a certificate is issued, it would have the effect of treating the IVA as fully implemented for the purposes of rule 8.31(1) of the Insolvency (England and Wales) Rules 2016 (IR 2016).[14]

12.06 Default may take various forms, from a failure to make assets or money (whether as a single transaction or by way of instalments) available to the supervisor for distribution under the IVA or a failure to comply with any other

---

11 [2017] EWCA Civ 111, [2017] BPIR 430.

12 See *Re TXU UK Ltd* [2021] EWHC 758 (Ch), a CVA case involving multiple uncrystallised mesothelioma and pension claims after 16 years, where ICCJ Prentis applied *Re Danka Business Systems (In Liquidation)* [2013] EWCA Civ 92.

13 See above [1.39].

14 See Standard Conditions, para 10 (see above [4.49]).

material obligation under the terms of the IVA, to a failure to cooperate with reasonable requests made by the supervisor.[15] It has already been noted that good faith and transparency are required of the debtor in putting forward a proposal. A material misrepresentation, or the provision or omission of material information so as to give a false or misleading picture of the debtor's true position, in the documents supplied or made available to the creditors when seeking their approval of the proposal or any variation may itself constitute a default.[16]

2. Termination

There are no statutory provisions that provide any guidance as to the circum- **12.07** stances in which or the mechanisms and procedures by which an IVA may be terminated prematurely by reason of the debtor's default, other than to a limited extent in the context of petitioning for the debtor's bankruptcy. In each case, it will depend on the terms (express or implied) of the arrangement. Some IVAs spell out explicitly in what circumstances and how the arrangement may be terminated, while others may be less prescriptive.[17]

Commonly the IVA will require the supervisor, in the event of default by the **12.08** debtor that is capable of remedy, to serve a notice on the debtor requiring the debtor to remedy the breach forthwith or within a specified time and such a notice may also require the debtor to provide a full explanation for the breach.[18] The breach may, however, be irremediable or the terms of the IVA may require strict compliance, such that the opportunity to remedy will not apply. Thus, in *Clarke v Birkin*,[19] the failure to pay instalments at regular intervals was held to have been an irremediable breach. Where the breach is not remedied (within the time allowed) or is incapable or being remedied, either under the terms of the IVA or for practical reasons, the IVA may empower or even require the supervisor to issue a formal notice or a certificate of termination (CoT) and/or present a petition for the debtor's bankruptcy. Whether or not the supervisor has a discretion in this matter or is mandated to take such action will depend on the wording of the IVA. Alternatively, the IVA may require the supervisor to seek a decision of the creditors as to whether to take one or both of those steps or to overlook the breach (for example, if it is not

---

15 See Standard Conditions, para 70(a) and (c).
16 See Standard Conditions, para 70(c). Cf. below [12.17].
17 For an example of the former, see the Standard Conditions, paras 11, 70–71.
18 See Standard Conditions, para 71(1).
19 [2006] BPIR 632.

particularly serious) or to allow the creditors the opportunity to vary the terms of the arrangement (assuming variation is permissible).[20]

12.09   Where the supervisor concludes that it is necessary to issue a CoT, or is required to do so (directly by the terms of the IVA or by a creditor decision), this should be done promptly; the terms of the IVA (or the creditors' resolution) may specify a more precise period within which it must be done. The supervisor must then serve such notice on both the debtor and any creditor bound by the IVA as soon as reasonably practicable.[21]

12.10   Where the terms of the IVA so provide, expressly or by necessary implication, the service of a CoT will itself bring the IVA to an end; in some cases, however, the formal termination may only occur once further steps have been completed, such as the issue of a bankruptcy petition or the making of a bankruptcy order.[22] The terms of the IVA may be such that, on their true construction, although the IVA will cease to have effect upon the service of a CoT, the process of termination might not be fully complete until the supervisor has completed all the steps necessary to bring the IVA to a conclusion (including filing the necessary reports and petitioning for the debtor's bankruptcy); this might allow the supervisor to seek directions from the court, within the 'twilight' period between the service of the CoT and the fulfilment of the ensuing steps, as to whether to seek a decision from the creditors on varying the terms so as to allow the debtor in effect to rectify the breach, thereby breathing sufficient life back into a moribund IVA to enable a successful outcome after all.[23]

3.   Effect of termination

12.11   As noted above, termination of the IVA does not mean that the IVA simply disappears or that its provisions cease to have any effect; nor do the provisions of IA 1986 in relation to the arrangement automatically cease to apply. In particular, the supervisor's role does not abruptly cease. For example, the supervisor is required to serve certain notices and provide a final report following termination.[24] Moreover, the supervisor's standing to present a default petition persists even after the IVA has come to an end.[25] In addition, there may be significant outstanding issues in relation to distribution of funds held by the

---

20   See Standard Conditions, para 70(3).
21   Thus, explicitly, in Standard Conditions, para 71(4)–(5).
22   See Standard Conditions, para 11(1).
23   *Franses v Hay* [2015] EWHC 3468 (Ch), [2016] BPIR 355.
24   See below [12.32]–[12.33].
25   See below [12.26].

supervisor under the terms of the IVA and the supervisor may need to seek directions from the court in relation to those or any other outstanding issues.

Where the terms of the IVA provide for moneys or other assets to be paid **12.12** or transferred or held for the benefit of the IVA creditors, this will – unless precluded by the terms of the IVA – create a trust of those moneys or assets for those creditors that may survive termination.[26] The effect upon such a trust of the failure of the IVA and any subsequent bankruptcy of the debtor depends on the terms of the IVA itself: if the IVA made specific provision for what should happen to that fund in the event of termination and bankruptcy, then the courts will give effect to those provisions; if not, the trust would nevertheless continue under its own terms. In circumstances where such a trust exists and survives a bankruptcy order, the trust fund does not vest in the trustee and will not be available for distribution in the bankruptcy. Instead, the IVA creditors would be entitled to any relevant distributions out of the trust fund in accordance with its terms and would also be entitled to prove for any shortfall in relation to the sums they would have been due from that trust (but for the failure of the IVA) in the bankruptcy.[27]

C. BANKRUPTCY PETITIONS ON DEFAULT

1. Overview

(a) Procedure

IA 1986 expressly provides that, in certain specified circumstances, the super- **12.13** visor of an IVA or any person bound by the IVA, other than the debtor, may petition for the debtor's bankruptcy.[28] In all but one of these circumstances, they essentially amount to where the debtor is in default in some way.[29] The exception is where the debtor has died during the course of the IVA.[30] This procedure provides the court with an opportunity to consider how best to deal with the consequences of the debtor's inability to implement fully the terms of the IVA and to wrap up the IVA in an orderly way by providing a transition into bankruptcy where that is the most appropriate course. In many cases, it is the act of presentation of such a petition or even the making of a bankruptcy order upon such a petition that will formally bring the IVA to an end.

---

26   *Re NT Gallagher & Sons Ltd* [2002] EWCA Civ 404, [2002] 1 WLR 2380; see above [2.16].
27   *Re Bradley-Hole (A Bankrupt)* [1995] 1 WLR 1907; *Re NT Gallagher & Sons Ltd* (above), especially at [54].
28   IA 1986, s 264(1)(c).
29   See below [12.16]–[12.17].
30   See below [12.18].

12.14 Ordinarily, a creditor's petition must satisfy certain jurisdictional conditions;[31] in contrast, no such jurisdictional test applies to petitions presented under section 264(1)(c).[32] It suffices that the debtor satisfied the jurisdictional requirements to enter the IVA; there is no additional jurisdictional hurdle relating to a section 264(1)(c) petition. This would remain the case even if the debtor could demonstrate that, since entering the IVA, they had moved their centre of main interests (COMI) out of England and Wales and even if (at the date of the hearing of the petition) they were neither domiciled in England and Wales nor, within the preceding three years, had had a place of residence or carried on a business in England and Wales.[33]

12.15 Unless the debtor has died,[34] the form of the petition and the applicable procedure are, in effect, governed by the rules applicable to ordinary creditor petitions (*mutatis mutandis*).[35] The court to which the petition should be presented will usually be the court in which the interim order was made (if there was one) or the appropriate court (where the alternative IVA procedure was followed).[36]

(b) Grounds

12.16 There are three different grounds on which such a default-based petition may be brought, although the petition may seek to rely on more than one ground. The most obvious and straightforward of these, and by far the most common, is that the debtor has failed to comply with one or more obligations under the IVA.[37] The default does not have to be intentional or repudiatory in nature, but the more serious the breach, the more likely the petition is to be granted.[38] The petition may also be presented on the ground that the debtor has failed to comply with reasonable requests for cooperation made by the supervisor.[39] In the vast majority of cases under either of these grounds the default will be a breach of express terms of the arrangement and may well factually overlap.

---

31 IA 1986, s 265, which, since 6 April 2016, applies only to petitions presented under s 264(1)(a): see above [1.22].

32 *Loy v O'Sullivan* [2010] EWHC 5383 (Ch), [2011] BPIR 181 (an application to annul a bankruptcy order made on a supervisor's petition; but the reasoning applies equally to an IVA creditor's petition).

33 On the facts in *Loy v O'Sullivan* (above), Mr Loy would actually have satisfied the s 265 test as at the date of the bankruptcy order (as would most IVA debtors), but that is irrelevant.

34 Where the debtor has died, a specific form of petition is required: see below [12.18].

35 IR 2016, r 10.6(3), applies Chapter 2 of Part 10 of IR 2016, with 'any necessary modifications', to petitions presented under IA 1986, s 264(1)(c). See, in particular, IR 2016, rr 10.7, 10.8, 10.10, 10.12–10.14, 10.18–10.23 and (where appropriate) 10.24(3)–(4) and 10.30(1), (3), (4).

36 IR 2016, r 10.11(6), (cf. r 8.20), unless r 10.11(2) applies.

37 IA 1986, s 276(1)(a).

38 See below [12.19].

39 IA 1986, s 276(1)(c).

The final ground is rather different in nature. Such a petition may also be **12.17** presented on the grounds that information that the debtor provided in the statement of affairs or the proposal or any other document supplied to the creditors under Part 8 of IA 1986, or otherwise made available to the creditors in connection with a creditors' decision procedure under that Part, was false or misleading in any material way or where some material omission from the information so provided gave a misleading impression.[40] In effect, this ground also represents a species of default, warranting immediate termination.[41] Petitions presented by IVA creditors are more likely to be brought under this last ground.

The above grounds do not apply, however, to a petition presented under **12.18** section 264(1)(c) where the debtor has died. This is due to the modifications made to IA 1986 in the event of the debtor's death by the Administration of Insolvent Estates of Deceased Persons Order 1986 (DPO 1986).[42] Instead, a specific form of petition is required, on which the ground is simply the fact of the debtor's death.[43]

(c) The court's approach

Upon a default petition, the court retains a discretion as to whether to make **12.19** a defaulting debtor bankrupt, but where the default is serious such as to prevent the proper implementation of the IVA, the court would only decline to make a bankruptcy order in exceptional circumstances.[44] When considering the degree to which the information supplied (or withheld) was misleading and whether to make a bankruptcy order on such a petition, the court may have regard to the cumulative effect of the erroneous information involved.[45] Where, following default, it comes to light that the debtor had not been entirely open or honest with the creditors, a bankruptcy order will usually be made.[46] If the terms of the IVA require payments to be made punctually and explicitly preclude that a breach of these terms can be remedied by later payment, the courts are most unlikely to accept an argument on the part of the debtor that the default was not sufficiently serious to warrant making a bankruptcy

---

40 IA 1986, s 276(1)(b).
41 Either expressly (see Standard Conditions, para 70(b)), or by necessary implication.
42 SI 1986/1999: IA 1986, s 276(1) is omitted by DPO 1986, Sch 1 Part II, para 8.
43 See above [3.14] and [3.18]. If the debtor dies between presentation and service, the procedure is as referred to above, save that IR 2016, r 10.15 also applies.
44 *Harris v Gross* [2001] BPIR 586; *Varden Nuttall Ltd v Baker* [2016] EWHC 3858 (Ch).
45 *Re Tack* [2000] BPIR 164.
46 *Varden Nuttall Ltd v Baker* (above).

order.[47] The fact that the default may not be the fault of the debtor personally is unlikely to be a sufficient reason to decline to make a bankruptcy order and cannot be so where the terms of the IVA make it clear that strict compliance with the relevant terms of the IVA is of the essence of the arrangement.[48]

12.20 On the other hand, the courts have sometimes been willing to stretch a point. In *Bonney v Mirpuri*,[49] the court accepted that there had been a sufficiently serious default by the debtor to justify the presentation of a petition, but nevertheless adjourned the petition on the basis that the default, consisting of a failure to realise a property within the time stipulated in the IVA, had been caused by a matrimonial dispute which had since been resolved, so that the property could now be sold and there was a real prospect that the adjournment would allow the creditors to be paid in full.[50]

(d) The order and the appointment of the trustee

12.21 Where the court makes a bankruptcy order on the petition, the form of that order follows that prescribed for bankruptcy orders made on creditor petitions generally, with slight modifications.[51] One difference is that, on a default petition, the court will need to make an order directing that any expense reasonably incurred as an expense of the administration of the IVA shall be a first charge on the bankruptcy estate.[52] This applies equally where the petition was presented in relation to a deceased debtor.[53] Another difference, applicable in most cases, relates to the identity of the trustee appointed by the court under this order.

12.22 The current standard form of order on a normal creditor's petition requires the court to acknowledge the appointment of the Official Receiver (OR) as trustee in bankruptcy.[54] This reflects the fact that, since 6 April 2017, unless the court orders otherwise, the OR automatically becomes the first trustee in bankruptcy.[55] In particular, the court may order otherwise where there is a supervisor in office under an IVA in relation to the bankrupt: in such circumstances it may appoint the supervisor as trustee.[56] To be able to make such an appointment,

---

47   *Clarke v Birkin* [2006] EWHC 340, [2006] BPIR 632.
48   *Re Keenan* [1998] BPIR 205; see also *Clarke v Birkin* (above).
49   [2013] BPIR 412.
50   See also *Franses v Hay* [2015] EWHC 3468 (Ch), [2016] BPIR 355, above [12.10].
51   IR 2016, r 10.31(1); see also rr 10.32 and 10.33.
52   IA 1986, s 276(2).
53   See above [3.14].
54   IR 2016, r 10.31(1)(f).
55   IA 1986, s 291A(1), inserted by the Small Business, Enterprise and Employment Act 2015 (SBEEA 2015).
56   IA 1986, s 291A(2); this replaced what had been s 297(5) prior to 6 April 2017.

however, the supervisor must have filed with the court a statement to the effect that they are an IP, qualified to act as trustee in relation to the bankrupt and that they consent so to act.[57] Where the petition was presented by the supervisor, this represents no special difficulties: the supervisor merely has to include these details in the evidence in support of the petition. Where the petition is presented by an IVA creditor, the creditor may apply for the supervisor's appointment and request the supervisor to file such a certificate; in any case, the creditor would need to put the supervisor on notice of the petition and, following such notice, the supervisor would have the opportunity to file a certificate.

Whether or not the court accedes to that request and appoints the supervisor **12.23** as the trustee in bankruptcy is always a matter of discretion and will depend on a number of factors. The appointment of the supervisor as trustee in bankruptcy makes perfect sense from the point of view of continuity and saving time and costs, and, where the court is asked to make such an appointment, it would only refuse to do so in the most exceptional circumstances.[58] Such circumstances might include objections raised by the creditors and/or complaints as to the conduct of the supervisor in relation to the IVA, but the complaints would have to be well founded and of a serious nature to warrant such refusal. Another more likely ground for refusal would be where the supervisor has been acting as trustee of the IVA assets: as the IVA trusts might well survive the bankruptcy and, if so, the appointment might place the supervisor in a position of conflict, it might not be appropriate for the supervisor to become trustee in bankruptcy.[59]

If the court does appoint the supervisor as trustee in bankruptcy, the order **12.24** must contain certain prescribed information (in so far as not included in the bankruptcy order already): the identification details of the proceedings; the name and title of the judge making the order; the name and postal address of the applicant and the capacity in which they made the application; the identification and contact details of the supervisor/trustee and a statement that they have filed the required certificate; an order appointing them as trustee and the date of the order.[60] Where there are to be joint trustees, the order must also specify the circumstances in which the trustees must act together and those in

---

57   IR 2016, r 10.71(2).

58   *Landsman v de Concilio* [2005] EWHC 267 (Ch), [2005] BPIR 829.

59   *Re Bradley-Hole* [1995] 1 WLR 1097, at 1102D.

60   IR 2016, r 10.71(3).

which one or more of them may act for the others.[61] The supervisor's appointment as trustee takes effect immediately.[62]

12.25 The court must deliver two copies of the order (one of which at least must be sealed) to the OR, who is in turn required to deliver a sealed copy of the order to the newly appointed trustee.[63] The supervisor turned trustee must then give notice of their appointment to the bankrupt's creditors (not just those bound by the IVA), or – if the court gives directions to this effect – advertise the fact in accordance with those directions.[64] The notice (or advertisement, as the case may be) must explain the procedure for establishing a creditors' committee.[65]

2. Supervisor's petition

12.26 In the event of serious default, the terms of the IVA may empower, or even oblige, the supervisor to present a petition for the debtor's bankruptcy. Whether or not the supervisor has any discretion in this matter will depend on a true construction of the terms. Where the breach is serious enough to warrant the making of a bankruptcy order, however, it is very unlikely the supervisor would exercise any such discretion in favour of the debtor, save in the most exceptional circumstances. In *Harris v Gross*,[66] it was held that the supervisor could present such a petition even after the expiry of the term of the IVA, provided that, at the date of presentation, they were still carrying out their statutory functions in relation to the IVA.[67] The reasoning behind this is that the statutory power allowing the supervisor to present such a petition is a necessary ancillary power analogous to that enabling the supervisor to apply to the court for directions.

12.27 The terms of the IVA will normally also provide that the supervisor may apply within the petition to be appointed as the debtor's trustee in bankruptcy. Even where that is not the case, the supervisor usually will so apply and, for reasons set out above, this request will normally be granted.

---

61   IR 2016, r 10.71(4), by reference to IA s 292(3).
62   IR 2016, r 10.71(7).
63   IR 2016, r 10.71(5)–(6).
64   IA 1986, s 291A(3).
65   In accordance with IA 1986, s 301: see s 291A(4).
66   [2001] BPIR 586.
67   Those under IA 1986, s 263(2).

3. Creditor's default petition

Where the supervisor does not present a petition, for whatever reason, it is **12.28** open to any one or more creditors bound by the IVA to present a petition instead. It is relatively rare for creditors to present such a petition on the grounds of a failure on the part of the debtor to comply with their obligations under the IVA or with reasonable requests for cooperation with the supervisor, as this is more usually the domain of the supervisor and creditors are therefore less likely to take on the cost risks.[68] On the other hand, it is comparatively more common for a creditor to present such a petition on the ground of false or misleading information.

Where the debtor has provided a misleading picture to the creditors (either by **12.29** providing false or misleading information or by a material omission), presenting a petition under this ground effectively provides the creditors with an alternative route to section 262 of IA 1986.[69] The standing to bring such a petition assumes greater significance where the window for the latter kind of challenge has already closed, either because the misinformation or omission only comes to light after the 28 days or because for some other reason the creditor missed that boat. In certain circumstances, the creditor may choose to attack on both fronts at once.[70] It is likely, at least where the ground related to misleading information, that a creditor bound by the CVA would still be able to present a petition even after the IVA had come to an end.[71]

D. SUPERVENING BANKRUPTCY

An IVA may also be brought to an end prematurely by means of a bankruptcy **12.30** order made on a petition presented by a creditor not bound by the IVA. This would include a creditor bound by the IVA in relation to a certain debt or debts but who has in addition a further debt that is not bound by the IVA; typically, this would be a debt that arose during the course of the IVA that was not a future or contingent debt as at the date of the approval.[72] There is nothing to prevent any such creditor (whether or not they are an IVA creditor

---

68   For an example of such a creditors' petition, see *Clarke v Birkin* [2006] EWHC 340, [2006] BPIR 632.

69   On which, see Chapter 9 above.

70   See, e.g., *Somji v Cadbury Schweppes Plc* [2001] BPIR 172 (CA), on which, see above [2.05].

71   Although the reasoning in *Harris v Gross* [2001] BPIR 586 (above [12.26]) related specifically to the supervisor's functions, there is no good reason to suppose this does not apply equally to creditors' default petitions.

72   See *Jules v Robertson* [2011] EWCA Civ 1322; [2012] BPIR 126; see above [2.27].

for the purposes of other debts) from presenting a petition in the normal way.[73] It should be noted, however, that the making of a bankruptcy order on such a petition will not necessarily bring the IVA completely to an end; whether it does or not will depend on the terms of the arrangement, properly construed.[74]

12.31 Just as with default petitions, discussed above, the appropriate court for presenting a creditor petition where there is a subsisting IVA will usually be the court in which the interim order was made or (where the alternative IVA procedure was followed) the appropriate court.[75] On such a petition presented against a debtor in IVA, the court is empowered to appoint the supervisor of the IVA as trustee in the same way and on the same terms as on a default petition.[76] Moreover, the same considerations in favour of such appointment would obtain and the same requirements and consequential measures would also apply.[77]

E. STATUTORY FORMALITIES AND RELEASE

1. Notice and final report

(a) At the conclusion of the IVA

12.32 Following either the successful implementation or the termination of an IVA, the supervisor must, within 28 days, certify the conclusion of the IVA and send notice to this effect to the debtor and every creditor bound by the IVA.[78] The notice must state the date the IVA took effect and must be accompanied by a final report that summarises all receipts and payments in relation to the IVA and explains any departure from the terms of the IVA as approved.[79] Within the same window, the supervisor must deliver copies of the statutory notice and the final report to the Secretary of State and, in an interim order case, also to the court.[80]

---

73   Pursuant to IA 1986, s 264(1)(a). See, e.g., *Re Bradley-Hole (A Bankrupt)* [1995] 1 WLR 1907.

74   *Re Bradley-Hole* (above). Note Standard Conditions, para 11(1)(b).

75   IR 2016, r 10.11(6), (cf. r 8.20), unless r 10.11(2) applies.

76   IA 1986, s 291A(2). This provision does not explicitly state that it applies 'whether or not on a petition under section 264(1)(c)', as did its predecessor, s 297(5) (repealed by SBEEA 2015 when s 291A was inserted), but the wording of s 291A(2) renders the omission unimportant.

77   See above [12.23].

78   IR 2016, r 8.31(1).

79   IR 2016, r 8.31(2)–(3).

80   IR 2016, r 8.31(4).

(b) Additional requirements on termination

In addition, where the IVA was terminated prematurely, in whatever way ter- **12.33**
mination was brought about, the supervisor must specify in the statutory notice
referred to above the reasons why the IVA was terminated.[81] This statutory
notice is to be distinguished from the CoT referred to above, although there
is no reason why, in an appropriate case, the two could not be elided into one
document. In practice, however, the requirement for the statutory notice to be
accompanied by the report will, at least in cases where a CoT is required to
terminate the IVA, mean that the two would be sequential.

2. Release of the supervisor

The supervisor is obliged to remain in office at least until the statutory notice, **12.34**
together with the final report, has been provided to the Secretary of State: it is
only once those reporting obligations have been completed that the supervisor
may vacate office.[82] Where the supervisor's role persists in relation to the distribution of funds held on trust for the benefit of the IVA creditors, the supervisor will not be entitled to step down until these functions are completed.[83]

It is customary in modern IVAs for the proposal to make explicit the terms on **12.35**
which the supervisor is entitled to obtain release. The Standard Conditions
employ the following formula: 'Upon the termination or full implementation
of the Arrangement and the Supervisor having dealt with the assets in his
possession in accordance with the terms of the Arrangement, the Supervisor
shall be released from any further obligations or liability in respect of the
Arrangement or any trusts created thereby'.[84]

---

81   IR 2016, r 8.31(3)(c).
82   IR 2016, r 8.31(5): strictly speaking, this only applies to the delivery to the Secretary of State, but in practice
     all the reporting obligations must be completed by the same date.
83   See above [12.04].
84   Standard Conditions, para 22.

INDEX